P9-CEX-888

The Tightwad Gazette III

The Tightwad Gazette III

Promoting Thrift as a Viable Alternative Lifestyle

Written and Illustrated by Amy Dacyczyn
a.k.a. The Frugal Zealot

Villard • New York

Published in the United States by Villard Books, a division of Random House, Inc., New York, and simultaneously in Canada by Random House of Canada Limited, Toronto.

VILLARD BOOKS is a registered trademark of Random House, Inc.

ISBN: 0-679-77766-0

Random House website address:
http://www.randomhouse.com/

Printed in the United States of America

A Word of Caution

Tightwads are by nature unconventional. We push the normal limits to make things last longer. We reuse things in unusual ways. We experiment constantly to find new, cheaper ways to do almost everything. Because this book draws upon the experiences of tightwads throughout the country, there is a chance we will inadvertently publish information that is technically illegal or not safe. On the other hand, all of the information in this book was previously published in a newsletter that was read by tens of thousands of people. Whenever any reader pointed out a concern, I thoroughly researched the question and then made a judgment as to the validity of the concern. These judgments are all incorporated in this book.

Based on this, to the best of my knowledge, all of the ideas in this book are legal. Likewise I believe that all of the ideas meet a reasonable level of safety. I pointed out any significant hazard I was aware of, but I did not point out safety concerns if the hazard was extremely remote. For example, when I suggested turning out the lights to save electricity, I did not warn you about the hazard of stumbling over your toddler's pull toy in the darkness.

You must exercise your personal judgment when using ideas in this book and take reasonable precautions.

Introduction

It's hard to believe that it's been almost seven years since that fateful night when I woke Jim up and said, "I have this idea for a home-based business—and I don't think it's bad!"

There was nothing in that small moment that provided a clue about the amazing years that were to come. After all, waking up my long-suffering husband at two A.M. with my latest brainstorm was nothing new, and a fair number of my ideas had fallen somewhere short of genius in application.

But the success of the newsletter—and these books—has been overwhelming. Though subscriptions rose and fell, the newsletter has had as many as 100,000 subscribers, and the *Tightwad Gazette* books I and II have collectively sold 475,000 copies. I've been interviewed about 750 times, including three *Donahue* appearances. I won the *Dateline NBC* Challenge by helping a family chop its grocery bills, survived an appearance on *Late Night with David Letterman*, and was even rendered in one of those little stipple drawings on the front page of *The Wall Street Journal*.

The financial success we've enjoyed—combined, of course, with frugality—has allowed us to retire early, which is why this will be the last compilation of articles from the newsletter. Closing down a successful business (i.e., killing the golden goose) is a mystery to most people, but I prefer the luxury of freedom from a job to the luxury of material goods. All along, I have pointed out that both earning and saving money should be means to an end, not ends in themselves. The "end" that I plan to pursue for the next several years is being a full-time mom to my six kids, and helping them realize—just as I have—that dreams can come true if you have the courage and determination to pursue them.

I also feel that, with the information in this volume, I have explored most of the ways in which the average American family can save money. If I have not covered a specific idea, I have at least provided a model that should allow you to figure it out for yourself. Magazines can plug along for decades by, essentially, repeating the same old articles, but I have always refused to do that.

And while most people might think a life of book tours and media opportunities is glamorous, it isn't all it's cracked up to be. It

was a minor thrill to meet folks like Danny DeVito, John Travolta, Tom Selleck, Glenn Close, and George McGovern—I even traded autographs with Gene Shalit and was smooched by Richard Simmons—but to be honest, I had more satisfying exchanges with people like the limo driver in Cleveland who told me all about how his company economized on cleaning supplies. While I've been happy to have the opportunity to disseminate my ideas, I never wanted to be famous. I look forward to regaining my anonymity, so that I can once again go to yard sales without the proprietor saying, "Hey! Aren't you the Tightwad Lady? Harry, bring the camera!"

But as I close out this part of my life, I will always treasure a fat file that I've kept, labeled "Success Stories." This three-pound collection consists of testimonials from readers who have followed the principles set forth in the books and newsletters and found that they really do work. They tell of conquering mountains of debt, buying a home when it had once seemed impossible, passing on important frugal values to their kids, and even turning back from the brink of divorce to a happy marriage.

I will also savor memories. One moment in particular that stands out occurred at a book signing somewhere in a month-long blur of cities. I felt a tap on my shoulder. I turned, and there was a woman. She said, "I just wanted to tell you that you changed my life." Then she walked away. She didn't want to take any of my time, or even ask for an autograph. She just wanted to tell me that. The exchange was so brief that I remember nothing else about her. Yet that woman has stayed with me as a mental symbol of all the unknown people who have been affected positively by *The Tightwad Gazette.*

I want to thank all those who have contributed to the success of *The Tightwad Gazette.* Its strength has always been the readers—not only have they encouraged me, but much of the content of the newsletter and books is based on their good ideas. Thanks also to the team of staffers who handled the everyday duties of running the business. This group changed over time, but in the last few years has included Pam Barker, Holly Wise-Copland, Blanche Hill, and Francis Page. A special thanks goes to my staffer Brad Lemley, who shared in much of the writing and researching during the last four and a half years. Were it not for his help, ideas, and especially his good humor, *The Tightwad Gazette* would have had a much shorter run.

Finally, I want to thank my family. Jim assumed all the duties of house-husband, has been an enthusiastic supporter of my work, and has patiently listened to a series of two A.M. brilliant-article-idea briefings. The children, Alec, Jamie, Neal, Rebecca, Brad, and Laura, who now range in age from thirteen to five, endured far too many television and magazine photo shoots, not to mention having a mother who was often so lost in a creative stupor that she could only be reached by waving a hand before her eyes. As much as I have enjoyed the last seven years, I hope to slow down the passage of time as I watch them mature to adulthood. I am grateful that frugality—and my readers—have given me that option.

The Tightwad Gazette III

DROWNING IN RISING EXPECTATIONS

The idea that the baby-boom generation has fewer opportunities and must struggle harder than previous generations is believed by millions of Americans. Specifically, they believe that it's almost impossible to afford kids on a middle-class income anymore.

A major reason I started the newsletter was that I believed this was false. It seemed to me that boomers were victims of their own inflated expectations, not the economy, and if they didn't live so extravagantly and planned better, they could easily afford what they really needed. But I lacked the statistics to back up my belief.

So now I am indebted to Karl Zinsmeister, an Ithaca, New York, writer and the editor in chief of *American Enterprise* magazine. He sent me some fascinating information, which will be included in an as-yet-unnamed book. His basic premise is that we are more fortunate today than we realize. Understanding this can be a great help to tightwads wrestling with the notion that "it's not fair."

First, why is this idea that boomers are worse off so prevalent? Zinsmeister says politicians can get lots of mileage from convincing people that they are hurting, and that a particular political plan will bring back opportunity. And news stories thrive on finding villains and victims. Stories built along these lines are more interesting than "gosh, everything is great" stories.

There have even been news stories that present statistics to back up the idea. Typically, a 1991 front-page article in *The Washington Post* stated that, adjusted for inflation, "young families with children suffered a 24% decline in median income between 1973 and 1987."

This information, says Zinsmeister, is just plain wrong. It's based on a statistical error in the way the figures were computed, and it's based on the idea that modern families are the same as those of the past. But families were, on average, 13 percent smaller in 1990 than they were in 1970.

When you correct those mistakes, a different picture emerges. A 1991 federal study found there was actually a 20 percent inflation-adjusted *increase* in the average family's income between 1973 and 1989. And when you factor in non-income "benefits" such as health care, which are about twice as generous as they were 20 years ago, you find that the real rise in family income is about 30 percent.

So why do people "feel" poorer than their parents? Zinsmeister says it's mainly because we have come to expect more. For example:

- The average American now

consumes twice as many goods and services as he did back in 1950. (Going back to 1928, when our grandparents were having children, the number of consumer durables bought annually per person has gone up ten times.)

• The number of motor vehicles per adult is 50 percent higher than it was in 1950. One reason is that it takes one *fewer* month's worth of family income to buy the average car now than it did then. Cars are cheaper to run, too. Today's biggest Ford, the Lincoln Town Car, gets the same mpg as Ford's smallest car did in 1975.

• Now, every year, 16 million Americans go to foreign countries other than Canada or Mexico. In 1950, the number was 680,000.

• Per-person spending on hobbies and home recreation has gone from $403 in 1950 to $1,149 in 1991, adjusted for inflation.

• In 1960, purchasing a refrigerator cost a family 145 hours of labor. Today it costs half that. As for what to put inside, in 1960, Americans spent 15 percent of their incomes on groceries, versus 7 percent today, and there are 12 times more items to choose from at the supermarket.

• In 1990, 42 cents of every food dollar was spent on restaurant meals—twice the amount spent by the previous generation.

• Only about 25 percent of the parents of baby boomers went to college. Half of all of the boomers themselves got to go, and by 1992, 62 percent of high school graduates chose and were able to go on to college.

Even if a boomer concedes all of the above, he'll still contend that housing prices have shot out of sight, and it is far harder for him to afford a house than it was for his parents. Although this is true in a few areas of the country, Zinsmeister says that, adjusted for inflation, the average price of new houses climbed 21 percent over the last 25 years, which is less than the rise in median-family purchasing power. And the price of existing houses—"used houses"—actually declined, adjusting for inflation. After factoring mortgage, utility, insurance, and other expenses, a Harvard University study found that home ownership is about 15 percent more affordable than it was in 1980.

The reason people feel priced out of the housing market, argues Zinsmeister, is because they want houses that are so much bigger and "better." Though the average family is smaller, the average modern, new house is twice as big as the average one built just after World War II. More than 75 percent of new houses have central air-conditioning, up from just 34 percent in 1970. Almost half have more than two bathrooms, up from 16 percent. In 1970, 58 percent of new homes had a garage; now 82 percent have them.

All of this would be pointless if boomers could not afford these places, but they can: 57 percent of married couples under 35 owned their homes in 1989, up from 43 percent 25 years ago.

And what about health care? Although this expense is rapidly escalating, the insurance of most families is paid for by employers. Thus, average out-of-pocket medical expenses have risen only slightly, from 5 percent of income in 1980 to 6 percent in 1990. And while health care costs are on the rise, that's because we expect more:

organ transplants, high-tech testing, cancer cures. Health care was cheaper when people died easier.

The one area in which boomer families have a legitimate beef, says Zinsmeister, is in taxes. Since 1948, the federal-tax-and-Social-Security bite for the median family of four has risen from 2 percent to 25 percent of income. (Taxes for people without dependents have stayed roughly the same.) As bad as this seems, it doesn't completely offset the gains in family buying power. Further, we probably do get at least some money-saving services from the government, even if indirectly. For example, previous generations bore more direct financial responsibility for helping elderly or unemployed relatives. Today these services are paid for with additional taxes.

You might argue that the boomers earn more only because women have gone to work, unlike the stay-at-home moms of the previous generation. But Zinsmeister's figures point up a fact that I've been stressing all along: If you are willing to live like people did in the 1960s, you can be a stay-at-home parent, too. Today's second income is often consumed by child care, extra taxes, and luxuries that our parents happily did without.

Zinsmeister's arguments are based on statistical averages. You might respond that they are interesting but they *don't* apply to you. You've examined your situation, and despite your hard work, you really are worse off than your parents were at your age.

I would respond that even if there is a financial inequity, complaining about it wastes emotional energy. You could use this same energy to be even more creative than your parents were. For example, our family expenditure for food and clothing is almost the same as what my parents spent for these items 25 years ago, and this *isn't* adjusted for inflation. There are many ways to save money today that didn't exist when I was a kid: yard sales, warehouse stores, and energy-saving appliances, to name a few. I feel that today it's easier than ever before to be a tightwad.

Zinsmeister's point, however, is that a great deal of modern complaining is baseless. There is more wealth, more luxury, and more opportunity. If you doubt it, sit down and have a long talk with your parents and grandparents.

MACARONI MIRACLE

In a newsletter article, I mentioned that we buy store-brand macaroni-and-cheese dinners for 25¢ each. Catherine Kenyon of Berwyn, Illinois, responded that at her local health/bulk-food store, she can buy the same kind of cheese powder that comes in the little packets in these dinners. She wondered if, at $4.46 a pound, it was cheaper to make macaroni-and-cheese with this stuff and bulk-purchased macaroni.

I admit, it seems hard to believe that the little boxes of macaroni-and-cheese could possibly be a good deal. Every tightwad has an instinctive distrust of convenience foods that come in tiny cardboard boxes.

So we checked it out. A 7.25-ounce box of macaroni-and-cheese contains 6 ounces of macaroni and 1.25 ounces of cheese powder. It is commonly sold as a loss leader for 25¢, but we have gotten it as cheaply as 20¢.

An equivalent amount of bulk-purchased elbow macaroni costs 12¢, and an equivalent amount of bulk-purchased cheese powder costs 36¢, for a total of 48¢.

I don't know that the cheese powder in macaroni-and-cheese dinners is the same as you would buy in a health food store. But with the exception of artificial coloring (and it probably contains less than the average hot-pink-and-purple Dacyczyn birthday cake), the ingredients don't appear to be "fake" food.

In short, the 25¢ box of macaroni-and-cheese is one of the few exceptions to the general rule that convenience foods cost more. I am the first to admit that this is probably not the most wholesome, nutritious meal imaginable, but we have found that by tossing in a can of tuna fish, it makes a satisfying last-minute meal.

THE KIDS' CLOTHING INVENTORY

I spend about $50 annually to dress six kids; that's an average of $8.33 per kid. This amount covers everything, including snow pants, boots, jackets, and mittens, which are essential for our cold climate. I buy clothing primarily for the older children, and to replenish the worn-out hand-me-downs for younger children.

Some of the clothing my children wear was given to our family. Socks and underwear are often purchased new, with a rebate. But well over half of what they wear comes from yard sales.

The kickoff of yard-sale season here occurs during Memorial Day weekend. During the next three months, I hope to buy most of the clothing our kids will need for the following year.

Managing the wardrobes of six children cannot be done without incredible organization. I found this difficult even when I had fewer children because I always shop a few years in advance. (Shopping in advance is essential if you hope to achieve the near-100-percent-secondhand wardrobe.) In the past, I wasn't quite organized enough. I bought duplicates of things I already had and overlooked a few gaps in my kids' wardrobes. Both mistakes are potentially costly, so I decided to be even more organized. Here's how:

I spent several hours in preparation in April. I went through my kids' bureaus and closets, and my clothing file (a box-storage system described in my first *Tightwad Gazette* book), and inventoried the contents. I tallied only school clothes, shoes, and outerwear, because there is always a way to improvise the rest of their apparel. Thus my inventories for the oldest boy and girl were more thorough than the ones for younger siblings.

Then I made up a chart for each child. Jamie's is shown at the bottom of this page. The first column shows clothing from her bureau that I anticipated will still fit the next school year, and the next two columns show clothing from the attic into which she'll grow. In categories with multiple items, like pants, I marked an *X* to indicate each item. In categories with only one or two items, I made specific notes as to the color and condition of the item. This will let me know that a borderline-worn-out coat can be replaced if I find a bargain, or if the colors of snow pants and a winter coat clash.

The purpose of making this chart becomes clear if you look at Jamie's shoe inventory. Previously I had bought four pairs of sneakers that ranged from size 5 to size 6½. They were great sneakers, most cost under $1, and she or one of her younger sisters will wear them someday. But this past year Jamie ran short of size 1 shoes. I want to ensure that gaps and unnecessary surpluses don't happen again.

In making an inventory, I saw that the manufacturers' sizes can vary dramatically. The shoes that fit Jamie are marked from size 2 to size 5. Additionally, the tags in used clothing are often faded or missing, making the sizes hard to identify. Thus I made notes as to the measurements in pants and shoes, the two items for which fit is most critical. I measured the waist in pants from side to side (which is really half of the waist size) and down the inseam. My measure for Jamie is size 8 (11 inches by 22 inches). I measured shoes from heel to toe. Her shoes are size 2 (8¾ inches). Boots generally have this same shoe measure, except any L. L. Bean–style or other bulky boot, for which you need to allow another inch. When shopping, I will rely more on my measurements than on tags.

Pre-buying pants is a bit tricky, since it's hard to predict how quickly children will sprout in a

JAMIE	SIZE 8	SIZE 10	SIZE 12
SHIRTS, WINTER	XXXXXXXX	XXX	XXXXXXX
SHIRTS, SUMMER	XXX XXXX	XXXXX	XXX
SCHOOL PANTS	XX XXXXXX	XX	XXXXXXX
SKIRTS	XXX	X	XXXX
DRESSES	XXXXX		XXX
LT. JACKET	LT. BLUE		
WINTER COAT	BLUE & GREEN / PINK		
RAINCOAT	GREEN & NAVY		
SNOW PANTS	PURPLE		LAVENDER
SNEAKERS	BLACK & PINK (2)	BLACK (3) WHITE (2½)	WHITE (5)(5½)(6½)(6½)(6½)
DRESS SHOES	LEATHER WEAVE (2) BOAT (5)	WHITE SANDALS (2½)	
BOOTS	BLUE (4)		GREY (5)

year. Most kids will grow between 1 inch and 4 inches per year, and half of that growth will be in their legs. Thus I try to have a supply of pants that are at least 2 inches longer than the child currently wears; 4 inches longer is better. So, while Jamie is size 8 now, I will buy size 10 and size 12 clothes this summer.

Naturally, when pre-buying pants, you run some risk that the kid will chunk up or slim down. But I've found kids generally remain husky, thin, or average through their childhoods, and anyway, if I guess wrong, I can resell the pants for the same price at a yard sale.

Wanting to forever resolve the mystery of pants and shoe sizes, I went through my extensive supply of kids' pants and shoes—toddler-sized through young-teenage sized—and measured each item. Although the measures for each size varied, I determined an average.

The clothing inventories give me a clear picture of what I need to shop for, but they are too cumbersome to refer to while I'm shopping. So I use them to make up a list of needs for each child. I put this information in a small spiral notebook. I also copy in my lists of pants and shoe sizes. I then file away my detailed inventories in case I need to refer to them.

As in the past, I will yard-sale with a tape measure and a list of sizes (now my list is far more precise).

At the sales themselves, I generally pay 25¢ per item of children's clothing. I pay more for new-looking shoes, coats, and snow

PANTS (waist and inseam measure)

Size 2 = 8½″ × 11½″
Size 3 = 9″ × 14″
Size 4 = 9″ × 16″
Size 5 = 10″ × 17″
Size 6 = 10¼″ × 18″
Size 7 = 10½″ × 20″
Size 8 = 11″ × 22″
Size 10 = 12″ × 24″
Size 12 = 12½″ × 26″
Size 14 = 13″ × 27″

SHOES (heel-to-toe measure)

Size 8 = 7″
Size 9 = 7¼″
Size 10 = 7½″
Size 11 = 7¾″
Size 12 = 8″
Size 13 = 8¼″
Size 1 = 8½″
Size 2 = 8¾″
Size 3 = 9″
Size 4 = 9¼″
Size 5 = 9½″
Size 6 = 10¼″
Size 7 = 10¾″
Size 8 = 11″
Size 9 = 11¼″

pants. I pay more for next year's needs, and less and less the further in the future the kid will wear the item. For example, one summer I paid $3 for L. L. Bean–style boots for then ten-year-old Alec. I paid that much only because it was August and he needed them for the following winter. But I would never pay more than 25¢ for a shirt he'll wear in four years.

Making up a clothing inventory required less than an hour per child. Considering the money I'll save by avoiding gaps and surpluses, it was time well spent.

A BOOK REVIEW

The blurbs on the back of the book are enough to set any frugal traveler's heart pounding:

Paris for $199!

Mexico City for $99!

Hong Kong for free!

The book is *The Insider's Guide to Air Courier Bargains,* by Kelly Monaghan. After reading it and speaking with the author on the phone, I am intrigued.

Courier travel grew out of a need companies have to transport stuff from country A to country B quickly. For lots of reasons, often the cheapest, fastest way to do this is to send it as passenger baggage. Freelance couriers give up their baggage allotment in return for a cheap fare.

It works like this: You start by calling around to the various courier companies. Monaghan's book lists dozens, which are concentrated in New York, Miami, San Francisco, and Los Angeles, though more cities are becoming courier take-off points each year. (If you don't live in one of these cities, figure out a way to get to one cheaply; call the companies about a week before you arrive.) Let them know when and where you want to go and return, and they'll tell you if they need a courier for those trips.

If you find an opening, you pay for it immediately. The prices vary widely, but tend to be about 25 percent of full-fare coach. Super-cheap or free flights happen when the courier company is desperate and needs couriers in the next day or two. If you are willing to go to a strange place on very short notice, this could be for you.

Then you go to the airport on the right day and meet a courier company representative, who gives you your ticket and some paperwork that must accompany the shipment. You fly to your destination, meet another representative of the courier company, hand him the papers, and hang around until stuff clears customs. The return flight works the same way.

Most arrangements require that you stay for a specific period of time. A week is typical, but it can be up to 30 days. You are responsible for your expenses during your stay. It's possible that you and your spouse can both travel as couriers, but you might not be able to travel on the same day.

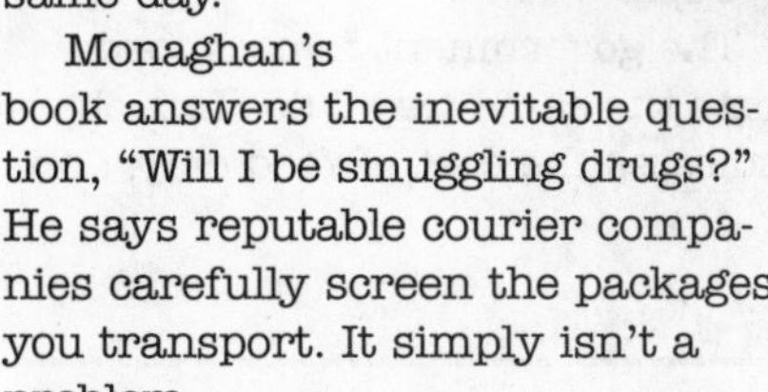

Monaghan's book answers the inevitable question, "Will I be smuggling drugs?" He says reputable courier companies carefully screen the packages you transport. It simply isn't a problem.

"The first time you do it, it's like playing James Bond," Monaghan told me. "After that, it's just another boring way to get from one place to another."

This concept is obviously ideal for the adventurous, single tightwad with a flexible schedule who lives near a large city.

The book costs $14.95, plus $3.00 shipping and handling. Call (800) 356-9315, or write:

The Intrepid Traveler
P.O. Box 438
New York, NY 10034

(Or check your library.)

HOW DOES YOUR FOOD BUDGET COMPARE?

Terry Lepire of Aurora, Oregon, sent me a newspaper clipping that includes a "Cost of Food at Home" chart issued in November 1993 by the USDA. I was fascinated, as I have always wondered if there is a way to accurately compare food budgets, given the varying sizes and ages of members of different families.

So I sat down with my calculator and was stunned to find our family not in the "thrifty" plan, but in the "low-cost" plan. After I moped around for several days, an employee double-checked my math and started laughing. The USDA chart, he said, "doesn't list the *monthly* budget, it lists the *weekly* budget!"

Oops.

The government figures food costs the same way I do. This chart indicates the cost of food only, and presumes that all the food is prepared at home—no restaurant meals. It shows the average of what people actually spend. It's not a recommendation.

According to the "thrifty" plan, my family could be spending $149.40 per week. We spend $41.53—just 28 percent of that. For laughs, we computed that under the "liberal" plan we could spend $282.10 per week!

I absolutely do not expect all my readers to duplicate what our family does, although some have reported they spend less than we do. But this chart does offer some way for you to compare. You should easily spend less than the "thrifty" plan.

This chart also shows us one of two things: Either the federal government is totally inept at gathering numbers to make charts, or Americans are totally clueless at the supermarket.

Or both.

		THRIFTY PLAN	LOW-COST PLAN	MODERATE-COST PLAN	LIBERAL PLAN
Child	1–2 yrs	$13.50	$16.40	$19.10	$23.10
	3–5 yrs	$14.50	$17.80	$22.00	$26.30
	6–8 yrs	$17.60	$23.60	$29.05	$34.40
	9–11 yrs	$21.00	$26.80	$34.40	$39.80
Male	12–14 yrs	$21.80	$30.40	$37.80	$44.50
	15–19 yrs	$22.60	$31.40	$39.00	$45.20
	20–50 yrs	$24.30	$31.10	$38.70	$46.90
	51 years up	$22.00	$29.50	$36.20	$43.40
Female	12–19 yrs	$22.10	$26.30	$31.80	$38.50
	20–50 yrs	$22.00	$27.30	$33.10	$42.30
	51 years up	$21.70	$26.50	$32.60	$39.00

BAGMAN AND RIBBON

Dear Amy,

Here's an idea for extending computer-printer-ribbon life. Pop out the cartridge after each use and place it in a Ziploc bag. With less exposure to the air, the ink stays useful longer. I haven't done a scientific experiment, but it seems to extend the life about two times.

—Katherine Malm
Austin, Texas

GUNK GETTER

Dear Amy,

When drains get sluggish, use this tested, inexpensive remedy:

1. Pour 1 cup of baking soda into the drain.

2. Follow the soda with 1 cup of vinegar.

3. Pour a pot of boiling water down the drain and follow through with the plunger.

This is safer, cheaper, and better for the environment than store-bought remedies, and it won't harm the septic system.

—Jan Mitchell
Salinas, California

(In some cases, boiling water alone is enough. FZ)

HANGOVER REMEDY

Dear Amy,

I don't have room in my house for a clothesline, so I came up with a "clothes bar" to hang over the tub. Drill holes through the ends of an old broom handle. Bend two wire clothes hangers and put the hook end through the holes. Hang this on two plant hooks screwed into the ceiling over the tub. I dry skirts, socks, pants, towels, etc. by hanging them on plastic hangers on my bar.

—Susan Hutchens,
Luquillo, Puerto Rico

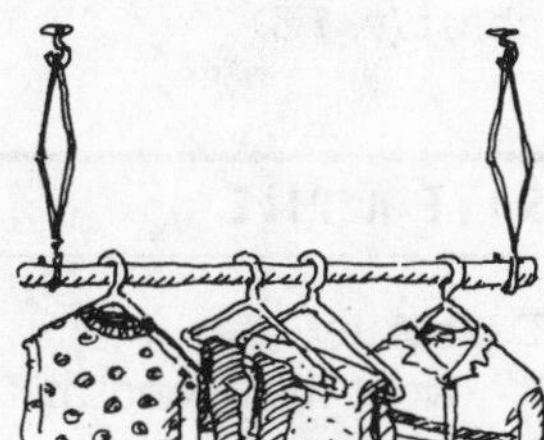

TURNIP AT SCHOOL

Dear Amy,

Investigate enrolling in a Master Gardener program offered through the county extension office in 45 states. You are taught every aspect of gardening by experts, and it is free. All you have to do is volunteer time back to the community on completion of your education.

—Beth Burrows
North Bend, Washington

GET IT FOR FEE

Dear Amy,

It may pay to buy a TV or VCR that was abandoned at a repair shop by its previous owner. I bought two VCRs this way. Generally, you are only charged for the cost of the repair.

—David Kaplan
Glen Head, New York

(One of my staffers recently bought a superb Hitachi stereo cas-

sette deck for $25; it had been abandoned at a repair shop. This buying strategy does not apply only to stereo equipment. Any place that repairs or services anything generally has some items around that the owner did not reclaim and can be purchased cheaply. FZ)

SAVE A PILE

Dear Amy,

Avoid the spendthrift mistake we made of having our new carpet professionally patched after a hot coal from the fireplace burned an unsightly hole in it. A 2-inch square patch cost us a hefty $75! I watched the repair and saw that all it took was an X-Acto knife, a scrap of our carpeting, and a hot-glue gun. We were really kicking ourselves after that one!

—Paula Ramm
Marysville, Ohio

DISCOUNT DUET

Dear Amy,

My neighbor and I save money by having our carpets cleaned, septic tanks pumped out, and furnaces cleaned at the same time. I start by calling a service company and asking if they will take $10 off if we both have the service performed at the same time. They agree, because they get two jobs and don't have to travel far for the second. This would probably work for other kinds of services as well.

—Deborah Maier
Copley, Ohio

HOME SUITE HOME

Dear Amy,

One time you asked for ideas for seniors. Here's one: We have put out the word to our scattered family and friends that we are available to sit with their house and pets. So far we have spent five lovely weeks in a new house in Florida with two cats; time in Kansas City with a young lady; and in the fall we are going to Arizona to sit with a dog and enjoy another new house. We will probably travel to Arizona on our railroad pass. This is a good way to travel and avoid the high motel charges. And it is fun.

—M. Helen Weaver
Ozawkie, Kansas

LOW-CHARGE NO-CHARGE

Dear Amy,

A great static eliminator is simple to make. Mix 1 part fabric softener and 20 parts water. Put in a spritzer bottle and spray just the amount that is needed. Works great and is much cheaper than commercial products.

—Elaine Hodgman
Ludlow, Massachusetts

CHEAPER CHOCOLATE

Dear Amy,

I'm fond of chocolate sprinkles on ice cream but find them prohibitive in cost. The supermarket has only tiny bottles (even so, it's synthetic chocolate). The cost figures

out to about $9 per pound! Then I discovered that a local franchised steak house with an ice cream bar is glad to sell them to me by the pound, at their cost: $1.66.

—Isadora Becker
Ithaca, New York

DENTED, DATED, AND DISCOUNTED

When we first moved to Maine, we were told to check out the wonderful salvaged-foods store in a nearby town. We went, with our price book in hand, and noted that the prices weren't as good as had been indicated. The convenience foods cost more than making foods from scratch. Other deals didn't beat buying loss-leader-sale items at supermarkets, or regular-price items at the wholesale clubs. As a result, we buy only a few items there regularly.

On a recent trip to Vermont, we visited another salvage store that had truly astonishing deals, but I was suspicious as to whether all the salvaged foods met state regulations. I called Vermont's health department and learned that this state, like many others, has no regulations governing the sale of these items. This store is located just over the border from highly regulated Massachusetts. Massachusetts has salvage stores like the one near me—the deals are unremarkable.

It occurred to me that this pattern probably holds across the country. If the deals in the salvage stores in your state seem paltry, check the situation just over the border, or in other states that you may visit regularly. The best deals are likely to be found in a store in an unregulated state that is just over the border from a highly regulated state, because the salvaged goods may be transported over state lines for resale.

Highly regulated states may prohibit the sale of any processed food that lacks a label. Such states may also require a special license to repackage foods that have damaged packaging. For example, if a clerk cut the inner bag in a cereal box when he opened the case, an unlicensed store couldn't repackage the cereal and sell it for a reduced price. (Incidentally, as I noted in *The Tightwad Gazette II,* a spokesman for the National Food Processors Association stated that

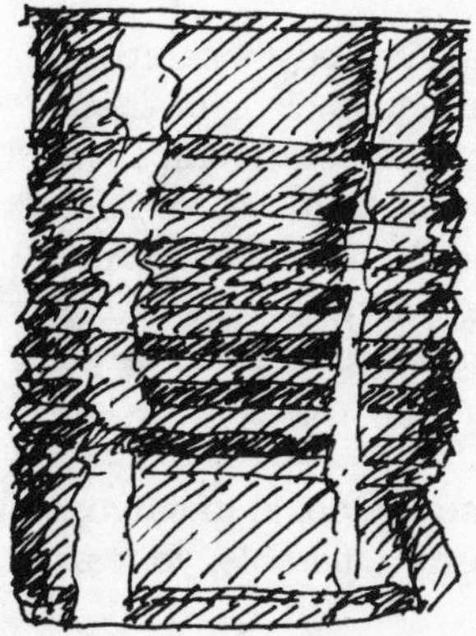

dented or rusty cans are safe as long as they don't leak or bulge.)

Oddly enough, even highly regulated states don't generally restrict the sale of outdated foods—that decision is made by individual stores. Consumers erroneously call the date on the packaging the "expiration date." Instead, this is a "recommended sell-by" date. While you probably wouldn't buy milk that's a week past the sell-by date, other products like canned goods and hard cheese would still be good beyond the date. Many foods that are outdated might be stale or have lost some nutritional content, but they aren't a health hazard.

With all this in mind, what might you find in an over-the-border salvage store?

Salvage stores specialize in damaged and discontinued items, such as cans battered in transit. The most remarkable deal we've found are "mystery cans." One store has a large bin of dented, unlabeled cans selling for 10¢ each, or $3 per box. Jim dropped the per-can cost to 5¢ by artfully fitting 60 cans in a box. The contents of the cans are guaranteed to be for human consumption; they are mostly vegetables and fruit.

We had only spotty success in determining the contents by comparing codes. So we just avoided small cans (less value) and large cans (probably pumpkin puree or tomato sauce, which our garden produces in quantity).

Mystery cans have become a major source of entertainment for our kids. They take turns choosing a can and guessing its contents. Once we open the cans, we plan meals to use them up, and this has resulted in some creative tightwad meals. On one occasion, we opened one can of baked beans and another of kidney beans. I combined these with some of our own leftover scratch baked beans and a few sliced hot dogs to create a tasty bean medley.

Aside from the cans, this store also sometimes sells cheese that's outdated by a few weeks. We've spent as little as 50¢ per pound for mozzarella and 75¢ per pound for cheddar. We found powdered milk at a $1-per-mixed-gallon price. A $1.39 bag of potato chips sells for 33¢. Oreo-like cookies sell for 50¢ a pound—the same cost as scratch cookies. We found good deals on canning supplies as well. While we can always find 33¢-per-pound spaghetti and macaroni in our area, other types of pasta cost more. This salvage store had a variety of cheap pasta—we even found lasagna noodles that weren't too badly broken.

Shopping in salvage stores is similar to other alternative strategies. You must:

- Bring your price book. Even in this good salvage store, most of the prices didn't beat other strategies.
- Look carefully at everything on the shelves. Salvage stores may have only a single unit of some products, like just one can of bug spray.
- If uncertain, buy a sample to test. We were suspicious of the freshness of the potato chips. We bought one bag, found the chips to be good, and then bought more.
- Even at salvage-store prices, nonnutritious foods should be purchased sparingly and hoarded as special treats.
- Because the deals in salvage stores are unpredictable, your sav-

ings will also be unpredictable. Go several times. Note the time and gas required for this out-of-the-way trip. Calculate your true savings as compared to other strategies. If the trip takes an hour and you save $20, you've netted a nice "hourly wage."

THE DRAPE ESCAPE

When poring over the Sears catalog in my quest for curtain ideas, I observed pages of "window treatments" featuring multiple layers of floral drapes, shades, and sheers, finished off with the latest styles of valances, ruffled swags, and tasseled tiebacks. You could easily spend $150 on one window. If you tried to duplicate this look for less by sewing the curtains yourself, it would still require lots of time, skill, and money.

So I turned to my stack of (trash-picked) *Country Living* magazines and found hope. Half of the windows featured had no curtains at all, and the rest had "minimalist" curtains. The simplicity appealed to me. Newsletter reader and interior decorator Sharon Cribbs of Jackson, South Carolina, expressed the same view. She wrote that most windows today are "overdressed" and suggested concentrating on simple treatments that use less fabric.

Whatever your taste, the first step in selecting a window treatment is to focus on your needs. Window treatments serve a variety of purposes. They hold in heat (only window quilts do this well), block out sunlight when we wish, provide privacy, and are decorative. Rather than spending your money satisfying a preconceived idea of what window treatments are supposed to look like, carefully assess your needs and preferences.

In our case, our home is secluded, so our privacy needs are minimal. I don't want to hide our nice woodwork, and to me curtains should be the background to our nice possessions, not the focal point of our rooms. I needed only ground-level privacy for one bedroom and a bathroom. So I sewed "café" curtains, which require little material or effort to make. I made these from white given-to-me sheets and hung them on trash-picked hardware; this window treatment was practically free.

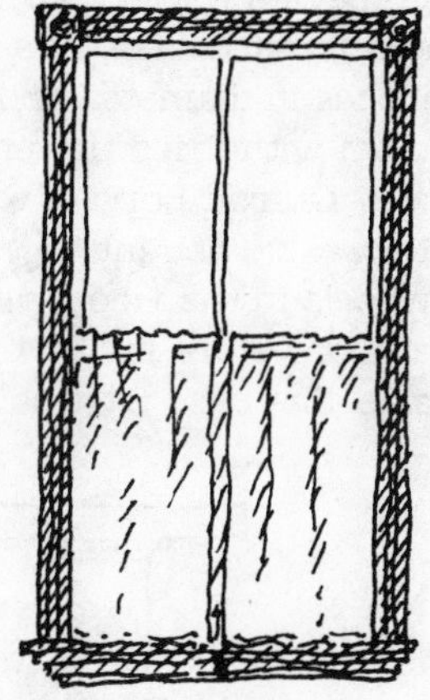

Readers who have greater needs for privacy and/or decoration have sent me a variety of ideas.

A decorative solution that uses little material is the "swag" style. It's simply a long piece of fabric that's draped over the window. The fabric is 18 inches or more wide, and the length, or the dis-

tance the swag hangs down, is optional. Swags are frequently combined with sheers or blinds and held by a bracket at each upper corner of the window. A pair of brackets typically costs $10 to $25. Readers offered cheaper hardware alternatives:

• Debra Meyers of Watertown, Connecticut, suggested draping the material over a nail and adding a grapevine wreath. These are easy and free to make. She made hers 7 inches in diameter and decorated them with dried flowers and ribbon.

• Lauren Bopp of Omaha, Nebraska, bought toy truck wooden wheels in the woodcraft section of a hobby store for 25¢ per pair on sale. She used 5¢ wooden spools

for spacers, and attached the spool/wheel combination to the window casing with a long screw. The wheel can be painted with wall or metallic paint, or stained. The cost per pair is 35¢.

• Jackie Stevens of Lake City, Florida, bought bicycle-storage hooks for $1.47 a pair. She wrapped the material around the hooks so they wouldn't show, and to create a pleasing effect.

• Merrilee Malcolm of Lawrenceville, Georgia, bought coat hooks for $2.50 a pair. She bunched the swag material and used rubber bands to make fabric "rosettes" to attach the swag to the hooks.

• Susan Abbott of Windsor, Connecticut, hammered a nail into the molding, leaving most of the nail showing. She bought inexpensive dime-store earrings, bent or removed the posts, and superglued the earrings to the nail heads.

Aside from alternative hardware, readers offered ideas for alternative fabrics:

• Julie Angotti of Madison, Wisconsin, pointed out that long cur-

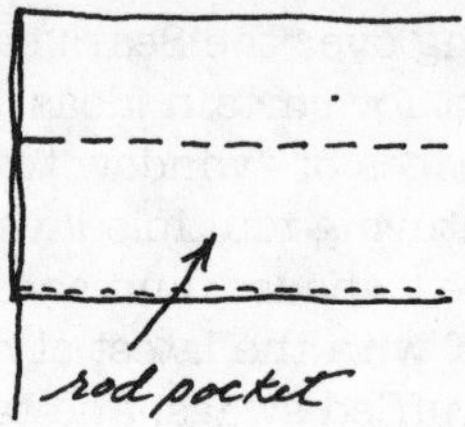

tains are easily made from twin sheets because the wide hem makes a handy rod pocket. You simply sew a straight seam through the center of this hem. Because you haven't cut them, they can be used as sheets in the future.

• Kim Connell of Yarmouth, Maine, suggested using either muslin or fabric from a mill store. One such store near me sells strips of sheet material that would be perfect for swags.

• Paula Martindale of Warner, New Hampshire, sent a magazine photo of a window decorated simply with a white, 48-inch square tablecloth

with decorative cutwork. This was hung over a rod and tacked on the inside of the window frame.

• Belinda Ford of Bad Kreuznach, Germany, says her husband

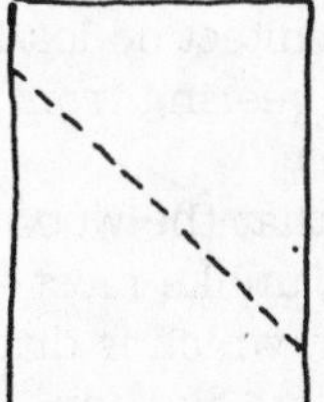

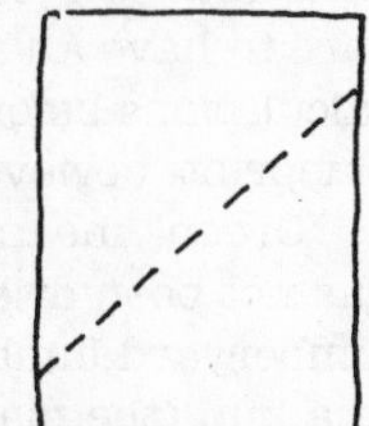

found dozens of discarded white tablecloths. She cut two cloths at an angle to make two pairs of diagonal curtains. She sponge-painted a border on these.

• A reader from Tucson, Arizona, sewed together small pieces of fabric to make curtains with a patchwork design.

• Earlene Giglierano of Iowa City, Iowa, suggested using cheesecloth, which is commonly available for 20¢ per yard. She saw this used in a magazine with lovely results.

Other readers offered these miscellaneous suggestions:

• Cindy Burns of Waco, Texas, duplicated the new, fashionable look of wide, expensive rods. She simply used her old thin rods and slipped a wide piece of poster board in the rod pocket.

• Mary Richardson of Saint Paul, Minnesota, needed miniblinds for her many odd-sized windows and found custom-made blinds were too expensive. She purchased standard-sized blinds at a discount store that were slightly wider than she needed. She cut a little off each side of the blinds, rounding the corners to make a "factory edge." Using a hacksaw, she cut the top rail and bottom bar. These came with caps that would cover the sawed edge. Each blind required one and a half hours to complete. Yard-sale blinds could be modified in the same way.

• An unusual privacy solution for a small window, such as in an entryway or bathroom, came from Denise Casey of Fayetteville, Georgia. She used Rubbermaid's clear contact paper to create a frosted look. Using a piece slightly larger than the window, she positioned the contact paper with a straight edge against the edge of the pane, smoothed it with a ruler wrapped in a washcloth, and cut the remaining three edges with an X-Acto knife. For this technique to look like real frosted glass, there should be no bubbles or uncovered glass showing around the edges.

One solution that no reader suggested is the un-curtain window treatment.

Sometimes instead of decorating with fabric, decorate with a collection of things. Most frequently people do this with hanging plants. Simple shelves attached to a window frame can hold your plants, colored bottles, or other collectibles.

WHERE THERE'S A MILL THERE'S A WAY

A growing worldwide demand for lumber combined with stricter environmental regulations has pushed lumber prices through the roof. Even here in Maine, where timber is abundant, lumberyards were recently selling an 8-foot spruce 2-by-4 for almost $4. Fortunately, there are alternatives.

Perhaps the best is getting rough-sawn, green lumber directly from a small sawmill. Patsy Hennin, founder of a house-building school called the Shelter Institute in Bath, Maine, says such lumber is from 15 to 50 percent cheaper than what's available at lumberyards, but Jim has realized larger savings. He bought 12-foot 2-by-12s from our local sawmill for $7.92 each. The best regular-lumberyard price was $17.39, so he saved 65 percent.

"Rough-sawn" means that the wood has simply been sawed—it has not subsequently been run through a planer, which makes wood smooth to the touch. As the name implies, it has a rough texture, but it is perfectly good for most applications. When we've used it for flooring, we've smoothed one side with a relative's planer.

Rough-sawn lumber can provide double savings. Not only is a rough-sawn 2-by-6 cheaper than a planed one, it is also larger, because it hasn't lost ½ inch in width and breadth to the planer. This means it may work in applications that call for a 2-by-8. (Be sure to have an architect do load calculations before veering from a blueprint, however.)

"Green" means that the wood has not been dried, unlike most lumberyard lumber, which is dried in a kiln (the marking "kd" on lumber stands for "kiln-dried"). Hennin notes that green wood is only half as strong as dried wood, but that the wood will dry on its own in from one month to one year, depending upon the climate. To air-dry it, it should be stacked under a cover with "stickers" (strips of wood about 1-inch square) between the pieces to allow air to circulate. As the wood dries, it will shrink about 3 percent in width, depending upon the type of wood.

While these independent sawmills are small, not all are rustic. An increasing number are computerized and can cut wood to extremely fine tolerances.

To find them, call your county extension agent for a list of small sawmills in the area. When you call the mills, in addition to asking about prices, be sure to ask about what is available—small sawmills often don't keep much stock on

hand. If the mill does not have what you need, it will have to be custom-cut.

For those who have their own trees, two other options deserve brief mention:

• Portable-sawmill operators will actually bring their rigs to your site, where they will fell, limb, drag, and cut your wood. These can be found in "shopper" type newspapers, the Yellow Pages, or by asking around at sawmills and lumberyards.

• For the ultimate do-it-yourselfer, there are "guide" attachments that convert a chain saw into a hand-held sawmill, allowing you to cut boards from logs. You'll find ads for these in woodworking and back-to-the-land magazines. The Shelter Institute has a subsidiary called Woodbutcher Tools, which sells two models: the Granburg Mini-Mill for $85, and the Haddon Lumbermaker for $63.50. For a free information sheet and list of shipping charges, contact:

Woodbutcher Tools
38 Center Street
Bath, ME 04530
(207) 442-7938

SAVE A WAD OF DOUGH

For his Sunday-morning birthday breakfast, Neal requested homemade doughnuts. So, Saturday night Jim whipped up a double batch of whole-wheat refrigerator dough. The next morning he made powdered-sugar and cinnamon-sugar doughnuts with some of the dough.

Sunday night Jim left town for two days, just as I was deathly ill with a cold. I didn't feel like cooking for my ravenous children, so Monday night I made tomato soup from tomato paste and milk (this quickie recipe appeared in *The Tightwad Gazette II*) and a dozen

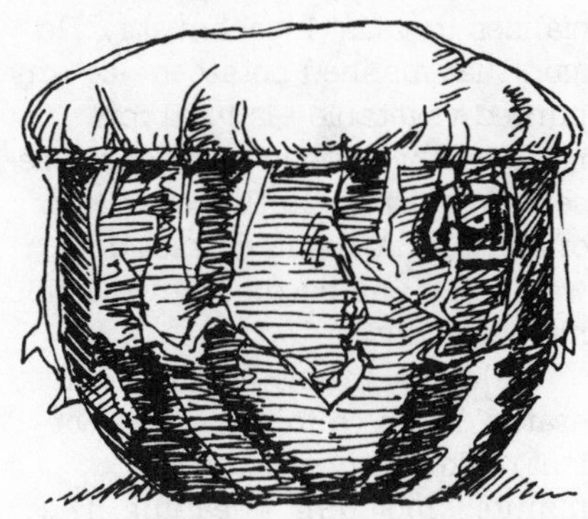

"cloverleaf" rolls from the same batch of dough. While I was at it, I rolled out and baked breadsticks for lunch boxes.

Thursday afternoon Jim used the remainder of the dough to make a dozen cinnamon rolls. Three of these went into lunch boxes the following Monday.

In short, refrigerator dough is extremely versatile and convenient. It's ideal for smaller families and for busy people who like fresh bread daily. You could make a large batch of dough on the weekend and use just a little at a time over the week.

The multipurpose refrigerator-dough recipe appears in all pre-1986 editions of *The Betty Crocker Cookbook.* (In some editions the recipe is called Potato Refrigerator Dough.) Jim has a version of the recipe that includes potato flakes.

Refrigerator dough includes mashed potatoes. To save time, Jim gets out potato flakes and other required ingredients to make 2 cups of mashed potatoes, then adds

the separate ingredients directly to the double batch of refrigerator dough.

What's the purpose of the mashed potatoes? We asked Lloyd M. Moxon, author of *The Baking Book* and a microbiologist who specializes in yeast biochemistry. He said that mashed potatoes—or any pureed vegetable—is vital for refrigerator doughs because it preserves moisture in the dry climate of a fridge. A regular yeast dough would dry and become unworkable more rapidly.

Making a double batch of refrigerator dough (a four-loaf equivalent) takes Jim exactly 19 minutes, including kneading. The dough is stored in a greased, covered bowl in the refrigerator. It's ready for use in eight hours, and lasts up to five days. (We've stretched this a few days and made sourdough-tasting rolls.)

The Betty Crocker Cookbook has directions for an amazing number of variations: brown-and-serve rolls, crescent rolls, pan biscuits, cloverleaf rolls, fantails, and Parker House rolls. Variations on other pages include raised doughnuts, hot-cross buns, and balloon buns. But this dough can be used in virtually any configuration, including braids, hamburger rolls, or sticks. It also makes a moist, heavy loaf suitable for toast and some types of sandwiches.

USED NEWS

Dear Amy,

We have many elderly people in our building who have difficulty disposing of their newspapers. A week's worth of papers is heavy, bulky, and hard for them to handle. We worked out a barter arrangement with our neighbor. She keeps her newspaper until she is finished with it—usually the day it is delivered. When she is done reading it, she brings it down the hall to us. We, in turn, get the complete newspaper for free. This saves us $13 a month.

—Sally Ennes
Independence, Missouri

HOW TO KNIT-PICK

Dear Amy,

I watch yard sales for buys on yarn. One problem with this yarn is that the label is usually missing, so you don't know if the yarn is wool or synthetic. A good way to test the yarn is this: Light the end of a piece of yarn with a match, then blow out the flame. If the residue is ashes, it's wool. If there is a little hard ball, it's synthetic.

This way you won't mix incompatible yarns when knitting afghans.

—Ann Zawistowski
Walpole, Massachusetts

KILL TWO BIRDIES . . .

Dear Amy,

The tightwad way to aerate your lawn: Wear your golf shoes while pushing your lawn mower. It works! I heard about this from a neighbor. I've tried it and it does open up the clay soil so the grass roots can grow and receive the water better.

—Jackie Steinberg
St. Peters, Missouri

LOW LIGHT

Dear Amy,

An inexpensive light box can be made this way: Obtain a piece of Plexiglas from your local hardware store. Remove one of the leaves from your dining room table and put the Plexiglas on top of the opening. Place a lamp (without the light shade) under the table.

—Maria Hester
Friendship, Maryland

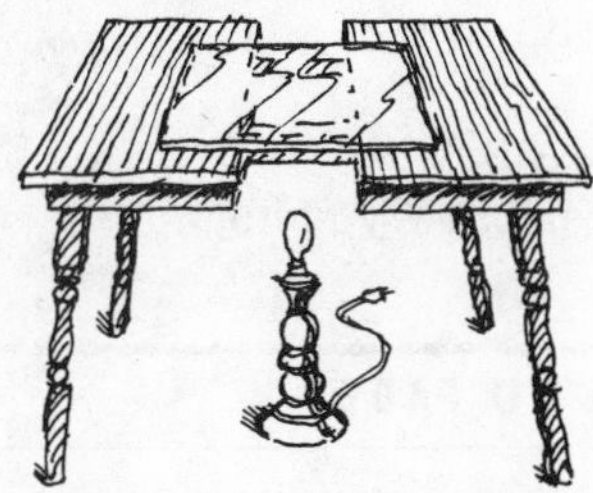

HAVE RUN, WILL RAVEL

Dear Amy,

A dab of nail polish stops runs in swimsuits. After about 25 wearings it might need to be reapplied, so check periodically.

—Debbi Heffern
St. Louis, Missouri

TYPO TIP

Dear Amy,

I use a Brother electronic typewriter and go through a lot of correction tape. During an idle moment, I tried to rewind the lift-off correction tape that I had just replaced on my typewriter. I noticed there was a lot of space left on the tape that could still be used for corrections. With a little patience, I rewound the tape and placed it in my typewriter. It works just fine the second time around. The tapes cost about $4.

—Laurie Spangler
Roanoke, Virginia

XEROCKS-BOTTOM PRICE

Dear Amy,

I need to make a lot of photocopies, and at 7¢ per copy (the cheapest price in our town) it was becoming very expensive. I found out that my copier store would charge me only 3¢ a copy if I bought my own paper. I was able to buy a 500-sheet package of Xerox paper from Wal-Mart for $3.48 plus tax. I figured that the copier store was charging me $20 for the same amount of paper. The people at the copier store were very nice. They loaded and unloaded my paper into the machine without complaint.

—Bonnie Andreani
Shawnee, Oklahoma

RETURN TO FENDER

Dear Amy,

While driving home from work one day this past winter, I failed to negotiate one of our infamous Rhode Island potholes. Needless to say, I lost one of my hubcaps. Upon doing some research, I found that new ones (plastic, no less) cost $90 each! Well, I had to buy it; then I got the idea to take off all my hubcaps, put my phone number and the word "reward" on the inside of each one, and put them

back on. Now if I lose another one, at least I'll provide the motivation for someone to return it for an amount far less than the $90 cost of a new hubcap.

—George Hadley
Lincoln, Rhode Island

GENIUS FLY TRAP

Dear Amy,

During canning season, I always get clouds of fruit flies in my house. I finally found the answer, thanks to the extension office's gardening expert. Take a plastic bag (a bread bag works great). Put banana peels, peach pits, rotten fruit, or whatever attracts fruit flies in the bag. Set it on the counter, wide open (cut the bag shorter if necessary). In a few hours, shut the bag with a twist-tie and throw it away. Repeat until the fruit flies are gone. Last fall I got rid of 99.9 percent of my fruit flies this way.

—Vicki Fisher
Clinton, Utah

SOAK AND SAVE

Dear Amy,

I love the stain-removal recipe (*The Tightwad Gazette I*) but I find the ingredients quite expensive to make each time I buy a garment at a yard sale for 25¢. To reduce the cost, I reuse the solution over and over. I keep it in a kettle in my cupboard, which enables me to reheat the solution on the stove.

—Donna Henderson
La Habra, California

SERIAL BOWL

Dear Amy,

My husband enjoys bowling through the winter months in our small town. We have found that for a small sign-up fee, he can bowl as a substitute almost every week. The regular for whom he is bowling is responsible for paying that night's fees. Also, this is a good time of the year to check with bowling alleys for used balls, bags, and even shoes. My husband brought home a used ball and bag for $15.

—Debra DeWitt
Edgerton, Wyoming

MADE TO FADE

Dear Amy,

I have found that if you add a squirt of dishwashing soap to the recipe for sidewalk chalk (in *The Tightwad Gazette II*), it cleans up more easily. This is important since we live in rental properties.

—Kym Reid-Reynoso
Boise, Idaho

NOT PALTRY POULTRY

Dear Amy,

The Hardee's in our area sells all its fried chicken for 25¢ per piece after 9 P.M. If you purchase only breast pieces, that's a pretty good deal. Sometimes my husband picks this up for his next day's lunch.

—Kristin McCoy
Mineral Point, Wisconsin

FOCUS BEFORE YOU FEAST

The diet-book author and the TV talk show host surveyed a banquet table of exquisitely prepared foods. The TV talk show host said that looking at the food made him hungry and he wanted to load his plate with some of everything.

The diet-book author, using this situation to demonstrate the premise of her book, had the TV talk show host do a mental exercise. She asked him to walk away from the table, close his eyes, and blank out the image of the banquet. Then she asked him to think about precisely what foods would satisfy him.

After a moment, the TV talk show host decided what he would like to eat. When he returned to the banquet table, the diet-book author instructed him to select the food he had imagined. From the vast bounty, the TV talk show host prepared a humble roast beef sandwich with mayonnaise and lettuce on a bulkie roll. Walking away from the remainder of the banquet, he began to eat his sandwich and admitted that it, alone, would satisfy him.

Had this diet-book author conducted the experiment with the studio audience, each individual would have selected different foods, or combinations of foods, and in different quantities.

The diet-book author's theory was that people often eat just because it's there. When we choose food this way, we will eat more, probably until we accidentally happen to consume the one item we really wanted in the first place. If, however, we can identify what food, and exactly how much of it, we need to feel satisfied, we will probably eat less.

The larger point is that, whether it is at the banquet table or the mall, you must decide what you want *first; then* look at the options. If you are confronted by options before you are firm about what you want, you'll be swayed.

As obvious as this sounds, a lot of people don't get it. In *Your Money or Your Life,* authors Joe Dominguez and Vicki Robin report that:

- 53 percent of groceries and 47 percent of hardware-store purchases are "spur of the moment" spending.
- When 34,300 shoppers in malls across the country were asked the primary reason for their visit, only 25 percent said they had come to look for a specific item.
- 70 percent of all adults visit a regional mall weekly.
- The number of U.S. shopping centers has grown from 2,000 in 1957 to more than 30,000 today. There are now more shopping malls than high schools.

Can you imagine what would

happen if all of these shopping-addicted adults blindly approached that banquet table and ate the same way they shop? It would be a carnage of Jell-O, taco chips, deviled eggs, potato salad, cheese dip, and those funny triangle things on the ends of toothpicks.

All of this points up the fact that there are two sides to frugality:

The glamorous side is the innovative and interesting strategies to get more for your dollars. Virtually everyone, including spendthrifts, is interested in getting more stuff for less money. They want to know how they can gorge at the banquet just as they've always done, but for, say, 50 percent of the money. Because there are hundreds, even thousands of such strategies, I tend to focus on these in the *Gazette.*

But the other side is about wanting and buying less. This unmagical aspect often disappoints people. They balk when they realize that achieving the lowest budget means they might also have to do without soda, designer suits, and first-run movies.

They need to understand that sometimes they're buying/eating just because it's there, not because they've determined it will bring sufficient satisfaction.

If people approach the banquet table with a clear vision of what they want, they will likely eat less and still feel quite satisfied, if not more satisfied.

Both aspects of frugality are important. If you buy something for half price and buy half as much, you've spent only 25 percent as much as the person who doesn't use either strategy.

SLACKS AX TAX

Anna L. Meenan of Cherry Valley, Illinois, wrote to say that for upper-income tightwads, donating used items to a charity to get the tax deduction will probably net a greater return than selling them at a yard sale.

To check this out, we called Barbara Shuckra, a public-affairs officer for the IRS, and Captain William Greenaway, administrator of the Salvation Army store in Portland, Maine. I also talked to John O'Malley, the CPA and tax consultant for our business, and Stephen DeFilippis, a member of the board of directors of the National Association of Enrolled Agents.

For this strategy to work for you, you must itemize your deductions and, as with any deduction strategy, your total deductions must exceed the standard deduction for you to save any money.

If you do itemize, obtain a list of the value of various items from your local nonprofit thrift shop (the shop to which you donate *must* have nonprofit status). Salvation Army stores will give you an IRS-approved document that lists the "high" and "low" thrift-shop prices for various types of clothing.

These amounts serve as your guideline for what you can deduct. Use them to determine if you could save more by donating to the shop, or by selling clothing at yard sales and consignment shops. For example: You can deduct between $15 and $60 for donating a man's suit. To be safe in the event of an audit, Shuckra suggest choosing a value in the middle. If you're in the 28-percent bracket and figure the suit's value is $35, donating it will

save $9.80 in taxes. If you are in the 15-percent bracket, it will save $5.25.

Even if you determine that consignment shops or yard sales will yield more, unsold clothing can still be donated. This is a good strategy if you lack storage space to stockpile yard-sale goods, or don't have the time or a good location in which to hold a yard sale.

O'Malley reminded me that there are some catches to this strategy. If your income is very high, you begin to lose deductions. In 1994, a couple filing jointly with an income over $111,800 would not get the total benefit of the deduction for the suit.

DeFilippis pointed out that if your noncash contributions exceed $500, you have to list your contributions on IRS Form 8283 and include it with your tax return. You need not list every pair of socks—"men's clothing" is sufficient—but you should have a list of every item in your files. He even recommends taking and filing a photo of your donated clothes.

You must have a receipt for deductible charitable contributions over $200, so be sure to get one when you drop stuff off. This receipt should list each item, although the thrift shop won't assign a value to the items; that's your job.

Finally, while I think this is a useful idea, keep in mind that you can often get the best value from your stuff by giving it to friends and relatives. Because what goes around comes around, giving things away ensures a steady stream of incoming clothes and favors. This is also the least time-consuming method, since buying and selling or donating (and getting the tax deduction) require time. Giving and receiving don't.

CRACKING THE DRESS CODE

The dress code here at *The Tightwad Gazette* is pretty lax—we all generally dress as if it's a day off. But having labored in the trenches of corporate America, I know that it can be challenging, and expensive, to dress up every day.

Some women, particularly those in urban areas, have written to me that they have had excellent luck getting top-quality business clothing at yard sales, thrift shops, and consignment shops. Because I'm tall and live in a rural area, I haven't been so lucky. After years of searching for outfits that I could use for speeches and book tours, I finally gave up and bought a $49, medium-quality suit at a discount store.

My need for business clothes is so minimal that I can get by with my Spartan wardrobe, but I know

my one-suit strategy won't work for most businesswomen. So here's a plan sent in by Patty Paulman of Randolph, New Jersey, for getting a month's worth of different business outfits at minimal cost.

Start with these nine pieces: two blazers, three tops, and four bottoms. Make sure that the blazers and bottoms all coordinate. This is easier if you choose solid colors and limit the number of patterns.

For example, Patty has a black blazer and a black-and-white checked blazer that match various shirts and slacks. The tops are blouses, sweaters, shirts, and T-shirts.

These combine as follows to make 24 different combinations:

Blazer #	1	1	1	1	1	1	1	1	1	1	1	1	2	2	2	2	2	2	2	2	2	2	2	2
Top #	1	1	1	1	2	2	2	2	3	3	3	3	1	1	1	1	2	2	2	2	3	3	3	3
Bottom #	1	2	3	4	1	2	3	4	1	2	3	4	1	2	3	4	1	2	3	4	1	2	3	4

WILL A DISHWASHER SAVE MONEY?

Calina Clarkson of Colorado Springs, Colorado, writes that she is curious about the cost of using a dishwasher versus washing dishes by hand.

I've known people who have purchased a dishwasher specifically because they believed that it would pay for itself in hot-water savings. This idea is supported by some consumer articles that have vaguely suggested a dishwasher will save you money. But these articles presumed that when hand-washing you rinse dishes under a running faucet, and they didn't factor in the cost of buying and maintaining a dishwasher. In fact, whether you would save depends on many variables. Let's use my situation as an example.

Most energy-efficient dishwashers use between 8 gallons (for china) and 14 gallons (for pots and pans) of water per cycle. I wash dishes by hand and rinse them in a dishpan. I use about 5 gallons for the breakfast dishes and about 7 gallons for the evening dishes (including all dishes accumulated after breakfast). If we used a dishwasher, we would run at least two loads per day and so would use about 6 more gallons of hot water per day.

The three energy experts I called agreed that the average cost of electrically heated hot water is about 1¢ per gallon at 8¢ per kilowatt-hour. (About 1¢ worth of natural gas will heat 5 gallons of water.) With our latest rate increase, we now pay 14.6¢ per kilowatt-hour, including tax. We have a well, so we don't have a water bill. So the extra hot water would cost us 11¢ per day.

In addition to the extra hot water, the energy to run the dishwasher could be another 4¢ or 8¢ for two loads.

We use $1.50 worth of liquid dishwashing detergent each month, or about 5¢ worth each day. A staffer says he needs to use 2 tablespoons of cheapo dishwasher detergent to ensure clean dishes; this amount costs 3.5¢ or 7¢ for two loads. So dishwasher detergent would cost me an additional 2¢ per day.

Various manufacturers and trade associations say that the average life span of a dishwasher is 11.5 years. The first repair averages at 8 years and costs $60. This means the purchase and mainte-

nance costs of a $400 dishwasher averages $40 per year.

So, in my case the extra cost of buying, maintaining, and using a dishwasher versus washing by hand would be $116.75 annually.

Compared to a frugal wash-by-hand method, a dishwasher doesn't save money. But does it save time? I believe so, but the amount is highly variable.

In some households, the cleanliness standard dictates that dishes must be clean enough to hold surgical tools, so when hand-washing, each item must be laboriously scrubbed and then rinsed under running water.

In my home, the standard is that dishes must not have visible food particles or be greasy. Thus we employ the speedier "dish-swishing" technique for washing and rinsing.

To determine how much time we would save with a dishwasher, I did all other related dishwashing activities first—putting away leftovers, washing countertops, scraping dishes, etc. After I assembled all of the dishes in one place, I timed how long the washing required. I repeated this experiment several times. I found that my actual dishwashing time was about one third to one half of the total after-meal cleanup—less than 30 minutes total each day for two washings. (Smaller families would use far less time.)

Because a dishwasher does save time, then it could, indirectly, save money. If I spend an extra 182½ hours per year hand-washing dishes and save $116.75, then my "hourly wage" would be about 64¢. Because there are other tightwad tasks that "pay" better, a dishwasher can be justified as a frugal purchase only if you are diligent about using the time you save profitably, not if you would use this time to watch a little TV.

Another point to consider is that dishwashers take up space enough to store a few 50-pound sacks of oatmeal. It seems to me that the same people who say they don't have enough time to be frugal also say they don't have enough space.

Some people think that because a dishwasher uses hotter water it kills more germs, so they will save money on their medical bills. A spokesman for the Centers for Disease Control said this was an improbable leap of logic. Germs are *far* more likely to be spread through the air or through hand-to-hand contact than by less-clean dishes. (I later theorized that since washing by hand also results in cleaner hands, this might offset the germ-killing benefits of hotter dishwasher water.)

Jim and I aren't planning to get a dishwasher. We don't mind washing dishes, partly because we use the time to watch the news on our small kitchen TV.

And within a couple of years the kids will assume this job. But my primary reason has more to do with aesthetics than frugality. I prefer not to put another modern appliance in my old-fashioned kitchen.

In short, if you already have a dishwasher, I won't discourage you from using it. If you don't have one, you should consider the variables in your situation carefully before getting one.

AVOID DEPTH CHARGES

Dear Amy,

To help stop water waste, I put a small piece of electrical tape on the bathtub to mark an appropriate water level for each child. Older ones get higher levels.

—Carla Matthews
Emmett, Idaho

NO-SPENDING CAP

Dear Amy,

I lost the gas cap off of my car. The next time I was at the gas station I asked if they had gas caps for sale. The clerk brought out a box of forgotten caps and let me choose one to fit my car for free. There was a large selection. I felt that I had donated mine to someone else, so I was happy to take him up on the offer.

—Dee Ann Dorman
Brookfield, Wisconsin

BUDGET BUMPER

Dear Amy,

I bought my daughter a used bicycle. It had a high bar between the handlebars. I was afraid she might fall and hurt herself. My husband suggested I get some pipe-insulation foam, which costs $2 for a big package. It was split along the side so we just had to cut the length. A friend saw it and said she paid a lot more for something very similar at the bike shop.

—Denita Bradley
Knoxville, Tennessee

MUSICAL SCORE

Dear Amy,

I decided at the beginning of November that I wanted an upright, second-loved piano for Christmas. I told everyone I knew that I was looking for one, that I had a very limited budget ($100), and, most important, that I would move it. I actually found *two* free pianos! One was in rough shape, but the other was in very good con-

dition and needed only a few repairs. After a week of coordinating the truck and the muscle, we moved it on New Year's Day. I am now negotiating with the piano tuner and repair guy to bring the cost within my $100 budget. So tell your readers to ask everyone they know if they're looking for something. You will never know what's out there if you don't ask.

—Carole Normandin
Gardner, Massachusetts

SWINGING WITH THE REIN

Dear Amy,

Here's a fun idea our kids love! Save an old horse from the spring-mounted-horse riding toy. Get some rope and string it from a tree branch. Makes a fun swing and extends the life of the toy. If the horse is plastic, make sure it is not cracking.

—M. L. Carson
Gainesville, Florida

I CAN DIG IT

Dear Amy,

We recently had our septic tank pumped and were charged $90 for the pumping and $30 to locate it and dig the dirt off the lid. They told us that next time we can do the digging ourselves (since we now know the location) and save ourselves $30. When buying a house, it would be worth asking where it is.

—Celia Byrnes
Crawfordsville, Indiana

FILL, FREEZE, AND FIT

Dear Amy,

A man the same size as my husband gave Bobby a pair of new boots. Bobby didn't wear them often until he got a new position at his job and had to dress up. One boot was a little too tight. Another man at his job gave him the solution: Put a garbage bag in the boot, fill the bag with water, and freeze. It worked. It stretched the boot just enough to fit comfortably.

—Cindy Burns
Waco, Texas

BOARD OF EDUCATION

Dear Amy,

My twin girls love to play school. For their ninth birthday they wanted a larger (classroom-sized) chalkboard. We found that they were outrageously expensive. My husband bought a sheet of plywood and some chalkboard paint at the hardware store for about $20. The same size chalkboard would have been about $200 if we had bought one. It hangs on the wall in their playroom and playing school is so much fun now!

—Beth Cape
Royston, Georgia

NOT STIFFED ON STARCH

Dear Amy,

My husband likes all of his shirts heavily starched. Instead of using the spray cans of starch, which cost 87¢ for 22 ounces, I mix 4 tablespoons of powdered

starch with 4 cups of hot water. Using a good spray bottle, I spray on the starch (shaking it often) and iron the garment as usual. One can of store-bought starch costs 87¢. An equivalent amount of homemade starch-spray costs 10¢.

—Pam Hoyer
Warrensburg, Missouri

BEAMPOLES

Dear Amy,

My neighbor built a pole barn out of used utility poles. Our local electric company gives the poles away for a onetime charge of $1. You must sign a contract that you won't hold them responsible for any damage, etc. The poles can also be used for landscaping and other uses.

—Mike and Cathy McDermott
Kokomo, Indiana

FLAPJACK SNACK

Dear Amy,

Kids love PPRs (Peanut-butter Pancake Roll-ups). I take pancakes left over from breakfast, spread them with peanut butter and a little honey, roll them up, and cut them in half. They stick together pretty well—good use for extra pancakes.

—Rose Sabel-Dodge
Portland, Oregon

HOW MUCH DOES IT REALLY COST TO RAISE A CHILD?

Now and then, in the midst of the daily mix of murders, muggings, and plane crashes, the newspapers run a story that's *really* scary. It's the latest government report on the cost of raising an American child.

A newsletter reader from Boca Raton, Florida, sent me an article from the April 1, 1994, issue of *The Wall Street Journal.* It says the U.S. Department of Agriculture determined that "the typical baby born to affluent parents in 1993 could cost as much as $334,600 to raise to age 18." The reader asked, "Are these costs real?"

To learn more, we called Mark Lino, the USDA economist who computes these numbers. He said that the figure cited in the *WSJ* is the maximum amount spent by the most affluent families, and that it assumes 6 percent annual inflation for the next 18 years. In other words, it's the USDA's highest kid-cost figure.

He went on to explain that the USDA bases its numbers on a survey of the spending habits of 20,000 families. He said all of its figures are based on the cost of raising the second of two children. And he said "to age 18" means from birth until the day before the child's 18th birthday, so it does not include prenatal or college expenses.

He also gave us a figure for a family-income range that is more typical of *Tightwad Gazette* readers and it was almost as scary as the "affluent parents" figure. He said it will cost families with taxable incomes of from $32,000 to $54,100 an average of $132,660, in 1993 dollars, to raise a child born in 1993. Add 6 percent inflation and the total rises to $231,140.

Each year we are both terrified and mystified by these USDA numbers, so I decided to dig into this further. I found that the USDA computes some of its numbers in a unique way that may not really reflect the cost of an extra child. Further, I found that when you consider the spending habits of a tightwad family, it's possible to come up with a dramatically lower number.

I want to make it clear that I am not coming up with an alternative number to refute the USDA number. All situations are different, and unlike the USDA, I can't do a detailed survey of the spending habits of 20,000 tightwad families. All I hope to show is that it is possible to raise a kid for much less than the USDA number would have us believe.

I'll use the real-life "Smith" family for my example. They are frugal friends of mine who already have one child, an eight-year-old son.

Kids cost more as they get older. According to the USDA's figures, the amount spent during a child's eighth year approximately represents the average cost per year over 18 years. So what the Smiths spend on their son now can provide clues about how much they would spend on another child.

The USDA figures costs in the following categories:

- Housing. The USDA figures per-kid housing costs by dividing the family's average monthly housing costs by the number of people in the family. A different, and perhaps more realistic, way to compute this number would be to determine how much housing costs would increase with an additional child. The Smiths already bought a three-bedroom ranch house with a yard because they didn't want to raise their son in an apartment. Based on other families in their neighborhood who live in homes of the same exact layout, the Smiths know they could raise three children in their 1,000-square-foot home. So their extra-child cost would be only for yard-sale furniture and utilities. This could easily be as little as $50 annually.
- Transportation. The USDA estimates that 40 percent of a family's transportation costs are work related. So they divide the remaining 60 percent by the number of people in the family to arrive at the per-kid transportation cost.

But the Smiths already have two cars, and each has a backseat, so an extra kid's transportation expenses would be zero when he accompanied the parents on family outings. Naturally, the Smiths

would make some special trips to shuttle the new kid around to doctors, schools, sports, etc. Annually this might cost an extra $50 in gas and maintenance.

Once every three years the Smiths take a plane trip to visit relatives. A ticket costs $400, so the annual average for the new child's ticket would be $133.

Transportation total: $183 annually.

• Food. The USDA says it costs an average of $1,316 to feed a kid annually, ranging from $870 for a 1-year-old to $1,750 for a 17-year-old.

Using the USDA chart on page 127, the Smiths determined that they can feed their family for 62 percent of the "thrifty" plan. This means the Smiths now feed their eight-year-old for $567 a year, so this would also be the annual average for the second child.

• Clothing. The USDA says this average annual cost is $603, ranging from $450 for a 1-year-old to $850 for a 17-year-old.

Through yard-saling, clothes-swapping, and other strategies, the Smiths spent $40 this year to dress their eight-year-old.

Some people claim that it's impossible to find good teenager clothing at yard sales, but I haven't found that to be the case. My 13-year-old Alec is a big kid, and I have had good luck stockpiling 25¢-per-item teen-sized clothing for him to wear in three or four years. The adult Smiths spend less than $50 apiece annually for clothing, and there is no reason that a teenaged Smith would cost more. So we'll put the annual clothing budget at $50. If, as teens, the Smiths' kids want something fancier, they will have to earn the money themselves.

• Health care. The USDA pegs this number at $470 annually, which covers the portion of insurance paid for by parents and any out-of-pocket costs for medical and dental bills. We accept this number as reasonable; indeed, this is one area in which people usually don't waste huge amounts of money.

• Child care and education. The USDA says this cost is $545 per year. As a result of making frugal choices and some creative job juggling, the Smiths have always had one parent at home. Thus they have never and would never pay for child care. Their son is in public school, as their next child would be. While the Smiths' son did go to a private nursery school, they probably would not do this again with another child.

As kids get older they need to buy school supplies or may want special lessons. So we'll estimate these costs to average $100 per year.

• Miscellaneous. Entertainment, personal care (such as haircuts and toothpaste), and school activity fees are all extremely variable. The USDA figures this to amount to $761 per year. The Smiths cut their son's hair. They spend less than $40 per year on presents, and $50 per year on entertainment for their son. Throw in some toothpaste, soap, laundry detergent, Q-Tips, etc. and the annual total is $110. Let's be generous and assume there is $60 worth of stuff we can't track down—we'll call the total $170.

So the average annual cost of raising this younger of two tightwad children would be $1,590. But

one factor that the USDA did not consider was the dependent income-tax exemption, which was $2,350 in 1993. The Smiths are in the 28 percent tax bracket, so their new kid would save them $658 annually in taxes, bringing the net cost to $932. Multiplied by 18 years, the cost is $16,776. Assuming 6 percent inflation, the total becomes $28,682, or about 12 percent of the USDA figure.

When looking at your own situation, you may find that our estimates are lower than yours. The point is that, at 12 percent of the USDA figure, even if we have forgotten some expenses and underestimated by a huge 100 percent, raising this second kid would still cost far less than what the USDA estimate indicates.

I'm not necessarily recommending that all of my readers rush off and produce another kid, but whenever one contemplates such a major step, it's handy to have accurate information.

TREND REVERSAL?

I get a great deal of mail, mostly from women, telling me that by applying the lessons of the newsletter they have been able to achieve their goal of quitting their jobs and staying home with the kids.

It turns out that these women are part of a nationwide trend. According to a study by Richard Hokenson, chief economist for the Wall Street brokerage firm of Donaldson, Lufkin and Jenrette, the percentage of women under age 30 in the workforce peaked in 1989 at 75 percent, after years of marching steadily upward. By early 1992 it had dropped to 71 percent. Since then it has crept back up to 72 percent, but Hokenson says indicators are that the long-term trend will continue downward.

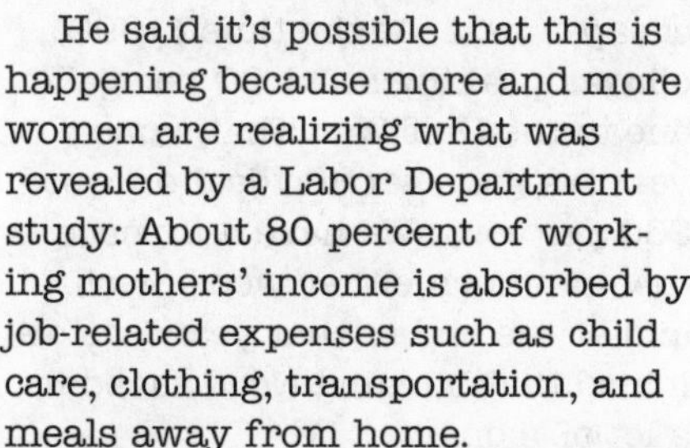

"Honey, I'm home... for good!"

He said it's possible that this is happening because more and more women are realizing what was revealed by a Labor Department study: About 80 percent of working mothers' income is absorbed by job-related expenses such as child care, clothing, transportation, and meals away from home.

This return-home trend explains an economic puzzle: Why didn't lower interest rates boost housing sales? Hokenson says it's because families didn't move. Instead they refinanced and used the money they saved to allow Mom to stay home with the kids.

It has never been my position that all moms should stay home, but I do feel that one of the great values of frugality is that it can allow moms—or dads—who want to stay home with the kids to do so. I asked Hokenson if he had any figures regarding whether more fathers are leaving the workforce and minding the kids, but he said he has no data on that.

LEARN BEFORE YOU BURN

In *The Tightwad Gazette* I wrote an article about how to compute whether wood or oil provides cheaper heat. At the time (1990), oil was peaking at $1.20 per gallon due to the Gulf War. That same year we got a terrific deal on wood: $60 per cord. We have a furnace that can burn either wood or oil, and at the end of that year I determined that burning wood saved us a lot of money.

But last fall Jim and I spent part of a weekend stacking maple firewood in our cellar. As I did this, I had time to wonder whether this wood, which cost $80 per cord, would provide cheaper heat than oil, which last year averaged 75¢ per gallon. The potential savings in the heating season ahead were not nearly so obvious as they were in 1990.

To help me fine-tune my ability to choose one or the other, I needed to know, precisely, the heating value of the maple. By making phone calls and going to the library, I was able to locate no fewer than eight different charts that listed the heating value of different species of wood. They agreed 100 percent on the "rank" of the wood species. Maple, for example, has more heat value than elm, which has more than pine. But they disagreed by as much as 25 percent about just what the heat value of a single species is. A cord of maple, for example, was listed as having the same heat value as between 132 and 188 gallons of oil. This difference would be enough to throw off any analysis.

As I investigated further, it appeared that the high figures represented oven-dried wood with a zero water content and the low figures represented air-dried wood with a 20 percent water content. I called Andrew J. Baker, a chemical engineer with the U.S. Forest Service's Forest Products Laboratory in Madison, Wisconsin, and he said that firewood stored under cover for a year generally dries to the 12 percent to 20 percent moisture range. He said you can tell if it has achieved this level by checking the ends—they should be cracked.

So, assuming that you are a true tightwad and you have taken care to let your wood season properly, here is the list of gallons-of-oil equivalences per cord that appears to be the most relevant. It is from the U.S. Department of Agriculture and assumes a 12 percent moisture content. In cases where there are several varieties within the

species (such as black oak, scarlet oak, water oak, etc.), this list shows the average of that species:

alder—125	hickory—206
ash—171	magnolia—149
aspen—117	maple—164
basswood—113	oak—202
beech—195	pine—142
birch—190	redwood—114
butternut—116	sassafras—140
cedar—116	spruce—119
cherry—152	sweetgum—158
cottonwood—111	sycamore—149
Douglas fir—146	tamarack—161
elm—152	tupelo—152
fir—115	walnut—168
hemlock—139	willow—118

Multiply these figures by 173.41 to get the equivalence in cubic feet of natural gas.

Basing my calculations on maple's 164-gallon equivalence, we would have to buy $123 in oil (75¢ × 164) to get the same heat we'd get from a cord of the wood. That seems to indicate that, at $80 a cord, maple is a good deal.

But it might not be for you. A final calculation has to be made based on the efficiency of your oil or gas furnace versus the efficiency of your woodstove.

According to the manufacturer, both wood and oil burn at the same level of efficiency in our furnace, so we can do a straight comparison like the one above.

But the efficiency of woodstoves ranges from just 20 percent for old Franklin types to over 75 percent for modern, airtight versions with catalytic combusters. Depending upon age, technology, and upkeep, the efficiency of oil furnaces ranges from 60 percent to about 82 percent; for gas, from 65 percent to over 95 percent.

If you don't know the efficiency of your stove or furnace, contact the manufacturer. Then determine the difference in their efficiencies and use that to calculate the actual difference in cost.

For example, supposing I have, as in the above example, determined that I would have to buy $123 in oil to equal $80 in wood. If I have an old oil furnace that is 65 percent efficient, and a new, high-tech woodstove that is 75 percent efficient, the 15 percent greater efficiency of the woodstove means that, for purposes of comparison, I can subtract 15 percent from the price of the wood. Wood, then, actually costs $68 per cord. Wood becomes an even better deal than my original calculation indicated.

As with all energy questions, there are, of course, other variables. Nadav Maline, managing editor of *Environmental Building News* in Brattleboro, Vermont, told me that if the ductwork of your furnace is leaky, or is uninsulated and runs through a cold space, your furnace may be far less efficient than its rating indicates.

Also, I have noticed an interesting behavioral effect of woodstoves. They tend to draw people away from cold parts of the house and toward the stove itself. So a woodstove does not necessarily have to crank out the same number of Btu's as a whole-house furnace to keep your family warm.

The bottom line is that it's a mistake to assume—as many people do—that wood is always a cheaper source of heat. While wood can be a good deal, you won't know for certain until you calculate all of the variables in your particular situation.

NO-GAIN OCTANE

Lisa Demick of Dublin, Ohio, asks, "How does one figure out which gasoline is the best deal? Is it ever an advantage to spend more for the higher octane?"

There is a "you-get-what-you-pay-for" notion that the more expensive "premium" gas will improve your mileage, give your car more power, and/or be better for your engine, so the extra expense is worth it.

Consumers haven't acquired this idea by accident. The ads of many oil companies have implied this. In fact, in 1992, Public Citizen, a consumer advocacy group founded by Ralph Nader, awarded Amoco the Harlon Page Hubbard Lemon Award, which is its award for the most misleading ad of the year. This ad suggested that cars with over 15,000 miles on the odometer—which includes most cars that are over a year old—could benefit from higher-octane gas, though automakers dispute this claim for all but a very few models. According to Public Citizen, the Federal Trade Commission cited Sunoco with making similar misrepresentations about higher-octane gas.

For the real story, I talked with David Solomon, editor of the *Nutz and Boltz* automotive newsletter, and William Berman, national environmental director for the American Automobile Association, and I did some library research.

First of all, Solomon and Berman said that higher-octane gasoline has no more power than low-octane gas. Higher-octane gas simply ignites less readily than the low-octane kind.

High-octane gas is needed in some kinds of engines. In these engines, the cylinders compress the fuel/air mixture so much that the resulting heat (pressure makes heat) can make the mixture explode prematurely—before the spark plug has a chance to ignite it. This premature ignition is "knocking" and it sounds like little metal balls rattling around inside your engine. It also means lost power, bad mileage, and, in some severe cases, engine damage. High-octane gas resists exploding prematurely.

But the chance that your car truly needs it is slim. Only 10 percent of the cars on the road were manufactured to require an octane that's higher than regular unleaded, which is 87 octane. Berman said that 20 percent of the gas sold in the United States is premium grade, so many drivers may be buying premium unnecessarily. That, according to Public Citizen, translates to about $3 billion in waste, or $95 wasted per vehicle per year.

Generally you should use a higher-octane gasoline only if your owner's manual specifies it.

There are also some rare cases in which cars begin to knock persistently and need higher-octane fuels as they age. But before you treat the symptom, try to cure the disease. Knocking can be due to a correctable carbon buildup. Solomon suggests trying a gas additive that can strip away carbon. He likes Redline SI One. Berman said several gasolines, notably Texaco's System 3, claim cleaning abilities, so you might try one of these.

If this doesn't work, try a tune-up. The average motorist uses 560 gallons of gas a year. If a $65 tune-up gives you the ability to run on regular, you will save about $112 on gas, for a total savings of about $47.

Berman believes that these steps will almost certainly solve any knocking problem, but if it persists, consult a mechanic.

If your car doesn't require high-octane gas, using it will not improve your mileage. In fact, it can actually *decrease* engine performance. GM Research and Development Center researchers say many premium gasolines are refined from lower-volatility (less readily combustible) feedstocks. The average car can't vaporize these heavier gas grades. They simply push the unburned gas out into the exhaust, wasting it and increasing emissions. This causes poor combustion, stalling, and hesitation. If you remain unconvinced, simply try filling up with various grades of gas and then calculate your miles per dollar.

One final consideration: Even if you're paying for high-octane gas, you may not be getting it. Berman said that, according to a government survey, when you get gas from a pump marked "premium," there's a 10 percent chance you're getting a lower grade. Some states now test octane levels; others have "hit-or-miss" programs; and a few have no regulations or testing regarding octane levels. "When you buy premium in those states, you have no idea what you are getting," Berman said.

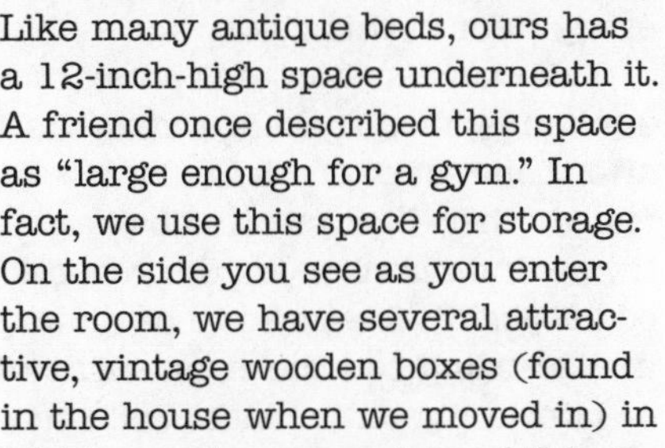

A TIME-SAVER OF SORTS

Like many antique beds, ours has a 12-inch-high space underneath it. A friend once described this space as "large enough for a gym." In fact, we use this space for storage. On the side you see as you enter the room, we have several attractive, vintage wooden boxes (found in the house when we moved in) in which we store a variety of things.

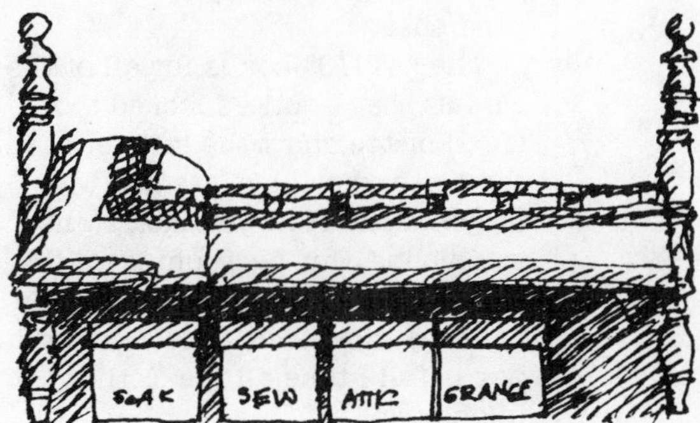

On the side you don't see, we have my time-saver four-box clothing-aid system. These four lidded cardboard boxes, marked "SOAK," "SEW," "ATTIC," and "GRANGE," are here because I sort the family's laundry on our bed and they serve as temporary storage for clothes that shouldn't go back into drawers and closets.

The "SOAK" box is for clothes that need to be soaked in the Clorox II/Cascade stain remedy given in the first *Tightwad Gazette* book. When this box is half-full of stained clothes, I know I have enough to make it worthwhile to mix up a batch of the stain recipe.

The "SEW" box is for any clothes that need mending. Once every couple of months, a rare intersection of two moods occurs: 1) I'm at a loss for something to do, and 2) I feel an urge to be pro-

ductive. When this happens I have a sewing afternoon and repair every item in this box.

This box also contains a bag of our unmatched socks. I sort socks after the rest of the laundry is folded. Then I get out this bag and try to find matches for the recently odd socks. I've learned to be slow in discarding odd socks, as sooner or later a match for most will turn up. (A sock can be lost for years if accidentally folded up in a seldom-used sheet.)

The "ATTIC" box is for all of the clothes that I noticed looked too small or too short the last time they were worn but are still too large for the next younger, same-sex sibling. Our bedroom is on the first floor and my clothing storage is in the third-floor attic. When this box is full I take all the clothes up in one trip.

The "GRANGE" box is for all the clothes outgrown by my youngest children and the adult-sized clothes we don't want to keep. I donate these to our church's thrift shop, which is run out of our town's grange hall. I'm happy to do this because we buy some clothes at the grange. When this box is full, I put it in the car to be dropped off on our next trip by. Before we moved to Leeds, this box was labeled "YARD SALE," and full boxes went into the garage, where we kept items to be sold at our next yard sale.

By putting the clothes into these four boxes as I sort laundry, I am assured that the clothing in my children's drawers is mended, has no stains, and is the correct size.

A FLUFFY FILLER ARTICLE

Jim and I each brought a pillow to our marriage. As our family grew, we acquired additional bedding from yard sales and older relatives who were breaking up households. But we've never seen pillows at yard sales or been able to get them from other cheap sources.

Which is too bad, because pillows are surprisingly expensive—from about $10 to $60 retail. We've reluctantly bought cheapo pillows for about $5 at a salvage store as we have needed more. Thus we've always had exactly enough pillows, unless company visits.

During one winter's flu season, then-two-year-old Brad got sick on an old fiberfill pillow. When I washed it, it came out in a trapezoidal lump. When I tried to pull it back into a rectangle, the casing material ripped.

After several months of making up Brad's bed with this mutant pillow, inspiration struck. I ripped it open, removed the fiberfill, and discarded the old casing. I shredded the fiberfill into marshmallow-sized fluffy pieces and filled up a white pillowcase (we have an impressive pillowcase surplus from the above-mentioned relatives). I also added some leftover batting scraps from quilting.

Once the pillowcase was full, it took just a minute or so to machine-stitch the end closed. Because a pillow needs to be shorter than a pillowcase, I folded and pinned the 4-inch hem inside before stitching. The result is an ever-so-slightly lumpy but quite serviceable pillow.

Flushed with this success, I recalled an old kid's comforter in our attic. Like most colored store-

bought comforters, this one became badly faded and pilled after a few washings. Also, the batting had become too matted to ever be reused in a quilt. Yet it always seemed like too much raw material to throw away, so I had saved it. Now, as I began to take it apart, the old threads tore easily. It yielded enough batting, once shredded, to make a second large pillow.

after

Making these two pillows from free materials required about 90 minutes, mostly in the shredding. It's a perfect activity for idle hands while watching TV. In addition to saving at least $10 on pillows, I was also able to avoid our $1-per-bag trash fees by not discarding the old pillow and comforter.

ROTTEN-BANANA IDEAS

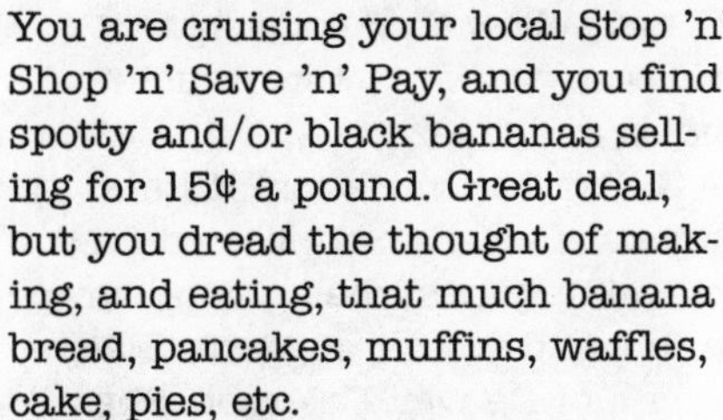

You are cruising your local Stop 'n' Shop 'n' Save 'n' Pay, and you find spotty and/or black bananas selling for 15¢ a pound. Great deal, but you dread the thought of making, and eating, that much banana bread, pancakes, muffins, waffles, cake, pies, etc.

But go ahead and buy them, because there are other ways to use this fruit, ways that are low in fat and sugar.

Bananas that can't be used immediately can be frozen. There are two ways to do this, depending on how you plan to use them.

- Bananas to be used in a frozen state: Peel and freeze whole, or sliced in a bag.
- Bananas to be used in a squishy state: Place bananas directly in the freezer without peeling or putting in a bag. To use, thaw completely, then cut off the tip and goosh the liquidy banana out. This sounds rather gross, but it's very convenient, because you don't have to mash the banana to use it.

Some frozen-banana recipes:

1. Banana "milkshake." In a blender, combine 3 frozen bananas, 4 cups of milk, a teaspoon of vanilla, and ¼ cup of sugar (optional). To make it even colder, add up to 6 crushed ice cubes. Maria Veres Homic of Austin, Texas, suggests that frozen bananas, with or without milk, make great "shakes" when combined with almost anything: other fruit, juice, coconut, yogurt, jam, cocoa powder. For creative tightwads, the possibilities are endless. Health-food stores and restaurants call these drinks "smoothies" and sell them for $2 to $4 a serving.

2. Popsicles. Same as above, except use thawed banana and add a little yellow food coloring to increase "wow" factor. Pour into molds and freeze.

3. Popsicle variation. If item number 2 is too complicated for you, simply peel the banana, wrap in foil, and freeze, suggests Gladys Harris of Denver, Colorado. She says this treatment improves the flavor and texture of overripe bananas.

4. Banana "ice cream." Debbie Mason of Virginia Beach, Virginia, combines frozen bananas with just enough orange juice to keep the mixture blending. For variety, she adds other fruits. She tops this with homemade granola.

5. Fruit salad dressing for those who like a banana/peanut butter combination. Combine 1 soft banana, 1 tablespoon lemon juice, ¼ cup peanut butter, ½ cup mayonnaise, 3 tablespoons milk powder, and ¼ cup water.

6. Banana toast. Frances Strauss of Victoria, British Columbia, suggests this simple recipe: Mash one limp banana and mix well with 2 eggs and 1 teaspoon cinnamon, or blenderize all ingredients. Dip bread slices into mixture and fry on both sides in oiled pan. Serve with fruit puree or syrup.

SLEEPWEAR SAFETY

Following a newsletter article about making pajama pants from hubby's old knit shirts, a reader wrote that she believed there's a law that says all children's sleepwear must be flame resistant. I investigated and found information that can be useful in helping parents choose both flame-resistant and cheaper sleepwear for their kids.

In 1972 the Consumer Products Safety Commission established flammability standards for children's sleepwear. These mandated that manufactured sleepwear be either polyester (which is naturally flame resistant) or, if a natural fiber, it must be chemically treated to be flame resistant. The standards govern only what can be manufactured and sold, not what parents can dress their children in for bed. They were passed at a time when most childhood burns from garments involved sleepwear and when about 60 deaths in the United States annually resulted from sleepwear fires.

In the years since the standards were established, the CPSC has gathered new data that indicates it can be safe to dress kids in certain kinds of flammable sleepwear.

The data shows that almost all sleepwear burns occurred when the children were playing before going to bed or after getting up in the morning. And almost all of the burns resulted from nightgowns, robes, and other flowing garments, which are more likely to come in

contact with fire. The point here is that children's clothing doesn't catch fire in bed. In keeping with this fact, there has never been a standard mandating that sheets and blankets be flame resistant.

Over the last two decades, sleepwear burns have declined so that they now make up only 8 percent of all garment burns. While the standards have contributed to the decline, the CPSC also attributes this to fewer fire hazards within the home. Cigarette smoking has declined in the last 20 years, and many fire hazards, like fireplaces, space heaters, gas stoves, and cigarette lighters, have developed improved safety features.

With this new knowledge, the CPSC staff is proposing to amend the standards to allow skintight pajamas and infant sleepwear to be made from fabrics that aren't flame resistant.

Upon learning all this, I asked CPSC spokeswoman Kathy Kaplan if a child who wore a T-shirt while sleeping was at more risk than a child who wore a T-shirt while playing. She said the risk would be exactly the same.

What does this mean for frugal parents selecting sleepwear for their kids? First, the common tightwad strategy of using an adult-sized cotton T-shirt for toddler sleepwear should not be considered absolutely safe. T-shirts are flammable and on a small child are loose and flowing.

Kaplan also said parents should assess the fire hazards in their home. In some homes, like mine, the fire hazards are almost nonexistent, so the flammability of sleepwear isn't a concern. However, parents in homes with hazards should choose sleepwear carefully. In the most hazardous situations one might even avoid flame-resistant gowns and robes, which still result in nearly all of the sleepwear burns.

In short, it's reasonable to assume that whatever is safe for your child to wear while playing is safe for your child to wear while sleeping. This can save you money, as it increases the sleepwear options for your children. Although most of my kids wear yard-sale-purchased traditional sleepwear, my older boys have been wearing no-longer-presentable sweatpants and correct-sized T-shirts.

BUDGET BUBBLES

Dear Amy,

My daughter's craft teacher gave me a great recipe for homemade bubble soap that's cheaper than the one in *The Tightwad Gazette* because it contains corn syrup instead of glycerin. Mix it ahead of time for best results:

6 parts water
2 parts Joy dishwashing liquid
¾ part corn syrup

This recipe costs 18¢ per cup, compared with 26¢ per cup for the glycerin recipe.

—Lori Evesque
Paw Paw, Michigan

AGED AD ADVANTAGE

Dear Amy,

I just bought a high-grade 6-foot picnic table (bolted instead of nailed) through the *Want Advertiser,* a classified-ad publication, for

$35. But I did not find it in the latest copy. I perused one that was a month old. Lots of items go unsold, and then you are in a stronger position to bargain.

—Susan Elliott
Milford, Massachusetts

OVER-CAPITOL-IZED

Dear Amy,

American flags that have been flown over the Capitol in Washington can be purchased very inexpensively from your senator or congressman. All flags come with a

certificate noting the date flown and, if requested, a person's name or special occasion. These make particularly nice and very special presents.

—Betsey Surmeier
Kensington, Maryland

(I wrote for and received an order form from my congressman and found that the least expensive option was a 3-foot-by-5-foot nylon flag for $6.76, plus $2.46 for postage. I called three suppliers in my area and found they charge from $28 to $31 for a 3-by-5 nylon flag.

Flags from your senator or congressman are available in both nylon and cotton, and range in size up to 5 feet by 8 feet. FZ)

POWDER YOUR JOES

Dear Amy,

I use instant, nonfat, powdered milk as a creamer in my coffee and tea. I pour it directly from the box. It does not dilute the flavor of the coffee, has no fat, and is inexpensive. It is far superior to the "creamer" products.

—Carol Collins
Greenville, South Carolina

CAN'T BEAT THIS WRAP

Dear Amy,

In order to save a substantial amount on waxed paper, aluminum foil, and plastic wrap, we buy the large, restaurant-sized boxes from our local restaurant-supply store. We just finished up a box of aluminum foil we bought six years ago for $10!

—Tina Hornsby
Allentown, Pennsylvania

(Warehouse stores also sometimes stock these big rolls. FZ)

SCOTCH ON SCOTCH

Dear Amy,

When I had a professional service clean stains from our sofas, I asked if they would spray my just-washed camping coat with spot

protector, as long as they were here. They did, and at no charge. I have priced cans of Scotchgard at $6.50, so now that I know about this, I'll have more items clean and ready to be zapped by them the next time I need the upholstery cleaned.

—Heidi M. Wright
Albuquerque, New Mexico

WORDS FOR WEAR

Dear Amy,

Have you ever mentioned "hand-me-ups"? We old parents wear our college kids' castoffs and work clothes. When anyone compliments our apparel, I mention it and no one has ever heard the term before. When my daughter moved out of her first rental home to get married, I got so many clothes my closet rod broke.

—Anne Hanna
Laurel, Maryland

SWEET AND LOW COST

Dear Amy,

Make your own brown sugar by taking 1 cup of white sugar and mixing it with 2 tablespoons of molasses. It tastes good on your oatmeal and in baked goods and is much cheaper. By our figuring, 2 pounds of the bargain brand of brown sugar costs $1.92, and 2 pounds of this homemade version costs only $1.00 (using bargain-brand white sugar at 35¢ per pound and molasses at $1.79).

—Clare Jones
Ogilvie, Minnesota

(The savings in this strategy is highly variable. We stock up on brown sugar when it hits 38¢ to 50¢ per pound. In our case, making our own brown sugar could cost slightly more; however, we use this strategy when we're out of brown sugar. FZ)

THE LEAST YEAST

Dear Amy,

I have enjoyed making "Cuban Bread" (from *The Tightwad Gazette II*). It is one bread that everyone loves, and it is quick and easy for me. However, I discovered that I needed only half the dry yeast called for in the recipe; that is, 1 tablespoon instead of 2. The bread does not taste as "yeasty," and the loaves turn out just as large.

—Carolyn C. Smith
Burlington, Connecticut

HANGER IN THERE, BABY

Dear Amy,

I had a baby daughter recently, and told my mom to put baby-clothes hangers on my shower list. She told me just to bend my wire ones, and it worked great.

—Nancy Waletzko
Zimmerman, Minnesota

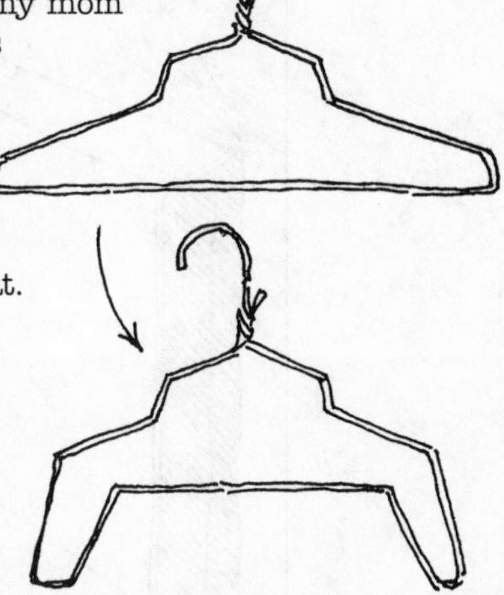

THE TUBE THAT BINDS

One of our best yard-sale finds was the *Reader's Digest Fix-It-Yourself Manual,* purchased for 25¢. Like all Reader's Digest books, it has excellent graphics and tells you just about everything you need to know about the subject. I thumbed through it and immediately found information I could use:

Months earlier, the covers had come off my 14-year-old, flour-dusted, batter-splattered *Fannie Farmer Cookbook.* I had been mystified as to how to reattach the covers of this essential hardcover book. The *Fix-It-Yourself Manual*'s book-repair section revealed the tightwaddy trick: a simple brown-paper tube.

You start by cutting a rectangle of grocery-bag paper that's slightly longer than the spine, and a ½ inch

more than twice as wide. Form a tube and glue together the overlapping edges. Cut the tube to the length of the spine.

If there's old backing on the spine, remove as much of it as possible. Apply white glue along the spine and let it dry. Glue the "un-overlapped" side of the paper tube to the spine

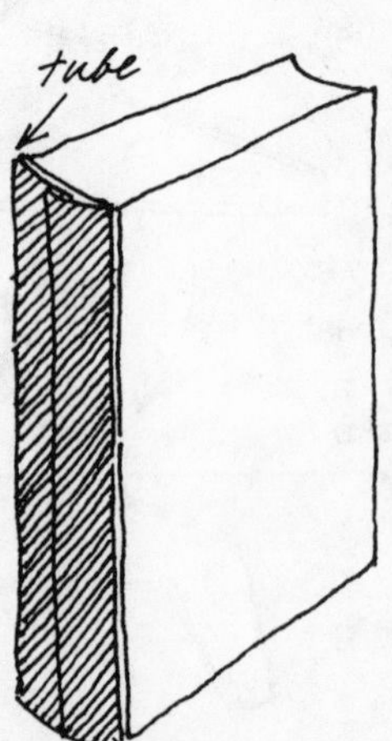

with white glue and smooth it down.

The manual then explains how to recover the spine and reattach the covers. The process involves gluing a cardboard strip to the exposed side of the tube, then gluing a piece of "book cloth" (available from bookbinding supply stores) over the strip and onto the covers.

But since I didn't have this special kind of cloth and don't care about the appearance of this book, I took the simple route: I used duct tape, pressing it firmly onto the tube and overlapping it onto the covers by about 1 inch to

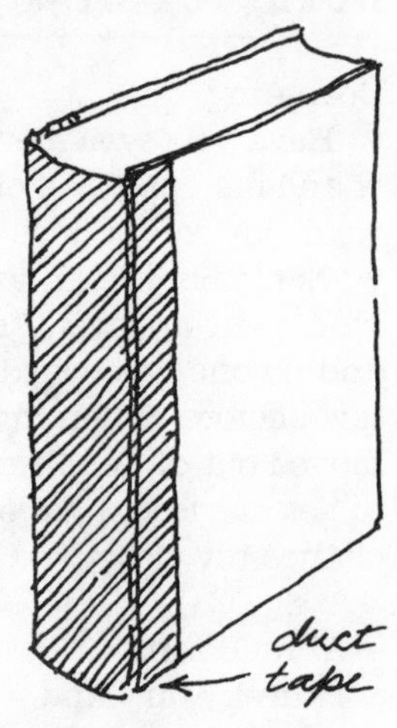

hold them in place. I also opened the front and back covers and pushed a strip of duct tape into the crease between the covers and the first and last pages.

This entire process took just 10 minutes, not including glue-drying time, and I look forward to another 14 years of flour-dusting and batter-splattering my favorite cookbook. Further, when my *Fix-It-Yourself Manual* expires someday, I now know how to revive it.

TOWARD SNEAKER IMMORTALITY

Whenever I point out that I spend less than $50 annually to dress six kids, frugal friends say that it generally seems possible, except when it comes to shoes. Even one pair of new, cheapo $10 sneakers per kid would put me over budget.

The secret is that I get their shoes at yard sales along with the rest of my kids' clothing. Last summer I picked up 16 pairs of shoes and sneakers and 3 pairs of boots, all in good-to-brand-new condition, for a total of $9.05. I'll concede that this required "power yard-saling," in which I hit at least 20 yard sales on each of 10 yard-sale days throughout the summer, but the point is that it can be done. This footwear comprises a small percent of my total haul, but if I bought only shoes, it would still be worth my time.

Getting yard-sale shoes has a couple of advantages aside from simply saving money. When my mother visited recently, she noted that the kids had many pairs of shoes lined up in their closets, and that if I were buying new shoes, they would have fewer pairs.

In addition to this, a new $10 pair of sneakers usually lacks style and quality. The brands I find at yard sales include Nike, Reebok, Etonic, and New Balance, which would cost anywhere from $25 to well over $50 new and would have that brand-new look for just a few weeks. My kids are not concerned if their shoes were previously owned, but they do prefer certain styles, and I can almost always accommodate them.

Kids are rough on sneakers. After a few months, these excellent-condition yard-sale sneakers can start to look ratty, and yard-sale season is over by then. So along with buying inexpensive sneakers, I also need to make them last and look good longer.

My first step is having the kids follow a strategy similar to my adult "Three-Year Sneaker Plan" outlined in *The Tightwad Gazette.* They reserve their best-looking sneakers for school and other occasions when they need to be presentable. As soon as they get home from school, they change into their "play" sneakers, which are often the "dress" sneakers that were worn by an older same-sex sibling.

Because the kids want to have good-looking sneakers to wear to school, they are happy to do this. In the summer my kids like to go barefooted, which happens to save wear on both sneakers and socks.

The second step is to continually refurbish sneakers for optimal appearance. Once you learn a few tricks, you can also visualize the possibilities in an old pair of sneak-

ers in a yard-sale "free box." Some basic tips:

• You can hand-wash vinyl sneakers by briefly submersing them in warm soapy water and scrubbing with an old toothbrush. Scuffs clean up beautifully with scouring powder and a damp cloth.

• Replace old laces with new ones. In a pinch, I've scavenged newer, snazzier laces from sneakers I purchased for a child to wear in future years. At the least, dirty laces can be added to your bucket of Clorox II/Cascade stain remover (see *The Tightwad Gazette*) while you soak other clothes.

• When Velcro fasteners become loaded with fuzz, hair, and dried grass, they look dirty and no longer adhere. Pick out this stuff with a sharp tool. Clip off all loose threads from the Velcro stitching and hand-sew any places it has become loose.

• Black leather or vinyl sneakers (as well as black patent-leather shoes and any black details on white sneakers) are easily spruced up with black permanent marker. In one yard-sale "free box" I found an excellent pair of black high-top sneakers. The only flaw was that the original owner crossed paths with some spray paint, leaving fine speckles of white. The black marker covered these perfectly.

• After the paint wears off white leather sneakers, I had thought they were hopeless. But a newsletter reader alerted me to a spray paint called Sneaker White Refinish by Kiwi. It enabled her to get an additional six months wear out of her old sneakers. We picked up a 4.5-ounce spray can for $2.98. It yielded enough paint to cover two pairs of badly worn, size-8 high-tops. The product lasts longer if used sparingly on lightly scuffed sneakers. You have to mask off any stripes and logos, but the paint covers the sides of the rubber soles nicely. (As a comparison experiment, I also painted a sneaker with regular flat white spray paint and another with gloss white. Neither produced a satisfactory finish.) Because the Kiwi paint costs about $1.50 per major overhaul, I would use it only for light touch-ups. This paint is a little hard to find but it's sold in some sporting goods stores.

• The downfall of vinyl sneakers occurs when they begin to crack where the toe bends. Once this happens the sneaker can deteriorate rapidly. The process can be slowed with Shoe Goo, a clear, flexible shoe-repair glue sold in sporting goods stores. I force a little glue under the crack while it's still small.

• Any top-stitched stripes that have become too loose or frayed to glue back into place can be removed altogether.

• Holes in the cloth tongue can be resewn. A fabric rim at the top of the shoe that has become separated can be repaired with a combination of gluing and sewing.

As a final note, if I were going to buy new sneakers for a boy, I would buy black high-tops for three reasons: black is easier to maintain than white; black sneakers can double for "dress shoes" in a pinch; and high-top sneakers are terrific for concealing those slightly too-short slacks.

CREATE A DINNER CASSEROLE

When confronted by an odd collection of leftovers, the typical tightwad response is to make them into leftover soup.

But Maria Kleinberg of Sterling Heights, Michigan, offers another alternative. This universal casserole recipe can use up a wide variety of ingredients, with impressive results.

1 cup main ingredient
1 cup second ingredient
1–2 cups starchy ingredient
1½ cups binder
¼ cup "goodie"
Seasoning
Topping

Main ingredient suggestions: tuna, cubed chicken, turkey, ham, seafood.

Second ingredient suggestions: thinly sliced celery, mushrooms, peas, chopped hard-cooked eggs.

Starchy ingredient suggestions: thinly sliced potatoes, cooked noodles, cooked rice.

Binder suggestions: cream sauce, sour cream, can of soup.

"Goodie" suggestions: pimiento, olives, almonds, water chestnuts.

Topping suggestions: potato chips, cheese, bread crumbs.

Thoroughly mix your combinations of the above ingredients. If it seems dry, add ½ cup milk or stock. Place in buttered casserole dish and bake at 350 degrees for 30 to 45 minutes.

In the Dacyczyn household we routinely concoct casseroles. We almost always use a white-sauce variation as a binder because it's cheaper than sour cream or canned soup. This can be found in any basic cookbook. The "goodies" are optional, as they are generally expensive foods.

DRIVE THE FREE WAY

As a general rule, the cheapest way to go from one city to another is by car, particularly for a group of people, or for one person with stuff to transport. But what if you don't have a car or, for whatever reason, you would rather not use your own car?

An excellent alternative is the "drive-away" car. Several companies with offices throughout the nation offer the use of a car free of charge to make a long-distance one-way trip.

Jinx Smith, owner of the A-1 Automovers office in Phoenix, Arizona, told me that it works like this: People who want their cars driven somewhere contact their local drive-away agency. Frequently these are retirees who will fly to their seasonal vacation homes and want their car to be there when they arrive. They pay a fee of about $300 for the service.

Meanwhile, potential drivers call these agencies to find out if a car

is available to be transported to the place and at the time they desire. If so, the person fills out an application to prove that he is a safe driver, puts down a deposit of about $200, and, at least at some agencies, he must also provide a reference from both the departure and destination cities.

To ensure that he uses the car solely for transportation between two cities, the driver is given a time limit. For example, from the East to West coasts, the trip must be completed in eight days. He also must not exceed the allowed mileage by more than 10 percent. The drive-away agency pays for the first tank of fuel; generally, the driver must pay for the rest. It is also the driver's responsibility to deliver the car to a specific address in the destination city.

If you consider this idea, be sure to carefully compare the costs of the gasoline and lodging against budget plane, train, and bus fares.

Drive-away companies can be found in the Yellow Pages under "Automobile Transporters and Drive-Away Companies."

SURPRISE PIES

Dear Amy,

My family does not care for cooked carrots, but carrots are often cheap and are high in vitamins. I now use well-cooked carrots to make "pumpkin" pie. My family loves it. I use four big carrots for a pie, and milk in place of sweetened, condensed milk.

—Lois Snyder
Peru, Massachusetts

SOFT-SERVE ICE BEANS

Dear Amy,

To cook beans quickly: Soak beans overnight. Drain. Then freeze in whatever quantity you choose. (I usually do some of 4 cups and some of 2 cups.) Freeze the beans. When you cook them, they will soften easily in about 20 minutes. The reason: When they are frozen, the water expands and breaks some of the cellulose strands that hold the cells together. This is the same action that occurs when you cook beans for hours. You can shorten the cooking time even more by putting frozen beans in a pressure cooker.

—Susan Burke
Santa Rosa, California

TIGHTWAD TURNOVERS

Dear Amy,

I have another way to use Jim's "Refrigerator Dough" (page 19). I make something my family calls "Bunches of Bunches" (family joke, don't ask). I take about ¼ cup of the dough for each person, roll it out into a circle, fill with a variety of ingredients, roll it up, and pinch the ends together. Bake in a 400-degree oven for 15 minutes. It's a good way to use up leftovers. The kids can even make up their own, using the "smorgasbord" method. Our favorite combination is ham, cheese, and broccoli.

—Kelly Miller
Virginia Beach, Virginia

GUTLESS WONDERS

Dear Amy,

As a first grade teacher, I have been interested in putting together a collection of puppets, but at $10 to $30 apiece the cost seemed prohibitive. I found a solution by buying stuffed animals at yard sales and thrift stores, making 4-inch incisions in the bellies or rear ends, and taking the stuffing out. Puppets seem to have far more play value than stuffed animals do.

—Kelye Stowell
Bellevue, Washington

DUCT TAPE 101

Dear Amy,

The University of Texas at Austin has evening "informal" non-credit classes on a whole range of subjects. Last year I began teaching a one-evening, three-hour course on frugal living, and I use material from *The Tightwad Gazette* as backup support.

—Janet L. Lewis
Austin, Texas

("Adult education" or "open university" programs are common in many cities throughout the country. Other readers who are black-belt tightwads might consider developing a curriculum and offering their services to teach a frugal-living course. FZ)

KEEP TABS ON GRIME

Dear Amy,

I use plastic bread tabs to get really stuck crud off pans (i.e., meatloaf remains in a bread pan) while doing dishes. They work, and don't scratch Teflon surfaces.

—Kim Jaworski
South St. Paul, Minnesota

MORE HANG TIME

Dear Amy,

With all six of us bathing once a day and my husband showering twice daily, and each of us using a fresh towel each time, we were generating a lot of laundry.

So we have installed a special towel rack in our bathroom with a peg for each person's towel. I brought out our store of towels, and everyone got to pick their own personal towel for the rack. The only rule was that everyone had to pick a different color so we could tell them apart.

This rack has cut our towel laundry from ten loads a week to one.

—Elizabeth Case
Belfair, Washington

MONEY-BACK KNACK

Dear Amy,

Most big-ticket items are sold with a guarantee. But many small-ticket items are also sold with guarantees that most people ignore because they figure it would be too hard to collect. The usual catch is that you must have the purchase receipt. Well, I simply have a file for such receipts, and about once a year I cull it for ones that are no longer useful. Recently I returned about 35 sprinkler heads that were of inferior quality and very clogged after one season, and got my money back. About four years ago my wife bought two washable throw rugs with rubber backing that had five-year guarantees. Imagine the surprise at the department store service desk when we came in with two frayed rugs and sales receipts from 1990!

—Jonathan Kennedy
Lancaster, California

MORE HANG TIME II

Dear Amy,

I used to hang shirts on the line with hangers, but they would blow off. My father-in-law solved the problem. He put a length of chain on the end of one of the lines. Now, I hook the hangers in the links. I can hang a lot of shirts in a small space, and they stay put until I take them down.

—Phyllis Wamack
Mt. Victory, Ohio

MOTEL SICKS

Dear Amy,

My husband needed arm surgery. The hospital was one and a half hours away over mountain passes. He needed to stay for 27 days. I stayed in his room for 20 days. If I had stayed in a hotel room across the street, it would have cost $68 a night, or $1,360 for 20 days. If your hospital does not allow this, maybe it's time to change their attitude.

—Thea Lou Seese
Mt. Shasta, California

A TALE OF TIGHTWAD TRANSFORMATION

Whenever *The Tightwad Gazette* examines everyday family life, the family that is examined is mine. Readers have, over the years, become intimately acquainted with how we live our frugal, happy life. Aside from little snippets that appear in reader letters, they generally don't get a peek into the lives of other readers.

I, however, frequently do see into the lives of these others, as people write to share the changes they have made in their lives. We have their letters in a fat file that we've labeled "Success Stories."

Readers say that what they've learned from *The Tightwad Gazette* has allowed them to, among other things, keep their homes despite a job loss, avoid bankruptcy, pay off huge credit-card debts, and/or cut their food bills in half.

I've refrained from publishing any of these letters because I

didn't want to appear to be patting myself on the back. But the downside of never highlighting success stories is that skeptical readers may not understand that the basic ideas in the newsletter work for others, and so could work for them, too. In short, I've been explaining the method, but I've never shown that the method works for anyone but us.

So I decided, just for once, to make an exception and highlight one successful reader's experience. Karen Lee of University City, Missouri, sent me a typical success story. Her letter is unusually rich in detail and outlines some of the basics that just about anyone can do to make a start.

She begins her letter by pointing out that, when she first came across my book and newsletter, she was "a miserable spendthrift, in debt, and a working mother." My book inspired her to "do the math" and discover that her working outside the home caused her family to simply break even, and sometimes even lose money. So she quit her job and incorporated many basic lifestyle changes that produced immediate results, such as:

1. Making school lunches every day.

2. Cooking from scratch. She also figures the cost of meals and records it on the recipes, next to each ingredient, with the total at the bottom. This allows her to record price changes of the ingredients.

3. Going to garage sales. She had never done it before, although she had shopped at thrift stores. She noted that thrift-store merchandise is usually priced higher than yard-sale stuff, so she keeps track of the stores' sale days and goes then.

4. Reusing common household items, including Ziploc bags, aluminum foil, and bread bags.

5. Using a price book for purchasing groceries. She also uses it to track prices of yard-sale merchandise and school supplies.

6. Using a freezer.

7. Buying in bulk.

8. Setting up and using a pantry under the basement stairs. Her husband made it from scavenged shelves, along with screws, nuts, and bolts that he already had or had scavenged.

9. Using the library much more. Children who met reading quotas at her library received the following, at no cost: a swimming party, a sleep-over at the library, a mini-circus with trained animals and birds, a carnival with horses and

pony rides, coupons for free fast food, a pizza party, a paperback of choice, and coupons for nearby theme parks.

10. Buying kids' shoes used.

11. Being more creative about birthday parties. For her daughter Christy's tenth birthday, Karen made pizza dough, used homemade sauce, had the guests top their individual pizzas, and then baked the pizzas in metal pie plates. The kids then ate a scratch cake decorated with frosting colored with paste coloring. Finally they watched a rented video and had a sleep-over. For the ninth birthday of her other daughter, Cassie, they went to a public-school-sponsored flea market. Each guest was given a small amount of money to spend. What they bought ended up as their party favors. Then they came back home for scratch cake.

12. Having her kids make economic choices. Karen and her husband provide what she calls "the basics of life," while her daughters figure out ways to come up with their own extras. If her kids want to buy something, they either work for the money or sell something of theirs.

13. Entertaining themselves, spending little or no money. Examples: free concerts, parks, garage-sale board games. They are also active in church activities.

14. Gardening.

15. Cutting her family's hair.

Karen goes on to list the benefits that she now enjoys as a result of making these changes:

1. She doesn't have to deal with the stress of working outside the home and putting her kids into child care.

2. Her family eats better, healthier, cheaper food. Their food bill has gone from $81 to $38 a week and continues to drop.

3. They are greatly reducing their consumer debt, incurred during her working years. She and her husband, Rudy, "no longer wake up in the middle of the night in a cold sweat . . . on those nights when we could get to sleep."

4. They enjoy family activities that they didn't have time for before.

5. She has learned how to cook (at age 38!).

6. Her kids have set new lunch trends at school. She says other kids try to trade store-bought granola bars, fruit snacks, and pudding cups for her girls' pineapple muffins, pumpkin bread, homemade granola, and oatmeal-applesauce bars. As she puts it, "This got so bad I had to pass out recipes to other mothers and make a rule about no trading."

7. Her girls learned quickly about cost and value. Now when they want to buy their own books, they get them at garage sales or at a specific, extremely cheap thrift store. After they've read them, they sell them to the used-book store for as much or more than they paid. If they want a brand-new outfit, they use their birthday money (from relatives). They keep their clothes, books, and toys nicer so they can sell them to the appropriate resale shop. And they can always do jobs around the house to earn money. They do not get an allowance.

8. Her daughter Christy no longer asks, "Are you babysitting me tonight?" and "When can we have an appointment?" Karen says that when she worked, she actually had to make appointments with

her girls and write their names in her appointment book.

9. Karen and her daughters will be able to drive to Florida this month and see Karen's mom.

10. They are happier and life is fun.

DISCONCERTING CONCERT

A brief note to add to your "We've Got a Long Way to Go" file:

Nancy Hallock of Delmar, New York, sent me a clipping from the *Albany Times Union* newspaper. It's a column by Fred LeBrun in which he contrasts the aftermaths of the Woodstock festivals of 1969 and 1994.

He writes that after the original Woodstock 25 years ago, "for the most part the ground was littered, after 500,000 passed through, with what is traditionally considered garbage and trash. . . . Very little useful gear, belongings, or food was purposely discarded. Waste not, want not was still ingrained and passed down to the great-grandchildren of the Depression."

But, describing the more recent Woodstock event, he writes: "I stopped counting at 200 the tents left standing and abandoned at Woodstock '94, a fraction of the total, many of them brand new, the boxes they came in ground into the clay alongside. Thousands of sleeping bags were strewn about, muddy and still wet but otherwise whole and reusable after a good cleaning. Duffel bags full of clothing, backpacks with keys and books, just left behind." He theorizes that the participants found it "too much work to lug all that wet stuff back again. So they left it. Mommy and Daddy will buy another."

It's a grim story, but there is, at least, one hopeful note. "By early afternoon and with the roads reopened, the locals were on the scene in growing numbers with pickups and vans, doing their own heavy-duty recycling."

Sounds good to me, I'll meet you the day after the closing of Woodstock III in the year 2019.

SKINFLINT SKIN CARE

When it comes to a "skin-care regimen," there are three basic approaches:

1. Using a vast variety of expensive astringents, toners, clay masks, scrubs, wrinkle creams, and other stuff, the benefits of which are heavily promoted by manufacturers.

2. Using homemade, "tightwad" alternatives to such products, such as cornmeal scrubs and banana/honey/egg-white masks, the benefits of which are heavily promoted by authors of numerous budget skin-regimen books.

3. Using a few basic, inexpensive products.

Personally, I follow number 3, but I'm the first to admit that I'm no expert and maybe I *would* look more "radiant" if I "sloughed off" those dead skin cells.

Some investigation led me to a book that has all the answers. It's *The Look You Like,* written by Linda Shoen (Marcel Dekker Inc., 1989). It was sponsored by the American Academy of Dermatologists and answers 500 questions about skin and hair care.

The bottom line? Shoen says

whole ranges of products that are marketed for skin care offer little or no benefit, and their "tight-waddy" alternatives are no more useful. In fact, the author expresses concern about homemade alternatives, which, she feels, are more apt to cause problems. Some of the ingredients used can be allergenic or irritating. These concoctions may also lack the preservatives necessary to control contamination by bacteria and fungus.

First, let's look at the products we don't need:

Scrubs. Also called exfoliators, these are designed to remove dead skin cells with a mild abrasive. They come in the form of abrasive cleansers, special sponges, or pumice stones. Homemade/alternative advocates suggest using oatmeal, baking soda, cornmeal, or sugar. The truth is that there is little evidence that these do more than can be achieved with a washcloth—the results are more psychological than anything else. If you use them too frequently, too vigorously, or have dry skin, scrubs can irritate your skin.

Masks. Traditional masks are made of clay products. They are said to help minimize wrinkles, improve texture, shrink and unplug pores, stimulate circulation, and smooth and refresh the skin. But the actual benefits are few. They may make your skin feel better, but only for a few minutes to a few hours. Clay masks do have some cleansing ability, but so does soap. Some "masks" marketed for people with dry skin are actually just lubricating films that have the same effect as moisturizers. As for the homemade masks, most of the ingredients are more effective when used in your muffins.

Astringents. Also called toners, fresheners, or clarifying lotions, these are supposed to be applied after cleaning your face to remove oil, or between cleanings to "refresh" the skin. Suggested cheap alternatives include witch hazel, cucumber, rubbing alcohol, and peppermint. One of the supposed benefits of astringents is that they "shrink" pores. Actually, they irritate your skin so that the area around the pores swells temporarily, making the pores appear to shrink. While astringents do remove oil, they don't stop your skin from producing more oil. Actually, astringents provide the same benefit as washing with soap and water. If you have extremely oily skin, you can use an astringent pad at times when it's inconvenient to wash, such as when at work. Because astringents contain alcohol, which dries the skin, people with dry skin should avoid them.

Wrinkle creams. There's no proof that any nonprescription cream, lotion, or gel will remove wrinkles. (The only topical product that appears to be of benefit is retinoic acid, which must be prescribed by a doctor.) Because wrinkles are primarily caused by exposure to sunlight, the best product to prevent them is a maximum sunblock cream, SPF 15 or higher.

Now, let's look at products that are useful:

Cold creams and cleansing lotions. These products are beneficial for removing makeup, especially the waterproof type. These are also useful for cleaning if your skin is too dry for frequent washing with soap and water. If you have oily skin, follow these with soap and water.

Soap and water. With the exception of the above uses for cold cream, soap and water are adequate for most cleaning. The choice of soap depends on skin type and personal preference. For some people, regular bath soaps are fine. Soap for oily skin is more efficient at removing oil, and soap for dry skin is less efficient. However, a moisturizing bar is not a substitute for a moisturizer. Bar soaps clean as well as expensive liquid facial soaps.

Moisturizers. Also called emollients and lubricants, these are said to speed cell renewal, improve "microcirculation," or retard aging. They don't. Instead, they do make dry skin smoother and softer by putting a film of oil on your skin to hold in the natural moisture. If your skin is oily, you may not need a moisturizer. If you do use a moisturizer, it need not be expensive. The September 1994 *Consumer Reports* magazine reveals that the cheapest moisturizers are among the most effective. Inexpensive body lotions may be harsher but can be used if your skin doesn't react negatively. Petroleum jelly also works, but it doesn't accept makeup as well as other kinds of moisturizers.

In short, despite the hype, you don't need a lot of money—or a lot of bananas—to have healthy skin.

THE PIE CHART

Pie-making is a "grandma skill" that I was determined to master. Even once I had, I still found making pies to be a bit time-consuming. I've found three ways to save time:

1. Draft help. I've taught Alec to make pies. He made his first lattice-top strawberry-rhubarb pie with almost no supervision when he was just ten years old.

2. Practice. People get discouraged by slow early attempts. Speed comes with practice.

3. Mass-produce. As with other frugal activities, you can save hours of labor if you do a lot all at once. In pie-making, for instance, much of the work is in the cleanup, and cleanup time is the same for 1 pie as it is for 12; I have made as many as 12 at one time.

Apply this basic system to the type of pie that is cheapest for you to make. I'll focus on pumpkin pies, because pumpkins are my free resource.

Crust mass production. Crust-making was my biggest stumbling block in learning to make pies. My humble

goal was a crust that wouldn't fall apart when I lifted it into the tin. For years, I would ask every successful pie-maker what the secret was, and each offered a different answer. I finally found that the

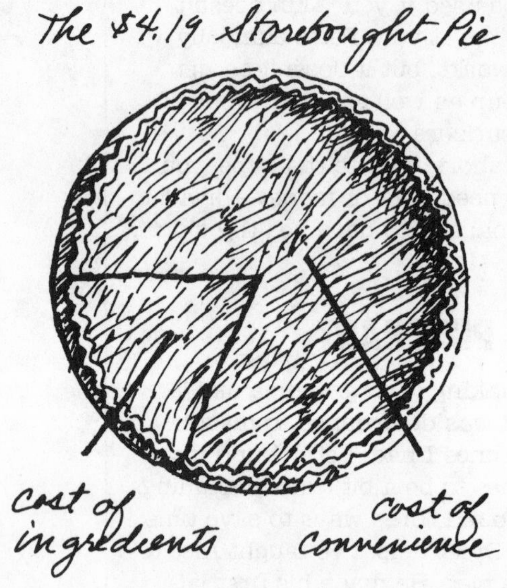

trick was to avoid overmixing the dough. I do this by mixing the dough with two knives in a scissor-action until the pieces are the size of small peas. It should also be just moist enough to hold together. I use Fannie Farmer's basic recipe and Crisco shortening, though I know others who have had success with oil or lard.

I always make enough crusts for at least four one-crust pies. I either use them all immediately or I freeze the surplus as one-crust-portion balls of dough. You could also put the crusts into aluminum pie tins and freeze them. My grandmother has rolled out crusts, covered them with plastic wrap, rolled them up on empty paper-towel tubes, and stored them in her freezer.

I also have a bag in my freezer for pastry scraps. When I accumulate enough scraps, I make a tough-crusted quiche. (Rerolled dough is always tougher.) When I clean up my pastry surface, I scrape up and save the excess flour and dough bits to be used in my next batch of muffins.

Recently I made six one-crust pie crusts in 30 minutes, including cleanup time; that's five minutes per crust. The cost per crust was about 8¢. The cheapest ready-made frozen crusts we could find were 63¢ each.

Pumpkin puree mass production. We grow our own pumpkins and butternut squashes. When we harvest them in the fall, our freezer is already packed full, but they will store for many months in a cool, dry place. We lack the perfect place to store them, so they begin to develop soft spots by midwinter—about the time our freezer begins to empty out.

So that's when I crank up the pumpkin-puree factory. I cut the slightly soft pumpkins into big chunks with an electric knife. I cut up the harder squashes by whacking my big knife through them with a mallet. Then I cut the peel off the chunks, and cut the peeled chunks into 1-inch pieces. I fill my largest pot with pieces, fill the pot halfway with water, cook until soft, and drain. I puree the cooked chunks in my food processor, but you could also use a potato masher or a blender. Some people find it easier to bake or microwave raw, seeded pumpkin halves until soft, then scoop out the flesh. I freeze the puree in pint containers.

Last year I put up 16 pints in two hours of hands-on time. Throw

in another hour for gardening and handling time, and it takes about 15 minutes to produce a pint of pumpkin puree. A store-bought pint (a 16-ounce can) costs about 80¢.

Pie mass production. In the spring my freezer is emptier still, allowing me to store even bulkier items, so that's when I crank up the pumpkin-pie factory.

With six crusts and the proper amount of puree thawed, it takes me another 15 minutes to make pumpkin-pie filling, fill the crusts, put all six pies in my large oven, and clean up. (I bake pumpkin pies before freezing to help them "set up." Fruit pies can be frozen unbaked.) I use a standard recipe, except instead of evaporated milk I use either whole milk, or powdered milk made with half the usual water. The pie assembly requires 2½ minutes per pie.

A relative who worked in a school cafeteria collected a large quantity of used, tiny aluminum pie tins for me. I wash the tins and use them to make little pies for lunch boxes. I've made as many as 64 of these at a time.

Pie storage. I put the cooked, cooled pies in the freezer, uncovered. Once they are frozen, I wrap them in plastic wrap and stack them in the freezer. The little pies stack nicely in bread bags.

Pie economics. The bottom line is, how much time does it take, and how much money do you save, by making your own mass-produced pies as compared to buying them? The following costs-per-pie include the cost of baking in an electric oven at 12¢ per kilowatt-hour. The "hourly wage" figures are based on a comparison to a store-bought 9-inch pumpkin pie that cost $4.19.

1. Store-bought crust and store-bought puree: costs $2.09 and requires 2½ minutes per pie. Hourly wage: $50.40.

2. Homemade crust and store-bought puree: costs $1.54 and requires 7½ minutes per pie. Hourly wage: $21.20.

3. Homemade crust and homemade puree: costs 74¢ and requires 17½ minutes per pie. Hourly wage: $11.83.

These figures show that even extraordinarily busy people should consider making pies with ready-made components rather than buying a premade pie. But don't let these hourly wages confuse you. Strategy 3, the one with the lowest hourly wage, still saves you the most money per pie.

DIRECTORY RESISTANCE

If you want to list your phone number in the Yellow Pages, you have to fork over a hefty fee. But in the white pages, it works just the opposite way—it costs extra to have an *un*listed number. The fee is $1 a month in my area.

Two readers offered a way to get a free "unlisted" number: give the phone company a listing name that's not your real name.

Anthony Willett of Annandale, Virginia, says his family is listed under his wife's maiden name. He says an unexpected side benefit is that the sales calls always ask for someone with his wife's maiden name. (The Willetts' reply: "She's not here.") They also throw away, unopened, all mail that comes addressed to the wife's maiden name, reasoning that a junk mailer

picked the name out of the phone book.

Another reader, who asked to remain anonymous, made up the name of a fictitious "roommate."

Sally Pelletier, customer service representative for my local phone company, said most phone companies allow customers to choose any name at all, even a fictitious one, for their listing, as long as they give their real name for billing.

Pelletier could think of only one possible hazard of this practice. In an emergency (such as when a person is rendered unconscious or killed), police can quickly submit a subpoena to the phone company to get the person's number if it's unlisted in the traditional way. She said if the number is under a fake name, the police would have no way of learning the person's phone number, unless he carried it along with his other identification.

WHAT TO DO WITH . . .

A soda bottle. Make a drip catcher for a cooler that has a spout near the bottom. Cut bottle diagonally. Then cut a horizontal slot in bottle to fit over the vertical spout. (Marliss Bombardier, Great Bend, Kansas)

Bread tabs. Use to mark various electrical cords in remote places, such as behind the entertainment center. (John Cant, Blauvelt, New York)

Blank stamps that come on the end of a sheet of postage stamps. Use to label jars of homemade jelly. (Martha Farley, Evanston, Illinois)

Old magazines. Make a booster seat by taping a stack together and covering with fabric. (Marie Rippel, Grayslake, Illinois)

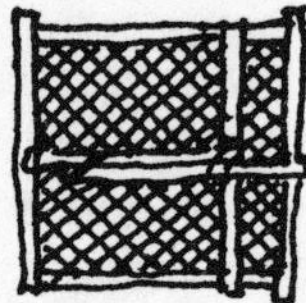

Old baby gates. Use for drying rack for sweaters that need to dry flat. Simply place over tub. (Debra J. Brock, Rialto, California)

A dead refrigerator. Remove adjustable shelves and drawers. Discard fridge. (Be sure to remove door first.) Reuse shelves and drawers for garage storage by mounting on wall. (Bonnie Finch, Pueblo, Colorado)

Fruit peelings and apple cores. Save in a bag in freezer. To make house smell great, put some of each type of peeling in a saucepan, cover with water, add a little cinnamon, and simmer. (Sheri Youngquist, Newark, California)

Squeeze containers that white glue and mustard come in. Use for cake decorating. The tips can be cut with a sharp knife to make different designs. (Maria Ferris, Bernville, Pennsylvania)

A large plastic toy-store bag. Use to make disposable painting smock for child. Cut head and arm holes. (Barbara Kaloydis, Fenton, Michigan)

A wine cork. Use to replace missing handle on pot lid. Attach with a screw. (Anne Hedian, Rockville, Maryland)

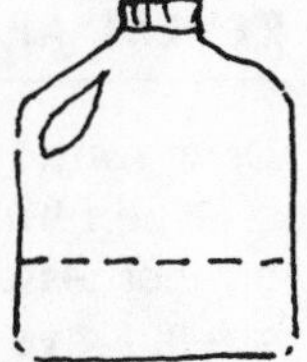

A milk jug. Cut off and discard bottom third. Use as a microwave splatter-shield. (Jean Fountain, Iowa City, Iowa)

A mesh onion bag. Use for storing cookie cutters. Dirty cutters in an onion bag can go on top shelf of dishwasher for easy cleaning.

Plastic tubing. Use to replace a missing handle on a lunch box. Attach by threading line through the tubing.

Old blue jeans. Make carrier for snow chains. Cut off pant legs to "shorts" length and sew legs closed. Put one chain in each leg. Make handles by putting rope or webbing through belt loops. Store gloves, tighteners, etc. in pockets. (Dorothy Jones, Seattle, Washington)

Old T-shirts. Cut into long strip 2 inches wide. Stretch this so that it curls to make a cord. Crochet into hot mats, doormats, and even baskets. Use colored shirts to create designs. (Heather Jack, Thomaston, Maine)

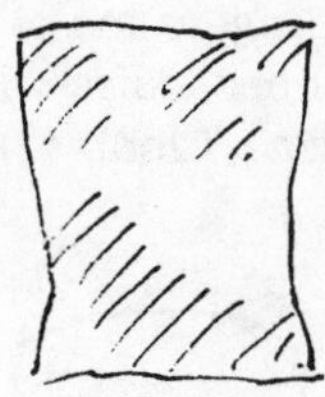

Used dryer sheets. Use as backing for embroidery instead of buying "stabilizers." Depending on the project, the sheets can be left in place or cut away. (Mary Frances Jablonskis, Westchester, Illinois)

Plastic bags of all types. Collect in burlap bag and use as an archery target. Plastic bags will stop the arrow, but allow it to be removed easily. (John Matejov, Story, Wyoming)

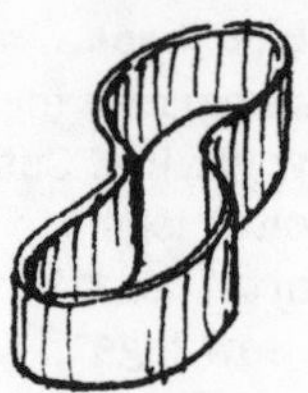

Broccoli rubber bands. Use for a jar or bottle opener. Place band on lid and twist. (Beverly Kendall, Seattle, Washington)

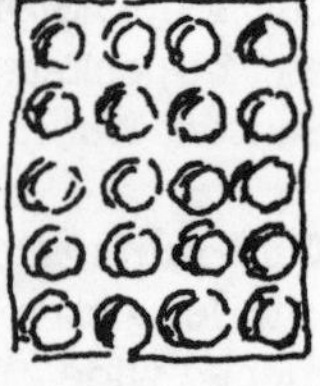

Bubble wrap. Those who spend their days on their feet can use sections for insole cushioning. Lasts about six hours and doesn't pop when walking. (Trish Luthro, Annapolis, Missouri)

Holey rubber gloves. Cut into sections, these make great rubber bands, which can be custom-cut for specific uses. Fingers make small ones, cuffs make large ones. (Norma Tabbi, Amherst, New York)

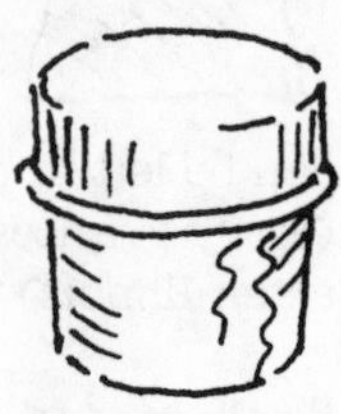

Dried-up oil-based paints in paint-by-number kits. If you don't have turpentine on hand, try a little vegetable oil. Adding too much will make the paint too thin. (Valerie Smith, Chicago, Illinois)

EYE A PEEL

Dear Amy,

I took this idea from restaurants that sell potato peelings as appetizers. Scrub your potatoes well and peel with a knife, trying to get large pieces. Place peels in a bowl and add salt, pepper, garlic, and onion powder. Grease a cookie sheet and place the skins on it. Bake in a hot oven at about 400 degrees for eight to ten minutes or until done. Remove from oven, sprinkle with grated cheese, then return to oven just until cheese melts.

—Sarah Flemming
Gulfport, Mississippi

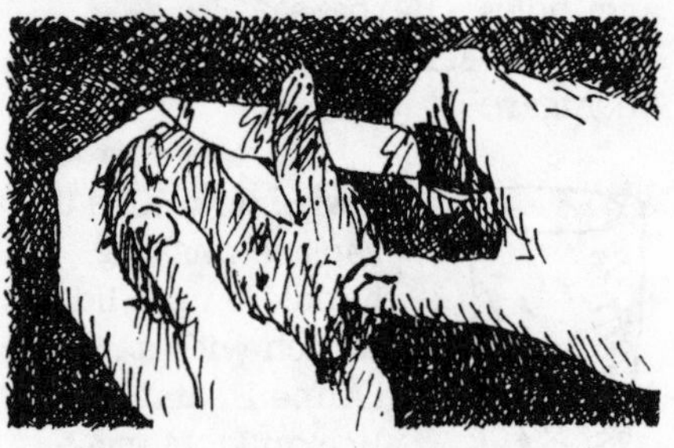

REVEAL APPEAL

Dear Amy,

When I hit a sale that has quality clothes in one of my children's sizes, I give the party "my card" (one half of an index card with my name, number, and "Garage Sale" written on it). I ask them to please give me a call the next time they are having a sale. You would be surprised how many "sneak previews" you get this way.

—Kris Jergenson
Hokah, Minnesota

ALL ON ABOARD!

Dear Amy,

If you live near a college or university, utilize their "ride board." It's usually hanging in the student center. Students hang cards indicating where they desire to go, or where they are driving. When I drive out of town, I share the gas expense with someone who needs an inexpensive mode of travel. I have met several wonderful babysitters by taking college students along when we drive to Grandma's house, three and a half hours away.

—Julie Minasian
Evanston, Illinois

STANKLESS STEEL

Dear Amy,

Many "kitchen gadget" stores carry a stainless-steel bar, which costs about $10, for a cook to use to rid his or her hands of pungent smells. I have found that *any* stainless-steel item does the trick. After working with garlic, onions, or fish, I rub my hands over a stainless-steel spoon under running water and the smells are gone!

—Jennifer Eldredge
San Rafael, California

LOW-PAY SPRAY

Dear Amy,

Do you like the convenience of spray-on cooking oil such as Pam but hate the price? Pam costs $2.69 for 6 ounces and contains only vegetable oil, grain alcohol, and lecithin. On sale, I can get a half-gallon (64 ounces) of vegetable oil for $2.69. I mix 5 ounces of oil with 1 ounce of vodka (because it is fairly odorless, tasteless, and clear), shake well, and spray. Use either a recycled Pam pump bottle or a purchased small spray bottle. It works like magic. My 6-ounce bottle cost me 49¢ to make.

—Penny Rapp
Louisville, Kentucky

(Some readers have suggested using plain oil in a spray bottle. Others have suggested adding some liquid lecithin from a health food store, but this raises the price considerably. Results may vary due to differences in spray bottles and the quality of ingredients. Try plain oil first and add other ingredients if you don't get satisfactory results. FZ)

CURE FOR SMALL BOX

Dear Amy,

When my husband needed to mail a new, small appliance recently, he took the item out of its original box, turned the box inside out, and taped it back together. He then had a plain cardboard box that was just the right size. The item came with plenty of padding, which we simply left in the box to cushion it.

—Maria Veres Homic
Austin, Texas

WALL-TO-WALL VOILA

Dear Amy,

We save big bucks on carpet cleaning by using our wet-dry shop vacuum instead of renting a commercial carpet cleaner, which costs $18 for four hours in our area. We buy the liquid carpet cleaner sold for the rental machines and mix according to label directions. Using a garden watering can with sprinkler head, we wet down the carpet lightly with the mix, then vacuum immediately with the shop vacuum set on "wet pickup." This works quite well.

—Cindy Kroon
Hartford, South Dakota

SOFA, SO GOOD

Dear Amy,

I work in an upholstery shop. I have learned that there is an awful lot of waste in this business. Through the years, people from the elderly down to Boy Scouts have asked for remnants for crafts and miscellaneous items. We ask them to bring by a paper bag, and when we are actually cutting, we conveniently drop scraps into the bag. The scraps range in size from 2 inches by 2 inches to 18 inches by 18 inches (we do this only when the customer does not want the scraps). All shops may not do this, but it doesn't hurt to ask.

—Mary Manly
Jacksonville, Florida

CLEAN YOUR PLATE

Dear Amy,

I am a dentist. I advise my patients to clean their removable partial dentures and complete dentures by soaking them overnight in vinegar and water and brushing them with baking soda in the morning. Obviously, this is cheaper than using Efferdent.

—Rose Mathews
Scottsdale, Arizona

REPOSE AND REPOSITION

Dear Amy,

I just purchased a new mattress and box spring—a major purchase, so I want it to last as long as possible. In the past, I've never been able to recall which way to turn it next. The mattress has four possible positions, so I marked the corners 1, 2, 3, and 4 with waterproof markers. I only have to see that the next number is in the corner near my pillow.

—Kathleen Hendrix
Goleta, California

(Another way to remember: "Spin in the spring, flip in the fall." FZ)

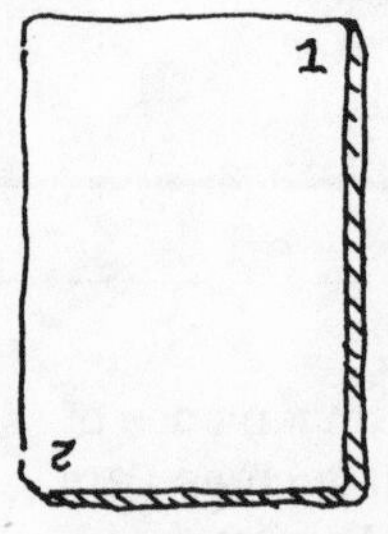

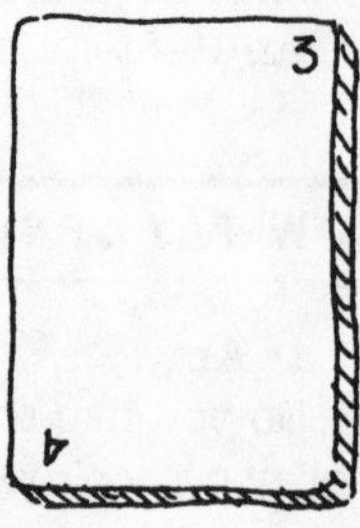

THE CLOVE COMPARTMENT

Dear Amy,

In place of sweet, sickening car air fresheners, I use cloves in the ashtrays. Any health food store that carries bulk items will have cloves. An ounce costs about 25¢. I have put cloves into each of my car's ashtrays for about 31¢ total. It is long lasting and very aromatic.

—Steven Lavender
West Palm Beach, Florida

ROUND ROBIN REDUX

Dear Amy,

With our six children spread all over the United States and in foreign lands, we used to use the "Round Robin" method of correspondence (explained on page 236) to keep in touch. For the past couple of years we have successfully used a variation; admittedly it's a little more expensive, but it's still reasonable and much more timely. Ours is the "Radiating Robin," and we, the parents, are the hub. The kids mail us a letter on the first Sunday of each month. We then make six photocopies of each and mail a set to each individual within the next week. I had a copy shop run off labels with the kids' addresses to make mailing easier.

—Gail Jackson
Blue Springs, Missouri

IMAGINING HOLIDAY PERFECTION . . . OR TRY IT, YULE LIKE IT

If I were the master of the universe, I would change all of the rules for holiday gift-giving. In my tightwad utopia, I would decree the following:

- Gifts shall not be given simply for the sake of giving a gift.
- Gifts shall be given only according to each individual's resources and inspiration.
- If an individual receives a gift from someone for whom he doesn't have a gift, no one shall care.
- The merits of a gift shall be based on thoughtfulness, cleverness, and appropriateness, not on the amount of money spent or whether it came from a store.
- If an individual is a regular recipient of a gift from a close friend or relative, it shall be acceptable for the recipient to suggest a gift idea that would be free and easy for the giver.

I am not the master of the universe, so the world will probably never be as I would like. I am, however, the "benevolent boss" of a much smaller realm: a company called *The Tightwad Gazette.* While we have no company policy on gift-giving, I've encouraged certain attitudes among my handful of employees. In the aftermath of one company party, I sat and viewed the explosion of wrappings, reflected on the gifts, and glowed. I thought, "This is the way everyone's Christmas should be." So, I want to share the specifics of what everyone did:

During the previous fall, I had suggested something that Elaine, our former business manager,

could do for me for Christmas. My great-grandmother knitted mittens for us every Christmas when we were young. I failed to appreciate them completely back then, but had become nostalgic for them in my adult years. A few years ago I came into the possession of a pair of child-sized mittens my great-grandmother had begun more than 25 years earlier. Although all the yarn was there, one mitten was only half finished. Elaine is an excellent knitter, so I asked if she would complete the mittens for me as my Christmas gift. She was pleased at my suggestion because it was an easy gift for her to give. So I received the completed mittens, and Elaine's work is indistinguishable from my great-grandmother's.

Elaine had a special relationship with my then five-year-old daughter, Rebecca. For Becca's previous birthday, Elaine had made matching yellow aprons for them to wear when cooking together at the office. Before Christmas, Becca wanted to make a present for Elaine. So I helped Becca make a pastel drawing of her and Elaine in their matching aprons, baking cookies. This was made to fit into an existing secondhand frame, which Becca and I also refinished. The picture now hangs in Elaine's office.

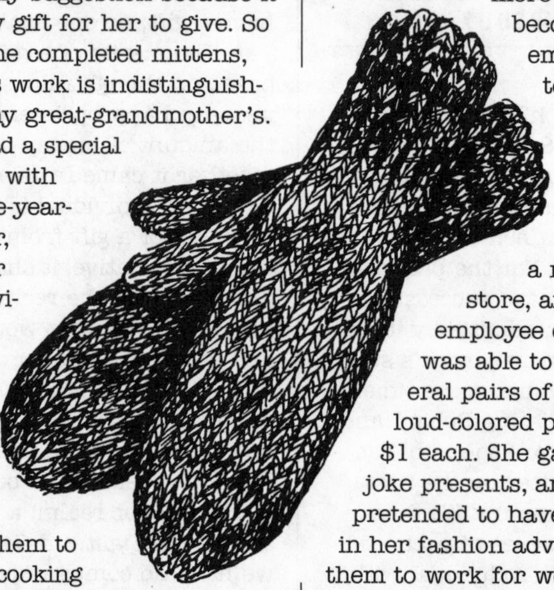

David, who ran our addressing machine, pleased and surprised us with simple, wooden, cut-out and painted ornaments of his own design, frugally wrapped in small brown bags.

I collect old blue-and-white dishes. Pam, a multipurpose employee, bought a lovely, large blue-and-white antique teacup at a yard sale as a gift for me. The cup has a rural scene painted on the outside; inside is a painted dog that resembles our own dog, Charlie. I love it.

In contrast to those of us who dress primarily for economy and comfort, Holly, our Generation X data-entry person, dresses far more stylishly. It has become an employee joke to tease Holly by asking her for fashion advice. Holly's husband works for a men's clothing store, and with his employee discount she was able to purchase several pairs of marked-down, loud-colored plaid socks for $1 each. She gave these as joke presents, and naturally we pretended to have complete faith in her fashion advice and wore them to work for weeks.

Frances, who opens our mail, came to me a month before Christmas and asked me if she could barter a few cuts of her home-grown beef, which she had in surplus, for newsletter subscriptions she could give to people on her list. The swap would have messed up our company bookkeeping, and the bartered cost of the meat exceeded the amount we customarily pay. So I declined and reminded her that in addition to a Christmas bonus,

employees are entitled to give away a certain number of free subscriptions. But I also subtly indicated that surplus beef makes a nice gift. We enjoyed ten pounds of her beef last winter.

Many of the adults gave our children yard-sale finds. Brad was thrilled with his recorder and tooted around the house for hours. Becca received an enormous pile of yard-sale jewelry from Elaine. Elaine, a lover of books, bought Jamie, my lover of books, a stack from a library-book sale. Pam picked up some coloring books at yard sales, which had just a few pictures already colored and some odd pencil markings. She carefully cut out the colored-on pages, erased the pencil markings, and gave my kids the like-new books. Alec received a new football-shaped soap-on-a-rope from a yard sale, and a carpenter's apron from a mail-order source which had discounted it to $1.

Blanche, another mail opener, gave our children a selection of small gifts she had purchased from a salvage store. She gave other employees homemade wreaths and craft items she had purchased at discount from a relative who makes them.

Pam likes old comic books. When Elaine went into the comic book store she found used ones for 25¢ each, and she bought a pile for Pam.

Frances is an excellent cook and gave various coworkers homemade jams, salsas, and pickles. Frances also made "jelly-bean prescription jars." The jars are filled with variously colored gourmet jelly beans and include "instructions." Each color is designated with a special cure that is relevant to the recipient, such as "Green is good for memory improvement."

Elaine gave Jim a volume of "Far Side" comics and another of "Doonesbury." These used books were slightly worn, but the jokes were still good.

One of the downsides of my minor-celebrity status is that I get spotted when I go to area yard sales. This is a problem, as I find it difficult to negotiate while blushing. As a joke present, Jim made me a pair of "anonymous glasses." He popped the lenses out of an old pair of sunglasses and then covered the frame with a huge rectangle of black felt. He cut tiny holes for me to see through. Then, because I have a tendency to lose earrings, he attached large brass fishing lures to the sides.

While I've highlighted some of the successful gifts, as with all gift-giving, there was, undoubtedly, a gift or two that missed the mark. But part of the pleasure of frugal gift-giving (and receiving) is that when the wrong gift is given, it's comforting to know that little or no money was wasted.

My situation may seem unique, but it really isn't. Every business, and every family, has one or two people who set the tone, either by domineering, or by (my style) gentle, kindly, unrelenting persuasion. I wish you success in persuading the people in your own "realm."

AN ITCHING, BURNING QUESTION

I have often written on the cost advantage of used shoes. People usually raise two objections to them. In *The Tightwad Gazette II,* I quoted experts who cast serious doubt on one of these objections: that used shoes can structurally damage feet. The second question concerns the possible spread of athlete's foot.

To check this out, I talked with Dr. Donald Greer, a professor in the department of dermatology and pathology at Louisiana State University. Dr. Greer might rightly be regarded as "Mr. Athlete's Foot." He has conducted several in-depth studies on the subject, and has been recommended by the National Institutes of Health as a leading authority.

He said that while it's theoretically possible to be infected by an athlete's foot fungus in a used shoe, "the probability is almost nil." And, he told me, a couple of simple precautions can eliminate even the remote chance of infection.

Dr. Greer said four conditions are needed for athlete's foot to develop: natural susceptibility (and no one knows what causes this), warm temperature, high humidity, and occlusion (being covered up, such as by a fairly airtight shoe). He said natural susceptibility is perhaps the biggest factor—if by age 30 you've never had athlete's foot, it's very unlikely you'll get it. If you are susceptible, chances are far greater that you'll reinfect yourself with your own shoes than with someone else's shoes.

He added that athlete's foot is quite rare in children, and so the spread through kids' used shoes is even more unlikely.

Dr. Greer said the organisms that cause athlete's foot can live in shoes, but only as long as the shoe remains relatively damp, as could happen over long periods in the humid Southeast. Once a shoe is completely dry, the athlete's foot fungus dies. This factor indicates why rented bowling shoes, which may swap owners within an hour, are sprayed; but why, at least in Maine, there are no laws governing the treatment of used shoes to be sold in thrift shops.

If you have any doubts about used shoes, Dr. Greer recommends these precautions:

- Run canvas sneakers through the washing machine and dryer.
- Spray the interior of leather shoes with a disinfectant such as Lysol, then dust with a drying powder such as Desenex.
- A tightwad alternative in dry climates is simply to unlace the shoe, pull back the tongue, and leave in the sun or in a hot, dry place.

Dr. Greer said he couldn't give any specific recommendations as to the length of drying time because there are too many variables. My guess is that any used shoes that have been sitting in the blistering sun on a summertime yard-sale day will be plenty dry enough.

THE PANTRY PRINCIPLE UPDATE

In my "Pantry Principle" article in *The Tightwad Gazette II,* I explained that to save the most money and time when buying food,

you should shop to replenish your pantry, not to make specific meals. That article prompted Karen Buckwalter of Palmyra, Missouri, to ask: "What must the tightwad pantry include?"

Because people have different needs, resources, and preferences, I can't prescribe "musts." Instead I offer this list of what's in our pantry and freezer as a general guideline; it's complete except for a few foods we purchase specifically for holidays and birthdays. It's as important to note what's *not* on this list as what's on it.

Baking supplies: Baking powder, baking soda, salt, cocoa, yeast, coconut, sunflower seeds, soy flour, eggs, bulk-purchased gelatin, cornstarch, vinegar, paste food coloring, colored sprinkles.

Breads: Whole-wheat loaves, bagels, English muffins, saltines. (We make other breads.)

Cheese: Parmesan, cream, and hard cheeses when the price drops below $2 per pound.

Cold cereal: Any cereal when price drops to 7¢ per ounce, frequently corn flakes, rarely presweetened cereal.

Condiments: Catsup, mayonnaise, mustard. (We make jams, pickles, and relishes.)

Fats: Corn oil, olive oil, margarine, shortening, no-stick spray.

Fruits: Apples, bananas, raisins, and, occasionally, other fresh fruits when on sale. Canned pineapple and other canned fruit as it turns up in "mystery cans" from the salvage store (see page 13). (We grow strawberries and acquire blackberries, blueberries, and pears from a relative.)

Grains: White flour, whole-wheat flour, rye flour, oatmeal, cornmeal, rice, popcorn, wheat germ.

Juices: Orange, apple, grape, lemon.

Legumes: Peanut butter, dried beans, dried peas, lentils.

Meats: Chicken parts, ground beef, ground turkey, whole turkey, tuna, ham, pork shoulder, bologna, hot dogs, bacon, salami, kielbasa, and other meats when sale price is low enough. (The article on page 105, "I Wouldn't Steer You Wrong," details my basic guidelines for meat purchases.)

Milk: Dry milk, whole milk.

Nonnutritious beverages: Tea, ground coffee.

Packaged dinners: Macaroni-and-cheese.

Pasta: Spaghetti, macaroni, and other pasta when the price drops to 33¢ per pound.

Seasonings and flavorings: A large selection of herbs and spices, wine and sherry for cooking, bouillon, soy sauce, Worcestershire sauce, artificial vanilla extract, maple extract.

Sweeteners: White sugar, brown sugar, confectioners' sugar, molasses, honey, corn syrup.

Vegetables: Onions, celery, potatoes, frozen french fries, instant mashed potatoes, tomato paste. (We grow a wide range of other vegetables.)

GET A PIECE OF THE AUCTION

I generally buy used household items at two places: yard sales and estate sales. In terms of saving money, yard sales are a better use of my time. But in terms of entertainment value, estate sales win hands down.

An estate sale is an auction of the contents of a home, usually of someone who has died. Because most people who die are older, their household effects frequently include antiques and collectibles. For this reason the term "estate sale" is generally synonymous with "antique auction."

Although some of these auctions offer only a selection of antiques from several estates, a true estate sale will include merchandise ranging from the very valuable to the very useless. In between you may find rakes, vacuum cleaners, and bedding—stuff that is rare at yard sales.

Ads for estate sales appear in the Sunday paper and include a partial listing of items to be sold. On-site sales (sales at the house instead of another location) generally have more nonantique items, but not always.

Having attended the auctions of several companies, I've found that it's hard to pick a good auction by reading ads. That's because it's the auctioneer, rather than the specific merchandise, that determines the quality of the auction. Some are more entertaining, more knowledgeable, and have more talent for putting together a good event. Attend sales of several companies before deciding if there's enough fun and/or savings to make this activity worthwhile for you.

I view estate sales

primarily as entertainment. I attend a dozen a year and purchase less than one item per sale. So to avoid hefty babysitting fees, Jim and I go separately, each with our auction buddies (good friends who enjoy old things and share a sense of adventure). We share the cost of gasoline and bring a "bag dinner." By doing this, we feel no disappointment when we come home empty-handed—we've had a good time for free.

When you go, arrive early to get a bidding card with your number and to preview the sale. Carefully inspect the merchandise for quality and condition, and note the item's lot number when similar items are to be sold. At this point, make a mental note as to the top price you'd pay for the item—you don't want to decide this during the bidding frenzy. Also learn the sales terms. For instance, some auctions tack on a 10 percent buyer's premium to the price you've bid.

It's a good idea to attend several auctions before you bid on anything. Not only will you get a good feel for how it's done, but you'll also get a sense of the price things bring at auctions and how common certain kinds of merchandise are. For instance, you might see an old treadle sewing machine sell for $50, which seems like a steal until you discover that every other sale has a $50 treadle machine. It's more likely a beginner will regret buying than not buying, so be slow to bid.

There's no surefire strategy to "psych out" other bidders. Just stick to the top price that you've already determined.

As for the merchandise offered, I've observed four categories:

Antiques and collectibles. Because about half of auction attendees are dealers, steals are rare. Generally, dealers will not bid more than 80 percent of any item's retail value, and their presence ensures that few valuables will sell for less than 50 percent of the retail value. Exceptions can occur when nondealers bid the price higher than this range.

So think of estate sales as a source of wholesale-priced antiques. A small oak table might

sell for $35 at an estate sale, $60 at an antique shop, and $90 at an antique show. However, since I'm extremely slow to buy antiques, I primarily view the sale of antiques as educational and entertaining. It's educational because I learn about the value of antique furniture, which will help me make more intelligent purchases, from whatever source, in the future. And it's just plain entertaining to see a Civil War diary sell for $675.

Nonantique valuables. These may include appliances, boats, and snow blowers; however, you'll more often find good-quality used furniture circa 1940 through 1960, before the scourge of particleboard overtook middle-class furnishings. Because most people attending these sales are seeking antiques, this stuff can go surprisingly cheap. One of my auction buddies purchased an "inoffensive," quality maple bedroom set, including a bed frame, full-size mattress, and box spring, a writing table, and two bureaus for $280. I've never seen any furniture remotely this nice at a yard sale.

If you're blessed with "unique" tastes, you can really clean up. Ugly furniture goes breathtakingly cheap. I've seen a massive, ornate, solid-mahogany sideboy sell for $50. Formica dinettes with chairs go for $10.

Box lots. A true estate sale in which the entire contents of the house are sold will have boxes of common household items such as bedding, tools, books, and kitchen utensils, as well as loads of stuff representing the worst of American taste. (You gotta wonder how anyone who owned a Chippendale highboy also decorated with "string art" and starburst clocks.) This stuff usually sells last, when the crowd has thinned dramatically, or at the "preauction." Often, whoever bids a dollar gets a whole box of stuff. Within this category I've seen merchandise exceed yard-sale prices, but I've also seen a garbage bag full of sheets sell for $1. If you want just one item in the whole lot and you don't win the bid, you can privately approach the buyer with an offer. Jim bought a 16-quart pressure canner for $6 this way.

The truly amazing. These antique and nonantique items reveal a side of human nature that boggles the mind. I've seen an 80 percent complete 1940s homemade airplane, in parts, that wouldn't sell for $1, but individual parts sold for a total of hundreds of dollars. A trunk of miscellaneous items sold for $2; a locked, unopenable one sold for $20. In one sale a large, rare wooden bowl sold for $150. The next bowl, identical except for a splash of original blue paint on the underside, sold for $300 (at which point the auctioneer yells to his helper, "Hey, Charlie, get out the can of blue spray paint!").

Like I said, estate sales are great, cheap entertainment, with the occasional bargain thrown in.

EEK! ANTIQUES?

After just reading about estate auctions, I imagine many readers are wondering, "What's so tightwaddy about antiques?" In fact, some antiques can be economical.

Many people think of antiques as what the Queen Mother lives with; all Chippendale, candelabras, and crystal. Or they think it's all like what's featured in *Country Living* magazine—severely countrified kitchens crammed with so many Indian baskets, painted firkins, spinning wheels, quilts, duck decoys, and crocks of wooden spoons that no grandma could turn around in one, much less bake a pie. When you price these smaller antiques, you know this look could be achieved only by spending a small fortune.

But there is a range of antique furniture that does make economic sense. It generally dates from 1875 to 1925. It was the middle-class furniture of its day. It's solid wood, and sometimes shows signs of use. It's appealing, but it was made to be lived with, not just collected and admired.

Even within this category there are exceptions for reasons of impracticality and price. For instance, antique sofas may be uncomfortable, bed frames may be of an odd size, and dining chairs may turn to kindling after a bit of abuse by children. And there are a few raging collectible trends, such as mission oak, that have pushed prices into the stratosphere.

The exceptions aside, these modest antiques can make sense for the following reasons:

- When comparing furniture of equal craftsmanship, antiques are frequently cheaper. It's true that many smaller antiques far exceed the price of their new counterparts, and so I seldom buy these things; instead I pick up look-alikes and collectibles at yard sales. But often the larger the antique is, the more competitive the price is when compared to new, quality furniture. At estate sales, large antique bureaus in good condition average $300. A same-sized but lower-quality bureau costs about $350 at Sears. A bureau with quality and aesthetic appeal equal to that of an antique can cost $750 at a contemporary furniture store.

Antique prices vary depending on the month, the affluence of the community, and the region of the country (although a West Coast auctioneer that I called told me that prices there are similar to what we see in the Northeast).

- Antiques appreciate in value, so if you ever change your mind, you should be able to sell the item for what you paid, if not more. Any minor wear and dings you've added won't matter. As witnessed at estate auctions, even quality contemporary furniture depreciates in value, and furniture of medium quality depreciates even more radically.
- Contemporary furniture will almost certainly look dated within a decade or two. The antiques my grandparents purchased in the 1930s look even better today.
- Often good antiques can be priced low because they require refinishing or repair. Sometimes hiring this work isn't cost-effective for dealers. Yet many visionless buyers will overlook these pieces.

Predicting how much refinishing or repair might be required isn't always easy. Sometimes an evening's worth of work increases the value of a bureau by $100. In cases where I guessed wrong, my hourly wage dipped to 73¢.

- Antiques provide entertainment as you hunt down hard-to-find items; we have casually searched for specific pieces for years. Because many antiques are unique, you have to educate your-

self about types of wood, construction, styles, and prices. But most important, it takes time to learn what you really like. Holding out for affordable treasures has always paid off. In the meantime, we've made do with scavenged furniture and had fun poking around antique shops and attending auctions.

Finally, if you don't love antiques, don't buy them. While they can be fairly economical if purchased intelligently, they aren't the cheapest way to furnish a house. Creative scroungers who aren't picky about aesthetics can furnish a house for free. But if you have already determined that you are going to own quality furniture that you love, antiques are an option to explore.

ETCH AND CATCH

Carol Stutts of Berea, Kentucky, alerted us to a unique method of saving on your automobile insurance and, as a side benefit, greatly reducing the chance that your car will be stolen.

It's simple: Using a kit (available by mail from Automark Corp.), you etch your car's federally registered vehicle identification number (VIN) onto each of its windows. In a study conducted in a high-theft area of Southern California, 6,955 vehicles were etched. Statistically, 133 of these vehicles should have been stolen during the next 18 months, but only 15 were stolen.

This works because when a valuable car is stolen for resale, the thief pops in a new dashboard vehicle identification number tag from a same-model junked car that he's purchased. Having to replace all the windows as well makes the operation too expensive. Medium-aged cars are often stolen for sale to "chop shops," where they're disassembled for parts. Chop shops don't want cars with etched glass because the doors, a valuable replacement part, become worthless for resale.

However, etching may not prevent the theft of an old car. These are usually stolen only for joyriding or for use in the commission of a crime. In this case, the thief plans to ditch the car within a few hours.

Because of the success of etching, several states have passed laws requiring car insurance companies to give discounts on the "comprehensive" portion of car insurance to car owners who etch their glass. Some insurance companies also have their own policies regarding discounts for etching. Call your state insurance commissioner and/or your insurer to find out whether your state and/or insurance company participates in these discounts. Automark will also be happy to provide you with up-to-date copies of legislation from states that require the discount.

The etching process isn't complicated. A kit comes with eight stencils, each of which is preprinted with your car's vehicle identification number. You peel off the backing and stick one on the bottom corner of each window in your car. You apply the etching gel and wait one minute. Then you peel away the stencil and the window is etched. The kit includes a decal warning crooks that identification numbers have been affixed to the windows, and it contains a certificate to send to your insurance

company verifying that you've etched your windows.

The regular price of the kit is $24.95 plus $2.50 shipping and handling, but *Gazette* readers get a discount. If you mention that you read about the kit in *The Tightwad Gazette,* the price is $11.95 plus $2.50 for shipping and handling. (If you order two or more kits, the total shipping charge is still just $2.50.)

Order from:

Automark Corp.
4323 Poplar Level Road
Louisville, KY 40213
(502) 452-9500

Along with your name, address, and number of kits desired, be sure to send the VIN(s) of your vehicle(s). You'll find it on your registration, or on a small metal plate on your dashboard.

Be aware that some automakers have begun etching car windows at the factory. Also, some glass companies, military bases, insurance companies, and police stations offer free etching. Check your windows and call around before ordering a kit.

BAG TO BASICS

Dear Amy,

All my life, I've loved my mother's Christmas wreath. It wasn't until I was an adult that I discovered she'd made it out of clear plastic bags and a wire coat hanger!

Start by snipping off the hook of a hanger and shape the remaining part into a circle, covering the joined ends with electrical or duct tape. Then cut about three dozen plastic bags into strips about 4 inches wide by 8 to 10 inches long. Tie the strips to the wire and fluff out the ends. Try to squeeze as many as possible onto the wire (but don't stretch the plastic in your effort to keep the knots small). The result is a fluffy, shimmery, silvery wreath, which you can then decorate with ribbons, ornaments, or whatever.

—Rebecca Nguyen
Alexandria, Virginia

ST. NICK TRICK

Dear Amy,

Take your own camera to the mall when your kids visit Santa. I've found that the Santa booths always allow you to take your own pictures. This tip saved me $7 per photo.

—Kim Lenart
Denton, Texas

BUDGET CUTTING GIFT

Dear Amy,

Here is a gift kids can make. Taking into account the interests of the recipients, collect these from newspapers: crossword puzzles, word games, cartoons, or bridge or chess problems. Make booklets of construction paper folded crosswise and sewn together through the centers. Paste clippings on pages; put solutions on the last pages.

—Mary B. Licari
Ft. Washington, Maryland

PHOTO FINESSE

Dear Amy,

While organizing my mother's "picture drawer" into albums, I decided that I would love to have some copies of these photos for myself and as gifts. But professional copies of old photos are very expensive if there are no negatives. So I lightly taped my favorite photos to a piece of typing paper and took them to a local copy shop to be reproduced on a laser copier. I was very impressed with the results. The charge was about $1.70 a sheet.

—Janet Bayless
Camdenton, Missouri

TIDEPOOL TIDINGS

Dear Amy,

Using twine, I tie a real, large, dried starfish to the top of my Christmas tree for a beautiful, inexpensive, natural "star."

—Sherry Brooks
Westlake Village, California

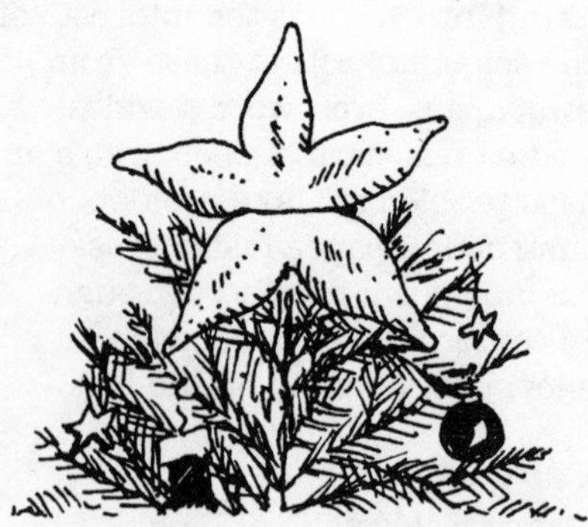

CHRISTMAS TREE CONES

Dear Amy,

These holiday treats taste good and look pretty:

6 pointy ice-cream cones
Lots of small pieces of candy, such as M&Ms, red-hots, sprinkles, etc.
2 cups powdered sugar
3 tablespoons soft margarine
1 tablespoon milk
3 teaspoons green food coloring
1 teaspoon vanilla

Mix sugar, margarine, milk, food coloring, and vanilla until creamy. Stand cones on plate or pan. Spread frosting all over cones with a butter knife or spatula. Stick candy on trees by pushing into frosting.

—Catherine Chavis
Florence, South Carolina

GOOFY GIFTS

Dear Amy,

My relatives and I give each other "goofy gifts." The rules are simple: It can't cost over a dollar, it must be clean, and it should be totally useless and/or as tacky as possible.

Garage sales and flea markets are the main sources. The trick is to turn your mind at garage sales to finding the worst thing, not the best. It's lots of fun to see the shock and amazement on the faces of the sellers, as they think, "I never thought *that* would sell!"

Through the years, we have exchanged stuff like beer-can bedroom slippers, tacky ashtrays, a

leather chewing gum dispenser, and several things we have yet to figure out.

Several of my friends have now joined my list, and some of the gifts get given again. It has turned out to be one of our favorite parts of Christmas, and we can't wait to see what will turn up next.

—Muriel Kupper
Downers Grove, Illinois

YANKEE SWAP

Dear Amy,

When family gift-giving becomes overburdened because there are too many kids or money is tight, a "yankee swap" is a creative alternative.

Each person brings one wrapped gift and puts it into a large container (we used a wicker laundry basket). Then everyone draws a number. Number One chooses a gift from the basket and opens it. Number Two then picks a gift, opens it, and can either keep it or swap it for Number One's gift. Number Three picks a gift, opens it, and can swap with Number One or Two, and so on. This keeps going until everyone has picked, swapped, and kept, amid laughing and joking.

—Nancy Wilson
Warren, Maine

(How about combining "Goofy Gifts" and "Yankee Swap" to make the gift-exchanging ritual even funnier? FZ)

'TIS THE SEASONING

Dear Amy,

I grow herbs and dry them. Then I package the herbs for friends and family as gifts. People who cook love to receive them. If you mail them, they are very lightweight for shipping.

—Laura Lipinski
Seven Valleys, Pennsylvania

FROM CHIPS TO STRIPS

Dear Amy,

I recycle Mylar popcorn and potato-chip bags into ribbon for wrapping and decorating packages. Just wipe out the inside of the bag with a damp cloth, then cut a long strip from it by spiraling around the bag. You now have a ribbon to curl like any other curling ribbon. Be sure to curl it so that the shiny side is facing out.

—Ellie Pett
Elmhurst, Illinois

THE UNMAGICAL TIME-MANAGEMENT METHOD

Because readers know that we have six kids and do time-intensive frugal activities such as gardening, canning, and quilt-making, they apparently feel there's a magical strategy that we've hit upon to squeeze more hours out of the day. "How do you manage your time?" and "Can you describe your typical day?" are among the most frequent questions I'm asked.

But the answer is that magical

strategies are few. Like saving money, most of saving time involves the making of choices.

In response to the requests to share a "typical day," I must say our lives vary quite a bit from day to day. However, there is a basic pattern:

We get up at 7 A.M. Jim makes breakfast while I prepare lunch boxes. Within an hour the six children are all out waiting for the school bus.

Then the houseperson (once it was always me, now it's usually Jim) divides the day into two parts. The morning is devoted to the routine household maintenance without which our lives would be completely chaotic. Each day the houseperson washes breakfast dishes, washes and hangs one or two loads of laundry, vacuums the downstairs, makes our bed, and generally picks up. Every two or three days a mountain of clean, dry laundry gets folded, floors get damp mopped, and bathrooms are cleaned.

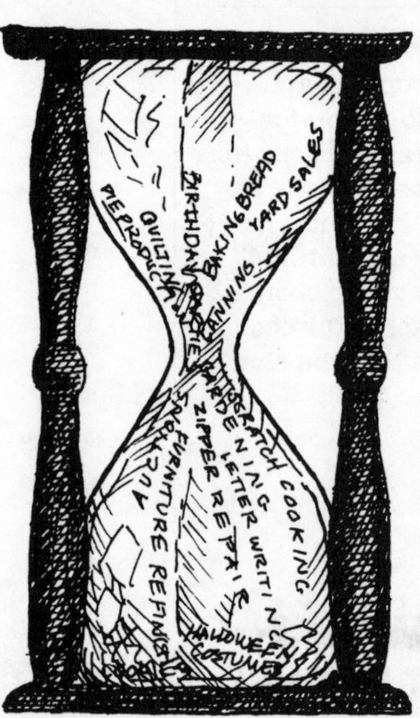

The houseperson compresses these boring activities into the morning so that the afternoons are freed up for more satisfying activities. These might include lawn work, gardening, cleaning the workshop, refinishing furniture, writing letters, home-renovation projects, Halloween-costume making, or baking cookies.

Jim usually makes supper. We alternate washing dishes. Aside from a continuation of the afternoon activities, our evenings consist of helping kids with homework, Scout-related activities, paying bills, giving baths, and occasionally going to estate auctions.

Sometime around 9 P.M., Jim and I crash and watch an hour or two of TV before going to bed. I may or may not be working on a project while watching TV.

If this routine doesn't sound remarkable to you, I agree. It isn't. If there's any "magical strategy," it's to be found in what we *don't* do. For instance:

- I don't blow-dry my hair and put on makeup, except on special occasions. I spend about the same time grooming as does my husband.
- I don't commute to a job.
- I don't have a spotlessly clean house, although it is generally tidy.
- I don't clean my children's rooms for them. They clean their rooms daily and aren't allowed to do anything else until their rooms "pass inspection."
- I don't prepare meals that would impress Martha Stewart.
- I don't chauffeur my kids to several places each day. If they want a friend over I will provide transportation two times a month. They are allowed one outside activity at a time.
- I don't insist on 24-hour togetherness with Jim. For example, he does the grocery shopping alone because my coming with him wouldn't speed up the process. Similarly, I yard-sale alone, attend school events alone, and sometimes even visit far-away relatives alone.

• I don't micromanage my kids' appearance. By age four, they choose their own clothes and dress themselves each morning. And I don't do complex hairdos—my girls have simple, straight hairstyles.

• I don't read more than one book a day to children.

• I have few volunteer commitments to organizations. Jim is a Scout treasurer but has no other commitments.

• I don't give my children a bath and shampoo each night. They get a bath as needed, or a minimum of once a week.

• I don't have an hour-long bedtime ritual for kids. Once I announce "Bedtime!" everyone is in bed in less than ten minutes.

• I don't drive my kids to get professional haircuts. Home haircuts save time as well as money.

• I don't read the newspaper every day. I occasionally read parts of the Sunday paper.

• I don't read novels, although I like them. I do read nonfiction when the information applies to work or to a personal project.

• I don't stop what I'm doing every time a child "needs" something. I say, with firmness, "I'm busy and can't do it now."

• I don't prepare sit-down lunches, although our family always eats breakfasts and suppers together. I will fix a sandwich or warm up leftovers for small children, and I make sure there's a selection of snacks and lunches that are easy for older kids to get for themselves.

• I don't socialize a lot, unless I'm combining it with a productive activity.

• I don't spend hours on the telephone. I average less than one social phone call per week, and even then I might wipe down kitchen cabinets at the same time.

• I don't watch TV during the daytime unless I'm doing a monotonous project at the same time.

• I don't work out . . . enough.

• I don't entertain my children. We place limits on television and leave them to their own devices after that.

• I don't have relatives who live nearby, so I don't spend time with them on a regular basis.

Within this group of "I don'ts" are things that others cannot duplicate easily. They are offered only as an explanation. Other "I don'ts" do provide genuine value to the lives of those who choose to do them. And there are some "I don'ts" that I could—and maybe should—make more time for. But I've arrived at these because they work best for myself and my family.

About half of these "I don'ts" others do because they feel it's part of "good parenting." But by omitting some of these I can include other activities that double as quality time with my kids. They have fun, learn, and feel accomplishment when they help me with my projects. Typically, when I was canning carrots one fall, five out of six of my children offered to help with washing, peeling, chopping, and filling jars. The other child, Alec, was helping Jim with a woodworking project in the workshop.

Further, I believe my kids benefit more from having a chaos-free home life.

There's an interesting parallel between those who claim they don't have enough money and those who claim they don't have enough time. In most cases, those who are short of cash are spending money on nonessentials. People

who claim they don't have enough time are usually choosing to give time to nonessential activities. In each case, it would be more truthful to say that they are *choosing* to spend money/time on other things.

The choices that you make won't necessarily be the ones I've made. But what's important is that whatever time-management strategy you use, you do it consciously. In my experience, most people who feel incredibly harried haven't made conscious, deliberate decisions about what is valuable to them and what isn't. Rather, they allow their time to be monopolized by whatever someone else demands of them at the moment, or whatever project happens to strike their fancy at a given time.

Successful time management means setting your own agenda and sticking to it. You can be flexible, but you must be willing to say "no" if there are too many obstacles between you and your goals.

PARSIMONIOUS PURCHASE POINTERS

Peggy Beals of Marshfield, Massachusetts, offers the following "Test for Value." Before making a purchase, she asks the following questions:

1. Can we do without it?

2. Does it do more than required?

3. Does it cost more than it's worth?

4. Can we do what it does with things we already have?

5. How often will we use it?

6. Where will we store it?

7. Will using it be more work than we're apt to want to do?

8. How many ways can we use it?

9. Have we checked with people who own one and with consumer ratings?

10. Would I be smarter to resist, and put the money toward another goal?

Peggy says this test has prevented her from buying a pasta machine, a bread-making machine, a word processor, joining a book club, and subscribing to several magazines.

While few purchases would pass all ten questions, it's safe to say that a wise purchase should pass eight or nine of them. Further, I would like to add another point:

11. If the item does not satisfy these criteria, can I at least resell it for the same price I paid?

This point means that it might be sensible to buy a secondhand item at a good price even if it does not measure up on points 1 through 10, because if you decide the item isn't worth keeping you can always recover your investment. Items in this category include expensive toys and sporting equipment for fickle kids, and marginal tools and kitchen gadgets for adults.

YOU CAN CAN . . . CHEAPLY

There's no shortage of written information out there about canning. Dozens of books and magazine articles give lengthy, specific explanations about how to can various vegetables, fruits, meats, and seafoods.

In this article we won't repeat any of this basic information, so it's essential that you pick up a comprehensive guide with the latest USDA recommendations.

One that I have read and highly recommend is *The Ball Blue Book: The Guide to Home Canning and Freezing,* which is available for $3.50 plus $1.00 shipping and handling from the Alltrista Corporation, Consumer Products Company, Consumer Affairs Department, P.O. Box 2729, Muncie, IN 47307. You can also write to the same address and sign up for a *free* lifetime subscription to Ball's excellent twice-yearly canning newsletter, *Consumer Newsline.*

Another up-to-date book is *The Kerr Kitchen Cookbook: Home Canning and Freezing Guide,* which is available for $3.50 plus 50¢ shipping from Kerr, P.O. Box 67961, Los Angeles, CA 90076. Kerr also has a newsletter free for the asking from the same address.

In this article we'll cover the tightwad angle on canning. Specifically, we'll dispel some myths and pass along some time- and money-saving pointers.

First, the myths:

• "Canning is difficult, tedious, and time-consuming." Several times I have run into modern, hip, '90s-type folks who have learned to can and they always say they are amazed at how easy it is.

People assume that canning must be difficult simply because it's unfamiliar; most of us are a generation or two away from anyone who's done it. But watching a pressure gauge isn't rocket science. If you can drive a car, you can can.

As for "tedious and time-consuming," canning can seem that way because you are generally processing a great deal of food at one time. But as you use that food day after day, you'll find it is actually a time-saver. For example, rather than making spaghetti sauce from scratch dozens of times in a year, you can cook up a year's worth of ready-to-use spaghetti sauce in just a few hours. If you're canning carrots, you'll do the same washing, peeling, chopping, and cooking that you would do over and over during the year. Canning is just one more simple step.

• "Canning is not economical." I have actually read this statement in "How to Can" books. The assumption is based on buying all of your equipment new and does not factor in that you'll reuse the same canner, jars, and rings year after year.

The reality is that when you're

canning free food such as surplus garden vegetables that would otherwise go bad, the only cost per quart is 7¢ for the lid, an insignificant energy cost, and the amortized cost of the canner, jars, and rings (which can be near zero; more on this later).

Naturally, the savings depend on what you're canning. Assuming the produce is free, and comparing home-canned to store-bought equivalents, the "hourly wage" for canning rhubarb jam is $15, but for canning pears it's just $1. The difference is in the time required to prepare the fruits.

In addition, canning can be an energy saver. The energy required to pressure-can 7 quarts of green beans is about the same as is needed to cook a single pot of fresh beans.

- "Canning is dangerous." It's important to acknowledge the danger of botulism in improperly canned food, but it's just as important to keep it in perspective. According to the Centers for Disease Control, in 1992 (the most recent year for which statistics are available) there were just 17 cases, and 1 death, resulting from foodborne botulism nationwide. ("Infant botulism" is more common, but it's a separate disease that infants can get from eating foods that are harmless to adults.)

Botulism outbreaks are most frequent in Alaska, Washington State, Oregon, and California, apparently because the *Clostridium botulinum* spores are more common in the soil there. Nonetheless, canners in all states should follow the rules to the letter. When they do so, canning is quite safe.

- "Canning is just for country folk with big gardens." It's true that it's seldom economical to can regular-price supermarket produce. But enterprising urbanites with some initiative can often buy cheap produce through informal arrangements with produce managers, can get it by U-pick and "gleaning" programs, or can even get it free from gardening friends. For example, I bought a bushel of "drops" at a U-pick apple orchard for $4. This made 21 quarts of applesauce. Including the lid, the cost of each quart was 26¢. That's about half the lowest price for store-bought applesauce.

- "Canning is only for people who love to cook." Kelly Frey of Readfield, Maine, loves to cook and hates to garden. Her friend loves to garden and hates to cook. They've worked out a deal in which Kelly cans her friend's garden produce and they each keep half the jars.

- "Canning is unnecessary for people who have freezers." Every canner I have ever known has also had a freezer. One reason is that many people, myself included, prefer the taste of certain canned foods, such as canned string beans, over their frozen counterparts. Home-canned foods are far better tasting and more nutritious than their store-bought counterparts.

Also, canning is a flexible method of dealing with surplus. Sometimes, after your freezer is full, you may come across an unexpected windfall—say you are offered four leftover turkey carcasses from a church supper. You could cook up the carcasses and can the resulting soup stock.

Further, compared to freezer food, canned food is more "immediate"—it doesn't need to be searched for and exhumed from the bottom of a freezer and it doesn't require thawing.

Another great advantage of canned foods over frozen is that they make wonderful, much-appreciated gifts. Home-canned salsa is great under the tree; frozen stuff is harder to give away.

Having dispensed with these myths, here are some tightwad tricks that we use.

• Get equipment cheaply. Avoid buying new jars and equipment. Because canning isn't as common as it used to be, chances are if you "put out the word"—either by asking friends or by taking out a free ad in a "shopper" publication—you will be able to get most of what you need for free. To buy some time in this process, try to borrow equipment as you need it.

Jim located our first pressure canner for $2 in a thrift shop and our second at an auction for $6 (it's handy to have two so we can do twice as much at once). Older canners generally use a dial-type pressure gauge; many extension service offices have equipment that tests these for accuracy. Also, if a canner has missing or defective parts, you can get replacements by mail order from the manufacturer. Jim got a new gasket for one of our canners for $8. That's a heck of a lot cheaper than a new, sale-priced $60 canner.

I also trash-picked an "applesauce mill." We even made our canning shelves from scavenged lumber and old bricks we found.

There's also no need to buy canning jars. We got virtually all of our canning jars free, some from older relatives who no longer used them and another 200 from trash-picking.

You can also use quart-sized mayonnaise jars, as these take the same-sized lid and ring as the canning jars made by Ball or Kerr. The USDA says these are fine for water-bath canning but tend to break in a pressure canner. However, every canner I know says that mayonnaise jars break no more often in pressure canners than the "proper" jars.

applesauce mill

There are two basic types of jars. One is the glass-top jar, which requires a disposable rubber ring. The USDA no longer recommends these, as it's difficult to tell if the jar has sealed. The other, called a "dome lid," uses a screw-on metal ring that holds a flat metal lid in place. This lid has a rim of rubber on the underside.

You can reuse the rings indefinitely if you remove them from the sealed jars and store them in a dry place so they won't rust. Removing the rings also allows you to put up hundreds of jars with just a few dozen rings.

In most canning, the only part that needs to be replaced is the lid. We watch for good deals on these and have found them at salvage stores. Some tightwads claim to

successfully reuse the lids; they say they simply remove them carefully to avoid denting them. But I don't reuse lids, and experts and manufacturers specifically advise against doing this.

It's common for canners to seal jars of jam or jelly with wax instead of a lid. This can be frugal, as the wax can be reused for years, but the USDA also now advises against this.

Some canning requires supplies like spices, pickling salt, alum, or sugar. It goes without saying that you'll look for deals on these things as well.

• Use the right-sized jar. Canning jars come in small-mouth and large-mouth quarts, and small-mouth and large-mouth pints. Small lids generally cost 7¢ each, and large lids usually cost 9¢. The obvious tightwad choice is to use small-mouth quarts whenever possible.

I use small-mouth quarts for all canning aside from jams and pickles. For these I use pints, because we just don't use quarts quickly enough.

• Save on energy. For foods that can be either pressure-canned or water-bath canned, we choose pressure-canning because it's so much quicker. Green beans, for example, can be pressure-canned in 25 minutes, versus three hours for water-bath canning. (The USDA no longer recommends water-bath canning for green beans.)

dome-type canning jar lids

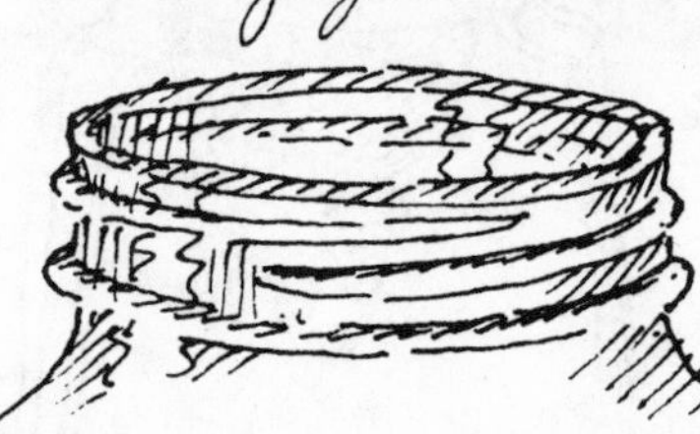

• Cut small, pack tight. The more food you can pack into a jar, the more efficient and economical the operation becomes. Unless you are willing to laboriously pack long foods like carrots and string beans into a precise, puzzlelike configuration, you'll be able to pack in another 15 percent if you cut things into small pieces so that they pack tightly. To test this, pack a jar with large pieces, empty the jar, chop the same pieces smaller, and refill. Be sure to remain within the official "headroom" guidelines, however.

• Use the hot-pack method when possible. Food shrinks during cooking, so filling jars with precooked foods instead of raw foods will save on jar space.

Finally, it's a mistake to think of the advantages of canning strictly in economic terms. While it can save lots of money, it also has psychological value. There's a great satisfaction in transforming the bounty of a garden into row upon row of canned fruits and vegetables. In my view, this is reason enough to give canning a try.

A TALE OF TIGHTWAD TRANSFORMATION UPDATE

Readers express their success with tightwaddery in a variety of ways. The following doodling appeared on the bottom of a letter from Jodi Peterson of Bloomington, Illinois.

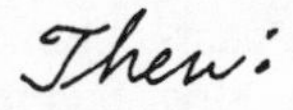

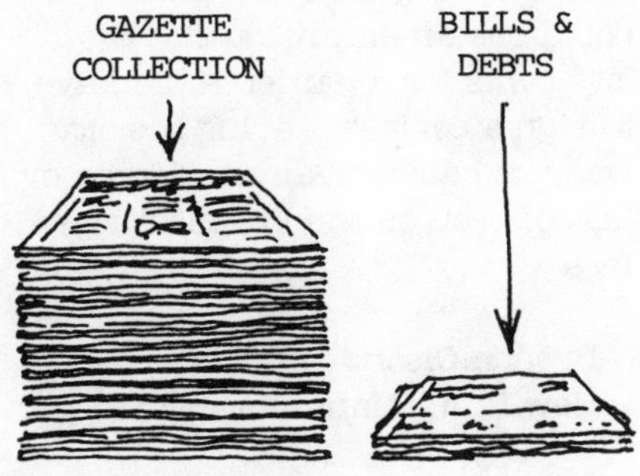

PAINT FOR KIDS

There are few more enjoyable activities for kids than painting pictures. Here are three recipes for kids' paints. The first two are from Rhonda Langley of Dayton, Oregon, and the third is from James and Earlene Giglierano of Iowa City, Iowa:

- Mix 1 teaspoon water and 1 teaspoon dishwashing liquid with ½ teaspoon liquid food coloring.
- Mix evaporated milk with enough food coloring to achieve desired hues. This paint is glossy when dry.
- Mix ⅓ cup powdered laundry starch with ½ cup cold water. Add 6 cups of boiling water, stirring constantly. Cool slightly. Divide into individual paint cups. Add food coloring, stir, and add more coloring until you achieve the desired shade. For prolonged storage, cover and keep in refrigerator.

To make each of these recipes even cheaper, I recommend the use of the paste-type food coloring sold in party-goods stores. It offers a far better range of colors and costs about the same per ounce as the liquid type, but it is much more concentrated, so it's cheaper to use.

PAINT FOR GROWN-UPS

Having recently had our house painted, I was astonished at the high price of quality latex paint. You are lucky if you can get it for $15 a gallon.

So I was intrigued by information one of my staffers gleaned from a back issue of *Organic Gardening* magazine. It's a recipe for whitewash, the stuff that used to cover practically every house, barn, and fence in America.

The mixture could not be simpler. Combine 10 pounds of ground limestone with 5 quarts of water, stirring until you get a smooth paste. A paint stirrer attached to an electric drill might make this easier. Then thin it until it is the consistency of milk.

For better, more durable cover-

age, add 1 pound of calcium chloride (available at farm-supply stores) dissolved in 1 gallon of water to the paste before you thin it.

The magazine says that one gallon of either mix will cover about 200 square feet of wood.

Unlike paint, whitewash bonds better to a wet surface, so start by scrubbing the surface to be painted with water. The stuff reportedly looks thin and fairly transparent when painted on, but is more opaque when dry.

I have not tried this, so I cannot vouch for how well it works. But in 1987, when this recipe ran in *Organic Gardening*, it cost just 30¢ a gallon. Even if today the price has zoomed to 50¢ a gallon, I'd say it's still worth a try, particularly on barns, sheds, and other buildings where you can tolerate a less-than-perfect finish.

FEELS LIKE A DEAL

Dear Amy,

The expensive carpet that our local carpet store installs is guaranteed 100 percent—even if the customer simply dislikes the color once it is installed. We let the store know that we would be interested in buying carpet that had been pulled up. We got beautiful carpet that was less than two weeks old, because the couple that bought it didn't like the way it felt on their feet. It normally costs $30 a yard. We got it for $6 a yard.

—Diane Rambo
Modesto, California

REACH OUT AND RECYCLE

Dear Amy,

I live about an hour from Salt Lake City. I wanted an SLC phone book, but I didn't want to purchase one at an outrageous price. So I waited until phone-book replacement time, went to the book recycling bin at the grocery store, and plucked the best-looking book I could reach. Most businesses I'd be interested in wouldn't change in a year's time.

—Beth Lisk
Harrisville, Utah

HIT PAY DIRT

Dear Amy,

I live in town, and our house is on a half-lot. That doesn't give us any room for a decent garden. I called the city hall and asked if I could use an empty lot that the city owns for a garden. I did have to sign a contract saying the city was not liable for any accidents or loss of crop on the lot, but it was free.

—Brenda Olson
New Ulm, Minnesota

DO THE WRITE THING

Dear Amy,

While in the hospital last month, I had a truly wonderful nurse. I wanted to do something special to express my appreciation. Instead of a gift, I wrote a letter to the director of the hospital, with copies to the nurse and her supervisor. I praised her work and positive atti-

tude, and suggested she be considered for a raise or promotion. The cost of this "gift" was under $1 for stamps and stationery, and it took no more time to deliver than a plant or candy. It occurred to me that a note to my principal from an appreciative student or teacher would have been far more welcome than many of the small gifts I received when I was teaching school.

—Karen Taylor-Ogren
West Trenton, New Jersey

SAVE BUCKS ON BUCKETS

Dear Amy,

Our community had a wonderful tightwad event this year: a toxic-waste turn-in and paint swap. Toxic wastes were safely disposed of and people acquired paints that others could not use, all for free! I brought home enough oil-based stain to completely restain our deck, and a brand-new can of paint, which I used to paint a bedroom. In addition, I got enough paint thinner to clean up the staining mess, two new paint-roller covers, an unopened tin of tile grout, and enamel paint to do the window trim in a bedroom.

—Tamara Kittelson-Aldred
Missoula, Montana

TAKE GREAT PANES

Dear Amy,

One of my favorite sources of bargains is the local demolition company. I got enough glass for a 6-foot by 6-foot greenhouse/porch addition on our house for $82. They also have everything to build with, as well as wooden carousel horses, hospital beds, marble pieces, and stained glass.

—Mrs. H. Smith
Mead, Washington

VASE VALUE

Dear Amy,

I recycle vases that come with floral bouquets by bringing them back to the florist's shop for reuse. I've also brought several from friends. The florist, in turn, sent a free bouquet to my aunt, out of state, when she was in the hospital.

I also save bags and hangers and return them to the local cleaners. In return, they give my husband a discount.

—Donna Ott
West Dundee, Illinois

USE FOR JUICE

Dear Amy,

While walking I spotted some beautiful oranges still on the tree. I knocked at the house and was told I could have some, but they were sour. I took some home anyway and juiced them. They were similar in taste to lemons, so I made "lemonade." My kids liked it. I also made frozen pops with it, which they are still enjoying. Other possibilities are key lime or lemon meringue pie, or orange marmalade. I thought I would pass this along for your Southern readers, because sour orange trees are fairly common in the South.

—Lynette Wayne
Middleburg, Florida

RUMMAGE FOR RUFFLES

Dear Amy,

Instead of making doll clothes for my two daughters' baby dolls, I buy "newborn" baby clothes for almost nothing at rummage sales. Usually the dresses that are all lace and ruffles have been worn only once or twice, and are my daughters' favorites.

—Joyce Eveler
Jefferson City, Missouri

A NEW WAY TO LOOK AT USED THINGS

It is strange, and sobering, to contemplate the odd beliefs that lurk in people's minds.

I ran into one such belief as I was being interviewed on a radio show. A listener called in and said, "I remember reading about you in *Parade* magazine, and I agree with everything you were saying . . . except for one thing: I couldn't believe you give your kids used toys for Christmas. Do you really do that? Kids *need* new toys on Christmas morning."

I responded by explaining that our kids do, frequently, get one special, new toy on Christmas morning. However, I also disputed her basic premise: that kids have a basic need for new stuff and will somehow be damaged if they don't have the experience of receiving new things.

The idea that kids—or adults, for that matter—have a basic need for new stuff is one that many people hold. Like this caller, even people who support the basic concept of frugality often still believe that people need some new things to be happy.

One reason this belief is so pervasive is that until fairly recently, the quality of used merchandise was poor. I remember, as a kid, going to the thrift shop in the small city of Fitchburg, Massachusetts, and finding the clothing selection truly pitiful. Thirty years ago there simply wasn't as much good used stuff floating around. Yard sales were just beginning, and people generally held on to their things until they got pretty ragged.

Because new stuff really was significantly better in those days, it was trotted out with great fanfare: "Look, honey, a *brand-new* bike from Santa!" By their enthusiasm, our parents taught us that new is better.

But then came the great boom in production, and the subsequent buying frenzy, which continues right up until the present day. A more recent development is the imposition of trash disposal fees, which make people very reluctant to throw away anything that someone else would take. The result is that in the 1990s there are tons of superb, used items available out there.

But the old attitude lives on. Even frugal parents who bring home yard-sale toys for their kids still give them only new toys for Christmas. The new merchandise is given with more honor and enthusiasm, even when the quality is the same. Kids *learn* that new is better, and their parents mistakenly conclude that this preference is "natural."

For the past 13 years I have been conducting what amounts to a social-science experiment to determine what would happen if kids were raised without receiving the message that new is better. Because I don't regard new stuff as superior, without consciously doing so I have offered used things to my kids with the same enthusiasm as new stuff. I also take my kids to yard sales and let them spend their own money.

The result: When I tell a three-year-old that I need to buy him a widget, he responds, "Need to get it at a 'Arrrd sale.' " When I tell a five-year-old that some people believe kids need new things to be happy, she giggles and rolls her eyes like she thinks I'm telling her a preposterous fairy tale. When I ask a ten-year-old if he thinks many other kids at school wear secondhand clothes, he responds, "I don't know. How can you tell?"

In other words, when children haven't been taught the faulty distinction between used and new, they don't presume that new stuff is better.

Conversely, it's also wrong to assume that used is always a better value. Each has benefits. Here are some guidelines:

THE ADVANTAGES OF NEW

• Sometimes you simply can't find exactly what you want used. This is why I usually buy each kid one new toy for birthdays and Christmas. For instance, Alec got a new Erector set for his birthday. While we find a lot of good used things for him, secondhand toys that come in sets of many tiny pieces are rarely complete. Similarly, expendable merchandise such

as lumber and fabric can be found used, but not always in the quantity or type you need.

• Sometimes new technology is so superior it isn't cost-effective to buy used things. For instance, most refrigerators and freezers should be purchased new because their old counterparts are energy-inefficient and therefore more costly in the long run.

• Sometimes the used alternative is simply overpriced, based on its life expectancy. Jim, who needs to buy tall-sized clothes, found thrift-shop flannel shirts for $5, but the elbows were worn. Instead, he went to Sears and bought new ones for $14.

THE ADVANTAGES OF USED

• Sometimes you can get the identical used item for significantly less. Jim hit the jackpot at a yard sale when he found a large bucket of Legos (including the miscellaneous wheels, hinges, and so on) for $1.50. This was a $100 value. Occasionally I wonder if people think my kids accept used toys because they're naïve. Actually, they're smart enough to figure out that this wealth of Legos is better than any $1.50 new toy.

• Sometimes used things are better for the environment. A friend bought a like-new $67 L. L. Bean jacket for $1 at a yard sale. He likes the savings, but he's also pleased to realize that if no one bought this jacket, it would have gone to the landfill and a new jacket would be made from virgin materials.

• Sometimes used things are more aesthetically pleasing and comfortable. This is part of the reason people value antiques so highly. Some manufacturers actually "distress" new furniture, to give it that worn, lived-with look. But it never really looks like a real antique. No one has yet figured out how to duplicate the honest, comfortable attractiveness that an object acquires through years of actual use.

• Sometimes, used things can give you important clues about their durability, whereas with a new item you simply have to guess. I know if I buy good-looking clothes at yard sales, they'll still look good after several washings.

• Sometimes used items are made better. At yard sales I buy older kitchen utensils with wooden or metal handles. I like them better than the new ones, which usually have plastic handles.

• Sometimes used things are more fun to acquire. I enjoy the "sport" of used-stuff acquisition. Anybody can grab something off the shelf at Wal-Mart, but it is an enjoyable challenge to hunt down, find, and bargain for a used item.

So both new and used items have their places in a frugal household. The important point is that your choice between them should be determined by the *actual value* to you, rather than some vague idea that one or the other is better, or necessary for good self-esteem. Of all of the big, sweeping frugal guidelines, understanding and appreciating the value of used stuff is one of the most important to master—for you, and for your kids.

AN AIRTIGHT CASE FOR FAMILY PACKS

Usually, the cheapest way to buy meat is through loss-leader sales at the supermarket. When buying hamburger and chicken, the two tightwad mainstays, the best deals are generally on the large "family packs." I have encountered many singles and couples who feel they can't take advantage of these because they can't eat that much. The fact is that these packs are too large even for a family of eight.

Here's how we handle it: When hamburger goes on sale for $1.19 per pound or less, and when chicken goes on sale for 39¢ per pound, we buy 20 to 30 pounds and individually wrap meal-sized portions.

The first step was purchasing a humongous, $7.99, 2,000-foot roll of 12-inch-wide clear plastic wrap from a warehouse store. One could make the argument that free bread bags are cheaper, but this wrap costs just 4/10ths of a cent per foot and allows a stretched-tight wrap that gives good protection from freezer burn. If this quantity is too much for you, we found that store-brand plastic wraps are 6/10 of a cent. (But be aware that name-brand wrap costs as much as 2 3/10 cents per foot.)

Next, if the chicken is in large pieces, Jim cuts it into small ones, removing the thighs from the legs, for example. Then he removes the skins (too much fat) and backs (too much bone), saving them in a big pot. He fills the pot with water to cover, and simmers it on the stove while he continues to work.

He then pulls out an 18-inch length of wrap, deposits a pound of hamburger (weighed on our kitchen scale) or a meal's worth of chicken pieces in it, and wraps it. Then he rotates the package 90 degrees and deposits it in the center of another 18-inch length of wrap. He folds this around, creating a double-wrapped, airtight package. When putting them in the freezer, he spreads them out as much as possible, to facilitate quick freezing. Once they are frozen, he gathers them into a single location in the freezer so they can be found easily.

After the chicken skins and backs are thoroughly cooked and cooled, we fish out the skins and bones. We chill the broth, then remove and discard the solidified fat. This broth and meat make several soup meals.

We discard the bones. Then we use the skins and other ookey soft stuff to make treats for our dog. Our vet says he's slightly underweight, so the chicken fat is good for him. To make the treats, I put a golf-ball-sized blob in the bottom of a bread bag, tie it off, add another blob, tie it off, and so on. I freeze these. To use, I snip off a section of the bread bag and thaw.

SOURDOUGH SIMPLIFIED

Ever since he was a kid, my staffer Brad has been in love with the taste of sourdough bread. When he was 13 years old, he lived in Alameda, California, and whenever his family would cross the Bay Bridge to visit San Francisco, they would buy a huge, crusty loaf of famous San Francisco sourdough. Brad ate at least half of it himself.

Brad has since learned how to replicate that bread. He has made over a hundred loaves of it, and relatives who come for dinner always clamor for more. Unlike other recipes for sourdough bread, which require the tedious creation of "sponges" and often call for added yeast, Brad's method is very simple.

Along with its distinctive taste, sourdough bread has a unique attraction for tightwads—it's the cheapest bread you can make, consisting only of flour, water, and salt. Brad's 24-ounce loaves cost 20¢ each.

The first step is to make a starter. The simplest way is to mix 1 tablespoon of yeast with 2 cups of chlorine-free water (allow your tap water to "air out" in a jug for a couple of days) and two cups of white flour. Combine these in a glass, plastic, or earthenware container—not a metal one. Cover loosely with plastic wrap and allow this mixture to sit at room temperature for at least 48 hours, until it foams and develops a pleasantly sour smell. Cover with plastic wrap and refrigerate. You can also get starter from a friend who makes sourdough. (The sourdough books warn that if the starter turns orange, pink, or any other strange color, you should throw it out. In years of sourdough baking, Brad has never had that problem.)

To make two loaves of bread:

5½ cups flour (you can substitute whole wheat flour for 1 or 2 cups)
2 cups starter
1 tablespoon salt
1 cup water

Dissolve the salt in the water in a mixing bowl. (Some sourdough cookery books say you should not use a metal bowl, but Brad has used his metal KitchenAid bowl for years.) Add the starter, and then the flour. Stir, then knead into a ball. (Brad uses the dough hook on his KitchenAid.) Cover with a damp towel and let rise *overnight* at room temperature. The next morning, punch down risen dough and divide in half. Shape each half into a round loaf, make an X-shaped slash on each top, and place the two loaves on a greased baking sheet. Cover with a damp towel and allow to rise at room temperature for about four more hours. Place a pan of water on the bottom rack of the oven and pre-

heat to 400 degrees. Bake for 35 minutes.

Each time you remove some starter, you must "feed" it. Just add back 1½ cups water and 1½ cups flour, stir, cover loosely, and return starter to the refrigerator.

You'll notice that the rising times seem extraordinarily long compared to yeast baking. Brad sees this as an advantage. With yeast breads, you may have just a 15-minute "window" in which the bread has risen to the right size for baking. Sourdough bread is far more forgiving. The first "window" is about two hours long (depending upon how warm the room is). If you should happen to miss that, just knead the bread again and allow to rise again. The only effect will be that the bread is somewhat more sour and the texture is finer.

Brad uses his starter, fresh from the fridge, for weeks at a time. Eventually the loaves he makes start to rise a bit more slowly. Whenever this happens, he just leaves the jar of starter out at room temperature overnight to speed its fermentation.

You need not confine your efforts to loaves of bread. Brad uses this bread recipe to make homemade pizza. He allows the dough to rise once, divides it in half, and rolls it out to make two pizzas.

Troubleshooting tips:

• After this story ran in the newsletter, readers reported varying success with their starters. After much correspondence and experimentation, we determined that the variety of yeast used for the initial starter was crucial. So if your starter doesn't work, make another batch with a different brand of yeast.

• Sourdough baking is generally less predictable than yeast baking. Accepting the fact that sometimes rising times need to double or triple is part of the adventure of sourdough. As with yeast baking, temperature is crucial; if you set your dough over a pan of warm water, it will rise much more quickly.

• Brad believes one reason his sourdough is so successful is that he bakes twice a week, so his starter is fed frequently. If you are an infrequent baker, you'll need to drain off some starter and feed it at least once every two weeks to keep it alive.

• Don't feel bound by the notion that the initial rising must double the volume. Brad often lets the initial rising quadruple the volume. He feels this makes better bread.

• The starter separates in the refrigerator. This is normal. Always stir it well before using, and stir it well again when feeding.

GREAT QUOTES

"Budgeting is the art of doing that well with one dollar which any bungler can do with two."
—Arthur Wellington, British soldier and statesman (1769–1852).

"Economy is the art of making the most of life."
—George Bernard Shaw (1856–1950)

"Any fool can waste, any fool can muddle, but it takes something of a man to save, and the more he saves, the more of a man does it make of him."
—Rudyard Kipling (1865–1936)

LET'S GARDEN WITH JIM

A newsletter reader from Manhattan, Illinois, asked, "How do frugal people garden? I always feel that by the time I buy my seeds, seed potatoes, tomato plants, fertilizer, and insect killers, I could have bought a whole lot of vegetables."

In response, I can't speak for all types of gardeners and gardens. Jim uses a basic system that works well for our situation, and we have determined that it is, indeed, a money-saver.

First, some statistics: We have four garden plots totaling about 8,700 square feet. We spend an average of seven hours a week over our four-month season to garden and process the food. We grow about 95 percent of the vegetables we eat.

To estimate the economy, I'll use exact figures from our 1994 gardening year. Jim spent $108 on gardening supplies and gas for the rototiller. It's difficult to calculate the amortized cost of the rototiller itself, which we bought used for $575. We don't know how many years it will last, and we also rototill gardens for a few other people, and get some benefit when favors are returned. In any case, a rototiller isn't necessary for smaller-scale gardening.

We froze or canned 317 quarts of food from our garden. In addition, we stored away a hard-to-measure quantity of unprocessed foods such as dried beans, carrots, beets, pumpkins, and squash. We also ate and gave away an unknown quantity of fresh food during the summer. I conservatively estimate we grew about 500 quarts of food. So, not including the cost of the rototiller, each quart cost about 22¢, plus about 8¢ per quart of processed food. It's clear, then, that gardening *can* save money.

Figuring the "hourly wage" for gardening is a bit trickier. Assuming, very arbitrarily, that a quart of store-bought vegetables costs $1.00, our gardening efforts are worth $2.91 an hour. But we feel that the improved taste, nutrition, and quality family time we spend together in the garden boost the value higher.

Further, the main thrust of our gardening style *isn't* to gain the highest hourly wage. We grow cheap stuff, such as carrots and cabbage, to have more variety and because we like them. It's conceivable, then, that by gardening more selectively you could have a higher hourly wage, or by gardening under less than ideal circumstances or gardening less frugally you could have a much lower hourly wage.

Here are some strategies to make gardening more profitable:

• Buy gardening supplies cheaply. All of our tools were purchased secondhand or acquired for free. We borrowed a rototiller until we found a used one.

• Shop around for the best price on seeds. Jim found that Fedco seeds were about half the price of the major seed companies. (For a catalog, send $1 to Fedco, P.O. Box 520, Waterville, ME 04903. Their

seeds are suitable for gardens in the northern half of the United States.)

• Grow from seeds whenever possible, as they can cost one tenth the price of nursery seedlings. If you have a short season and a light-filled south-facing window, you can start your seeds indoors. But trying to extend the season outdoors with hoop houses, row covers, "Wall-o'-Water" protectors, and other devices drives up the price of gardening considerably.

• Choose the right vegetables. Get varieties that do well in your climate. If your time and space are limited, bear in mind the expense of the store-bought counterpart—potatoes and carrots tend to be cheap to buy, but lettuce and strawberries are expensive. Choose vegetables based on their yield as compared to the space and effort required. A large, sprawling brussels-sprout plant may yield enough for just one meal, while bush beans and lettuce require comparatively little effort and space for the yield. Keep in mind how they will be preserved—carrots can be stored for months in sand, so although they're cheap to buy, I still think they are worthwhile to grow.

• Don't buy garden paraphernalia, particularly the obscenely overpriced stuff in catalogs. Egg cartons can be seed starters, plastic milk jugs can serve as mini greenhouses, and scavenged lumber and old windows can make cold frames in regions that get little snow.

• Design your garden based on your space. We use the row method, but those with minimal space will get higher yields from the square-foot gardening method, outlined in the book *Square Foot Gardening* by Mel Bartholomew.

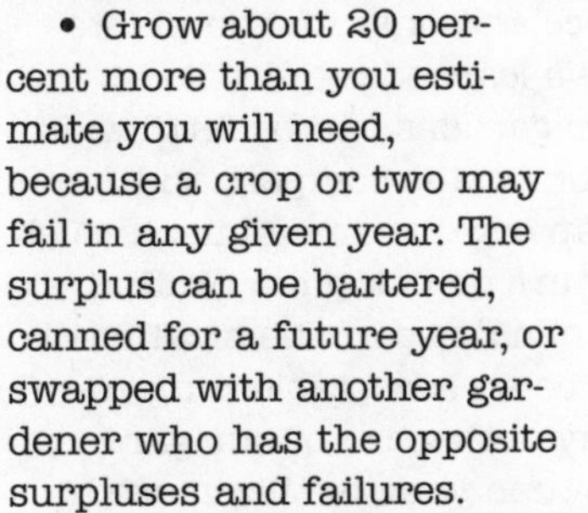

• Grow about 20 percent more than you estimate you will need, because a crop or two may fail in any given year. The surplus can be bartered, canned for a future year, or swapped with another gardener who has the opposite surpluses and failures.

• Manage weeds correctly. The key is to never let them get big. Simply disturb the soil once a week so that new weeds can't get rooted. You can use a hoe, a push-type cultivator, or a rototiller. You'll still have to weed by hand between plants, but the aisles can be easily maintained. If time prevents you from tending the weeds all summer, concentrate on the first few weeks. Once the plants grow taller than the weeds, the plants will do fine. The year the twins were born, we had an awful-looking but abundant garden. For a variety of reasons, including appearance and expense, we don't use straw mulch or black plastic to control weeds. Finally, keep in mind that weeds will be abundant the first year and diminish thereafter.

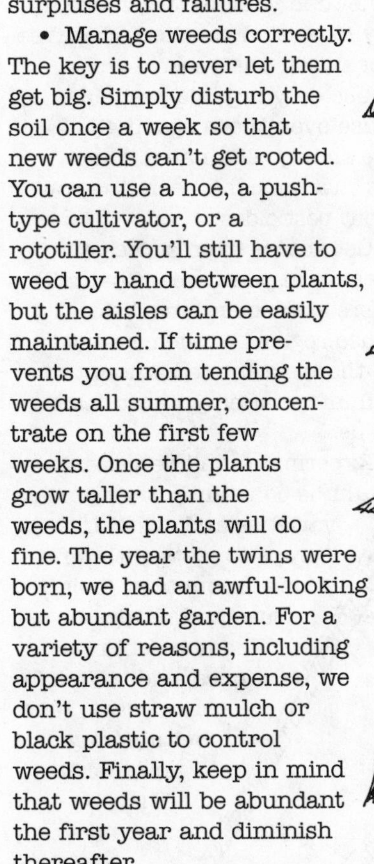

• Fertilize inexpensively. Because our soil is so rich, Jim uses just 40 pounds of 10-10-10 fertilizer each year. He gets it from the local farmers' co-op for less than $8. He waits until the plant is firmly

rooted and doing well, then hand-sprinkles and hoes in a circle of fertilizer around it. He does this just once and only for the plants that he's learned require it. Smaller gardens can be fertilized with homemade compost and free or cheap organic amendments such as manure or fish guts. We find our minimal use of chemical fertilizer to be an acceptable compromise given the size of our garden. To fine-tune your fertilizer needs, many extension services offer free or cheap soil analyses.

- Use only organic pesticides, and use even those sparingly. We've simply eliminated some crops that we can't seem to grow without pesticides.
- Get advice from successful gardeners in your area. Chat with farmers at farmers' markets. Because regions of the country vary, there's a limited amount of useful information you can learn from us.
- Experiment and be patient. Jim is constantly trying new varieties and switching crops to plots with differing amounts of moisture and shade.

Thomas Jefferson once said, "Though old in years, I am but a young gardener." There's always more to learn, and if your first year was dismal, you at least know now how *not* to grow certain items. Keep asking, trying, and refining, and eventually you'll succeed.

WHEEL SHARP TIP

Dear Amy,

As a quilter, I use a rotary cutter for speed-cutting my pieces. I used to have to replace the blade at least once for each quilt. At $5 per blade, it's expensive to use. Then I found that I could sharpen it with my sharpening stone. Keeping the blade in the cutter holder, I hold it at a 30-degree angle while sharpening. The Olfa blade has numbers, so I can keep track as I rotate and sharpen each section.

—C. Dong
Wayland, Massachusetts

RATE REDUCTION

Dear Amy,

It pays to keep your auto insurance company advised of your driving habits. The premium on the car my husband drives was cut 5 percent when I told them he carpools to work. The company cut 14 percent off the annual premium for my vehicle when I informed them I no longer worked full time and had become a stay-at-home Mom.

—Diane Ogle
Kent, Washington

UNDER ONE CONDITIONER

Dear Amy,

My husband and I use inexpensive hair conditioner in place of shaving cream. A little bit goes a long way, and it does not dry your skin like soap often does.

—Barbara Davis-Pyles
Seattle, Washington

FIND YOUR MARBLES

Dear Amy,

You can easily make heart-shaped cupcakes. Line the muffin pan with paper baking liners. Place a small marble in each cup between the liner and the muffin tin. Pour in batter, filling halfway, and bake as directed.

—Nancy J. Martin
Wyoming, Michigan

HOT WASH, COLD RINSE

Dear Amy,

I learned from a former boyfriend, a health inspector, that rinsing dishes in hot water has no bearing on the cleaning process. I rinse in cold water I collect in jugs while waiting for the dishwater to get hot.

—Deann Landers
Georgetown, Texas

(Or you could simply fill your rinse-water dishpan as you wait for the water to get hot. FZ)

IT SAVES TO ASK

Dear Amy,

If you don't see something at a garage sale, ask. I've bought a pitchfork that the owner brought out from a shed after I asked. Sometimes other garage salers hear the question and know where you can find the item.

—Jan Jacquet
Olympia, Washington

APPROVAL OF STAMP

Dear Amy,

Don't buy gummed and sticky address labels. I invested $5.95 in a rubber stamp, which can be reused, possibly indefinitely, with a few drops of ink. I ordered mine through a mail-order house.

—Nancy Brockmeier
Yorba Linda, California

(The Tightwad Gazette *can testify to the durability of these self-inking stamps. We bought one for our business nearly five years ago. Every once in a while we add a little more stamp-pad ink to its reservoir. We know that this one stamp has been used tens of thousands of times since then. FZ)*

READ THIS ARTICLE AND SAVE $150,000

The Guinness Book of World Records contains two interesting facts: The weight-loss record is held by a woman who lost 917 pounds; as you read on, you find that this same woman holds another record—the highest weight ever for a woman. She weighed 1,200 pounds.

I'm sincerely happy that this woman lost weight, and I don't mean to make light of a serious medical problem. However, I instantly saw her situation as a way to illustrate a hard-to-grasp flaw I routinely see in advertising, in consumer reporting, and even in the way tightwads discuss saving money. In each case, they emphasize the amount a strategy theoretically could "save" without focusing on the amount that was actually spent or might have been spent.

It's important to understand this flaw because sometimes to "save" the most, you have to spend the most. In the case of this woman, she was able to lose so much only because she weighed so much in the first place. Further, at the time of publication she still weighed 283 pounds, so whatever strategies she used may not apply to those of us who struggle with 10 unwanted pounds.

If this woman wrote a diet book and marketed it on the claim that she lost 75 percent of her weight, you'd immediately conclude she must have weighed a lot before the diet. Unfortunately, when fuzzy claims are made about how much *money* can be "saved," we don't always grasp the implication.

The term "saving money" can mean one of two things:

- In the tangible sense, we "save money" when we literally put money in the bank.
- In the theoretical sense, we "save money" when we use one strategy versus another. In this case, to use this term responsibly we must specify the comparison strategy and, at best, give specific numbers to show how we arrived at the claim. The following are examples of how I have seen the term "saving money" misused in the theoretical sense.

First, let's pick on advertisers. Long ago, advertisers learned they could get a consumer to spend money by claiming he could save money. This commonly occurs when a store has overpriced merchandise and then marks it down "on sale," thereby appealing to the consumer's lust for spending and his need for feeling that he is saving money. Amusingly, one advertiser turned this around to his advantage. In a pre-Christmas ad, a low-cost jewelry shop said a competing shop had marked up its diamonds and then advertised customers could save 50 percent at its sale. Typically, an overpriced $2,000 diamond was marked down to a more reasonable $1,000. The low-cost jeweler said you could buy the same-quality diamond in his shop for $750, although you wouldn't, ahem, "save" as much.

The same strategy can be used when marketing save-money ideas. Say, for example, an author writes a book on how to renovate a house cheaply. In it, he shows how a ranch house can be fixed up for $10,000. But this isn't sufficiently sensational to sell books, since most people with common sense know how to do this. So he finds a brain-dead home renovator who

spent $50,000 to fix up a similar house. He can now market his book on the claim that he saved 80 percent on the cost of home renovation. Although he does reveal how he arrived at his savings claim in the book, you have to buy the book in order to learn this. For this author to increase his savings claims to 90 percent, he just has to find a $100,000 home renovation.

Second, let's pick on consumer reporters. Sometimes consumer reporters throw out a statistic that a product or strategy could save X percent, or X amount of dollars without specifying the basis of their claim. They may do this because it's a fast way to express an idea. Unfortunately, the claim may be misleading.

For example, a magazine contained this typical claim about coupons: "By combining coupons and rebates you can save up to 60 percent of your grocery bill." As usual, nowhere attached to this claim were the other important pieces of information. For this statement to have any meaning, we must know the amount of the grocery bill either before or after the coupons are deducted.

Personally, I "save" about 1 percent on my grocery bill by using coupons. Because my percentage of savings is so much smaller, this might lead you to assume I'm not a very good shopper. But I spend $190 a month to feed a family of eight. I challenge anyone to show me how coupon use can save me 60 percent and knock my food bill down to $76 a month. In researching this previously, I know that such claims are based on extremely high starting grocery bills.

As an example of how focusing on "coupon savings" instead of spending is misleading: I buy store-brand cold cereal only when it goes on sale for $1 per box. Instead, if I apply a $1 coupon toward a $4 box of name-brand cereal in a double-coupon store, I would spend $2. In this case, to "save" 50 percent on cereal I'd have to double my spending.

Now it's occasionally possible to get name-brand cold cereal for free by using coupons and rebates. If the *only* cold-cereal option I had was a $4 box, it would be fair to say that if I got a free box I "saved" $4. However, since store-brand cold cereal can be purchased for $1, my true savings would be only $1.

SAVE 50% on all overpriced merchandise

Although coupon use can save money, after a certain point the only way you can increase your "savings percentage" is by increasing your after-coupon grocery bill.

Third, let's pick on tightwads. Sometimes out of simple enthusiasm we quantify the value of a bargain by focusing on a theoretical savings rather than on the amount we realistically would have spent. For example, a tightwad acquires ten free movie posters discarded by the local video store. Since large posters at Wal-Mart cost $5, he claims that by picking up these free posters he "saved" $50. In this case, the savings claim is misleading since he wouldn't have purchased ten $5 posters in the first place. As tightwads, we all delight in such freebies, but even if we collected 1,000 posters, it wouldn't result in more money in the bank.

In contrast, another tightwad claims she saves $7 each time she cuts her son's hair. Since she doesn't want her son to have a ponytail, one way or another he must have a haircut. Her only other option is a $7 haircut. In this case, her claim is accurate.

To be honest, I'll bet you could find a time or two when I have specified the value of a strategy in terms of a savings rather than the amount spent. But overall I do laboriously and tediously give a basis for any claims I make about money-saving strategies.

By focusing only on a theoretical savings, you may buy products you don't need, use too many coupons, or expend a lot of energy running around picking up free movie posters. In short, thinking about saving money in this way is nothing more than fake frugality. To "save money," in the tangible sense of putting money in the bank, you have to focus on the amount of money you actually spend.

To me, the basis of this article is pretty obvious. Yet, I am amazed at how often I see intelligent people get the "save money" concept backward. Surprisingly often, for example, reporters try to strong-arm me into quantifying the value of my book by asking, "If people used every idea in your book, how much could they save each year?" And what a great marketing opportunity it would be for me to enthusiastically gush, "If you buy my $12 book and use every idea in it, over the year you could save $10,000!"

But making such a claim would be unrealistic and misleading. Instead, I make my point by responding, "Gee, I dunno. That depends on how stupid those people were last year." We both laugh, and then I redirect the conversation to a discussion of how little money we spend on specific areas of our budget.

Oh, yeah, about that tip on saving $150,000: Don't buy a Rolls-Royce.

READ THIS ARTICLE AND SAVE $150,000 UPDATE

After the previous article ran in my newsletter, Patty Furlong of Mt. Pleasant, South Carolina, sent me what may be the best illustration of all. It's a joke she found in *The Best of the Good Clean Jokes* by Bob Phillips (Harvest House, 1989):

A man staggered into his house panting and exhausted. "What happened, honey?" inquired his wife.

"It's a great new idea I have," he gasped. "I ran all the way home behind the bus and saved fifty cents!"

"That wasn't very bright," replied his wife. "Why didn't you run behind a taxi and save three dollars?"

BOXES FOR BONBONS

Dear Amy,

I usually give homemade candies as gifts for all occasions. I solved my packaging dilemma by purchasing 50 white Chinese-food containers for $3, or 6¢ each. We decorate them with markers or rubber stamps and ink. Preprinted boxes sell at Hallmark for 69¢ each!

—Jeanne Buchanan
San Mateo, California

RETREADS RECONSIDERED

When Nancy Kish of Monroe, Connecticut, needed a new set of tires, she carefully researched all of the options and decided that in her case, retreads were the best value. I investigated and concluded that retreads are a worthy option to explore.

The information that follows is based on industry literature, and on my talks with Ken Collings, the manager of the Federal Tire Program; Dana Arnold, an environmental protection specialist with the EPA; David Van Sickle, director of automotive engineering for AAA; Rene Therrien, owner of a tire retreading shop here in Maine; and Harvey Brodsky, managing director of the Tire Retreading Information Bureau.

The technology of retreading has improved dramatically. Years ago, new treads were simply vulcanized onto old tires. Since then, retreading has evolved to a computerized business that uses the latest manufacturing technology.

A huge number of vehicles use retreads. In 1993, truckers purchased 16 million retreads and just 11 million new tires. Retreads are widely used on school buses, U.S. mail trucks, private delivery vehicles, even aircraft; about 80 percent of commercial jets use retreads.

Still, average motorists remain skeptical. When people see hunks of tread littering the sides of highways, they assume these peeled off of retreads, "proving" retreads aren't durable.

But when Probe Scientific Laboratories of El Paso, Texas, sampled roadside tire pieces in several states, it found that about two thirds were from nonretreaded tires and a third were from retreads. Further, research indicates that these tire treads ripped loose because the tires were underinflated, overloaded, or were mismatched dual truck tires, *not* because of the type of tire they were.

Recently the magazine *AAA World* raised another possible objection to retreads: that the buyer has no way of knowing whether the original casings are identical, and that mismatched

brands could affect a car's handling. But the experts we interviewed, including a spokesman for AAA, told us that this effect would be noticed only in high-performance cars taken to "the edge" of their capabilities. They also said that this loss of handling would be no greater than what results when one tire has a pound or less air pressure than another, and that it would be unnoticeable in trucks.

So, are retreads cost-effective? It depends.

The benefits of retreads may be negligible for the average passenger car. Although car retreads are about one third cheaper than new tires, the casings of car tires aren't as sturdy as those of truck tires. So while you might expect 36,000 to 40,000 miles from a new car tire, a retreaded one may be good for only 25,000 to 30,000 miles. Based on that assumption, and on prices in our area, we determined that the cost per mile for each kind of tire was about the same.

Nevertheless, retreads can make sense for cars driven in pothole-strewn areas where tires are torn or punctured before they are worn down. They may also save money on an older car that might not outlast new tires.

The obvious savings begin when you move up to tires for larger vehicles, such as pickup trucks and full-sized vans. In these tires the casings are far more durable, so you can expect to get as many or even more miles from retreads as from new tires. Further, retreaded truck tires cost about half as much as their new counterparts. For example, a mounted, balanced, new tire for a three-quarter-ton truck costs about $120. A mounted, balanced, retreaded version costs approximately $60.

If you are teetering on the question of whether retreads are worthwhile for you, consider that retreads are the environmentally responsible choice. According to the TRIB, while it takes 7 gallons of crude oil to make a new passenger tire, a retread requires only 2.5 gallons. Further, retreading significantly slows the flow of tires into overcrowded landfills.

The best way to find out who sells retreads in your area is to call or write:

Tire Retread Information Bureau
900 Weldon Grove
Pacific Grove, CA 93950
(408) 372-1917

You can also find retread dealers under "Tires—Retreads" in the Yellow Pages.

Look for a dealer who buys from a retreader who belongs to either the American Retreaders Association and/or is an A-rated member of the National Tire Dealers and Retreaders Association. You should also insist on a warranty that's at least as good as the one offered for a new tire.

Nancy Kish researched—and rejected—one other cheap tire alternative: used tires from a junkyard. These are removed from wrecked cars. She found them to be roughly a third cheaper than retreads.

I called several junkyards and found that a typical used passenger-car tire costs from $5 to $30, depending on its condition. I also called several tire service centers and found they charge an average of $9 to mount and balance a tire.

So it's clear that used tires can have the cheapest initial cost; they could cost as little as $14 each for the poorest-quality used tires. But they have no warranty, are sometimes hard to find, may be aged or damaged in ways that aren't obvious, and require two errands: first to the junkyard, then to the tire shop. Van Sickle, our expert from AAA, agreed with all of these observations. He said he "wouldn't touch them with a 10-foot pole."

PROM 'N' AID

According to *Your Prom* magazine, the average cost of a prom date is $1,058: $585 for the girl and $473 for the guy. As in all areas of spending money, people mistakenly believe that because the average spending habits of most people are so high, getting by with much less is simply impossible. Some expenses, like tickets, are fixed, but letters from several readers prove that most prom costs can be beat.

FOR GIRLS

Kimberly Barbour of Wilmington, North Carolina, wrote that her daughter was thrilled with her consignment-shop prom dress, which cost $10. (Her daughter insists that anyone who pays mall prices is "like, a total dweeb!")

Judy Burkhardt of Wall, New Jersey, bought a pink Jessica McClintock gown that originally cost $100 for $5 at an end-of-the-season sale at Marshall's, and then saved it until the next season.

One teen, of West Alexandria, Ohio, wrote that after much fruitless prom-dress searching she realized that she already had the perfect outfit—in her mother's closet. She borrowed her mother's elegant evening dress, along with her matching shoes, purse, and gloves. She added her own necklace and had to buy only earrings. The total cost was $6.50.

Merrie Hallman of Livingston Manor, New York, sent a precise breakdown of the cost to outfit her daughter. A basic black gown from an auction cost $5. Two yards of fabric to update the bow on the dress cost $12. Black patent-leather shoes from Fayva cost $8.

Sale-priced fancy stockings cost $2.50. A comb with matching fabric flowers from a craft store cost $5. Gloves and shoe clips were donated by her grandmother for no cost. So the total cost of her daughter's outfit was $32.50.

FOR GUYS

In *The Tightwad Gazette II* we published a reader letter in which a mother related how she outfitted her two sons for $15 each. She bought thrift-shop tuxedos and cummerbunds. She borrowed shirts and bought new black ties. Each ensemble cost $15 and still fit a year later.

Another reader, who asked to remain anonymous, wrote that she makes corsages for her son's dates. She buys florist's tape and ribbon to make bows. She substitutes quilting pins and recycled wire for their professional counterparts. She either uses a flower from her garden or buys a single flower and uses greenery from her houseplants. For presentation, she buys a plastic see-through salad container from a deli, places the corsage on a bed of Easter grass or exotic paper cut in strips, and ties a ribbon around the container.

MINOR MIDASES

Dear Amy,

Our bank offers "junior savings accounts." The kids get incentives all year long because if they make a deposit they can get a gift.

Just before Mother's Day they get a free mum plant for depositing money. Other holidays also yield gifts.

During the year they have received a special day at the movie theater, which included popcorn and a prize (like a Frisbee or squeeze bottle). We get coupons every few months for free french fries, discounts at the skating rink, free breakfasts, and so on. Aside from the freebies, the children are learning to save money.

—Julie Schulte
Dubuque, Iowa

GRASS ACT

Dear Amy,

Here's a cheap thrill for kids: When we mow our lawn (we live on a farm and have 2 acres to mow), we cut a "maze" in the lawn for our kids to play in. They love running along the paths and trying to beat one another to the end. We've done this all summer and they have yet to tire of it.

—Valaree Stodola
Shellburg, Iowa

TOWELS WITHOUT SCOWLS

Dear Amy,

As a lifeguard/swim instructor, I'd like to suggest a free source of towels. At the end of the outdoor swim season, the lost and found often has some wonderful but "not matching" towels. Of course, this is after reminding the users to review the lost and found for their missing items.

—Ebie Morris
Villa Park, Illinois

A GOOD IDEA, I TINK

Dear Amy,

We like to play with Tinkertoys, but we needed more sticks. Using a hacksaw, Mom cut a dowel the lengths we needed and put slits in the ends.

—Heather Melton
Lucas, Texas

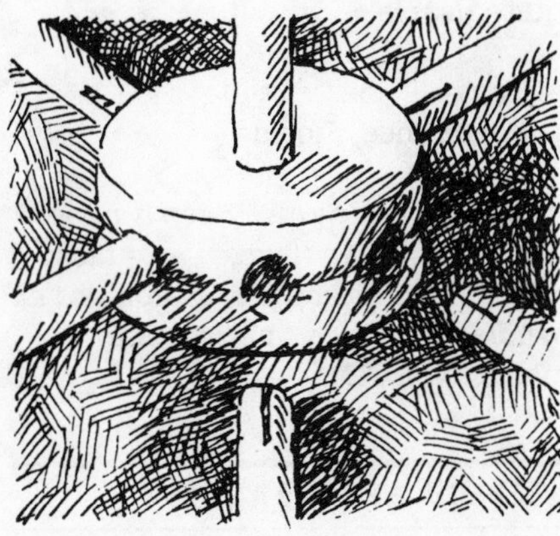

(I used this idea because the yard-sale Tinkertoys I purchased were short on sticks. Jim used the band saw to make more from ¼-inch dowels. It took him 40 minutes to make 64 sticks; the dowels cost $1.91. FZ)

LABOR AND SAVOR

Dear Amy,

We give a frugal baby shower that we call a "casserole shower." We give it about three weeks before the baby is due. All the guests bring a casserole as their gift. The mom-to-be just puts them in the freezer until the baby arrives. Then, during those hectic postpartum days, she just has to pop a casserole from her freezer into the oven and dinner is ready! These showers are fun, easy, cheap, and a godsend if you're the mom-to-be!

—Jane Kiel
Kalamazoo, Michigan

TAGS FOR TOGS

Dear Amy,

I use homemade, numbered cardboard markers on the hangers holding my office clothes to indicate whether the garment can stand another wearing or is due for washing. I can tell at a glance whether I have enough ready for my work week, and as I usually handwash these garments separately, it allows me to wash them more efficiently.

—Deirdre Angus
British Columbia

PUNCH AND MUNCH

Dear Amy,

The cracker recipe [in the first *Tightwad Gazette* book] is great. But instead of cutting them, use a comb to "dot" them and break apart when done. You can also sprinkle them with onion or garlic powder, powdered cheese from macaroni-and-cheese in a box, or sugar and cinnamon.

—Pam Ristaino
Lindenwold, New Jersey

READ 'EM AND WEEP

Dear Amy,

For my parents' 35th wedding anniversary, I got the idea to write letters to all of the people who were in their wedding and to some of their close friends, asking them to send a card and their well-wishes. Everyone wrote back, many with letters that included a recounting of funny things that happened during that time. I wrapped the letters like an ordinary present and when my parents opened it, they were so surprised! My mom tried reading the first letter, but became so choked up she had to hand them over to my father, who finished reading them aloud to the family. What fun it was watching the smiles on their faces!

—Jan Chase
San Jose, California

WHAT'S CHEAP, DOC?

Dear Amy,

Check with your local hospital to see if they have an in-house printing department. We use the hospital for much of the printing needed for our business. They are happy to do it to fill their excess capacity. The cost is less than half of what we used to pay a commercial printer.

—Barbara J. Durflinger
Benton Harbor, Michigan

ROLL OUT THE SAVINGS

Dear Amy,

I normally buy the single rolls of 1,000-sheet toilet paper, which sell for 50¢ to 60¢. Today I went to the local paper products factory in my town and purchased a case of 72 rolls of the same kind of paper for $14.25. This is about 20¢ per roll. These were "seconds"; they were not perfectly round, but are quite usable.

—Karyn Price
Kissimmee, Florida

(While you may not have a paper factory in your town, many factories do sell directly to customers at wholesale prices. It's worth a phone call. FZ)

KEEP UP APPEARANCES

Dear Amy,

My husband's white gym socks lose the elasticity in the tops before the bottoms wear out. I buy elastic "thread," wind it into the bobbin of my sewing machine, and stitch around the cuff about three times to restore the elasticity.

—Carolyn Pollock
Hunt, New York

CREATE A BREAKFAST MUFFIN UPDATE

In *The Tightwad Gazette II* I published a sort of universal muffin formula. This was one of the most well-received articles I've published. Well, I've found an improve-

ment on the technique I suggested for using cooked grains (such as leftover oatmeal, rice, or cornmeal mush) in muffins.

In the original article I passed along a common cookbook suggestion: If you're adding cooked grain, you should separate your egg, add the yolk directly to the batter, beat the white until stiff, and fold it into the batter. I assume this was suggested to offset the heaviness of the cooked cereal.

Personally, I found beating egg whites to be too laborious at 7 A.M. So, despite frequently having several small containers of leftover cooked cereal jammed in my freezer, I've tried to find other ways to use it up.

I've experimented and found that I could use cooked cereals in my muffin batter with the aid of my blender. First, I mix all of the dry ingredients in a big bowl. Then I put all of the wet and moist ingredients in a blender. These could include: cooked grain (about ½ cup per batch), egg, milk, honey or molasses, peanut butter, pumpkin puree, applesauce, and/or banana. I've even added unused cookie dough and pastry scraps. I don't blenderize any moist ingredient that I want to retain its original texture, such as shredded zucchini.

Another possible addition to your blender of wet stuff could be small quantities of unappealing dry leftovers, such as broken cookies, cornbread, muffins, or bread crusts. This stuff is hard to crumble in a blender alone, but it blends easily with wet ingredients.

After blending, I mix the wet stuff into the bowl of dry stuff.

I make a final adjustment to the batter by adding more liquid or flour.

The blender seems to whip up the egg sufficiently as well as helps to quickly combine hard-to-mix-in moist stuff.

If you still have a hard time working muffins into your busy morning routine, I have a final suggestion: Premix your ingredients the night before. Put your dry ingredients in a large bowl and cover. Put your wet and moist ingredients in a separate bowl or blender jar and put that in the refrigerator. Also, pregrease your muffin tins. In the morning it's a simple matter to combine the two bowls of ingredients to make your muffins.

I WOULDN'T STEER YOU WRONG

Three newsletter readers asked the following questions about meat:

• Linda Linden of Kettering, Ohio, asked, "Could you write down some of your 'rules of thumb,' such as the prices that you generally pay for meat?"

• Robin Mertz of Edgewater, Maryland, asked, "I have been toying with the idea of purchasing a steer and having it slaughtered for my family's consumption. Have you researched the cost to pur-

chase meat in this manner versus store-bought?"

• A reader from St. Paul, Minnesota, asked, "Shopping for chicken is frustrating. It can be bought in at least six different packages, all with different combinations. Are boneless breasts really that much more expensive when you consider all the bones and innards you throw away from the other packages?"

All of these questions come under the larger topic of my "protein philosophy."

Before going further, let me emphasize that this philosophy is mine. Meat consumption is a subject surprisingly loaded with political, environmental, and health beliefs. Our "less-meat" meals might not meet with the approval of vegetarians or hard-core carnivores. So you can make different choices based on your beliefs, health restrictions, or personal preferences.

That said, there are three basic ways to compare meat prices:

• Keep track of the prices of all the various cuts of meat. Unfortunately, there are too many types to track easily, and there are variables within each type, such as how much bone or fat are included. But simply purchasing meat on sale won't necessarily reduce your food bill either—filet mignon and lobster go on sale, too.

• Calculate the cost per gram of protein. *Sylvia Porter's Money Book* (Avon Books, 1976) has a chart to help you do this. It shows that because hot dogs have more fat and filler, chicken, even when it costs more per pound, could provide more protein for less money. But this method has two flaws. First, it's the most complicated way to compare meat costs. Second, we don't need to track our protein consumption, because most Americans eat far too much anyway. The average American eats over 100 grams of protein per day. The recommended daily allowance is 55 grams, and studies have shown that we need as little as 30 grams daily.

• Calculate the cost per portion, or the cost of one meal for your family. This is the simplest method, and the one that reflects the way people really eat. For example, a one-serving portion might be 4 ounces of turkey, but just 1½ ounces of cheese. So though the turkey costs less per pound, the actual cost of the meals might be the same.

When I was first trying to reduce my food budget, I tried and rejected the first two methods. Instead I began to pay attention to how much each type of protein meal cost. When we bought a pork roast, we would eat a meal and

then package the leftovers into family-dinner-sized portions. If the roast yielded four family dinners, I would divide the price of the roast by 4 and use that number for comparison with other protein sources.

From this I developed price guidelines, which with inflation have gradually risen over time. To answer the first question, we now pay up to 69¢ for with-bone meat and $1.19 for boneless. We often buy meat that costs much less than this, and just a couple of times each year Jim splurges above this price range.

By limiting ourselves to these prices, we still have plenty of variety. I detailed the types of meat in our diet on page 66, "Pantry Principle Update."

My guidelines largely eliminated the following meats from our diet: seafood, chicken breasts, most cuts of beef, deli meats, and pork chops.

It's true that the low-cost meats we've chosen aren't always the ones with the least fat and preservatives. Neither are we eating 100 percent organically raised meats. But we feel our choice is reasonable because we eat less meat than most American families. We usually use it as an ingredient rather than as a main course, and we average one pound per dinner for all eight of us. Further, we remove the skin from chicken and drain the fat from ground beef.

We use this exercise to keep us on the frugal-meat course: When we buy or are given a rare expensive cut of meat, we consider if the extra cost is worth the extra pleasure. For example, if sea scallops cost ten times as much as turkey, we ask "Did we enjoy this ten times as much?" The answer is almost always no.

To answer the latter two readers questions specifically:

When you buy a whole steer, you'll probably pay the wholesale price. This is less than the regular supermarket price for the same cuts of meat, but more than the supermarket's loss-leader prices. A supermarket sells some things below wholesale because they make it up when customers buy overpriced potato chips.

The problem with buying whole or half steers is that you lose the option of choice: You must buy the more expensive steaks to get the ground beef. But even if you would buy the steaks anyway, the steer may not be the best deal. To be sure, you must haul out your calculator and price book and determine if the cuts from the whole steer are as cheap as the sale prices you can get on the cuts at the supermarket.

To answer the last question, the amount of waste in cuts with fat, bones, and skin varies among types of meat, but it's fair to say that the waste might be about one third of the total weight. So if boneless costs one third more, it's about the same price as with-bone. The only reliable way to know is to buy both types and count how many meals you get, including soup stock.

FOR SALE BY TIGHTWAD

Our newsletter solicitation for readers' "For Sale by Owner" experiences received a large and, to me, fascinating response. We got 188 letters, and the consensus was overwhelmingly in favor of the FSBO route versus selling through a real estate agent.

In all, 130 readers said they had successfully sold their own homes, while just 10 said they had tried to sell on their own and failed. We also received a number of letters about readers' success with "compromise" strategies such as bargaining for a lower agent's commission. And we got a surprisingly small response, just six letters, from real estate agents warning that owner-selling is an awful idea.

Clearly, these letters are not a scientific sample of house-selling experiences across the nation, but I found them compelling. The lesson I took away was: If you are willing to study and invest some time, money, and energy, selling your own home can be one of the highest "hourly wage" activities a tightwad can do. Readers who supplied dollar figures said they saved from $3,500 to $31,000 by selling their homes themselves. At the least, many readers suggested, it makes sense to give owner-selling a try for a month or two before turning the task over to a real estate agent.

Our research revealed that owner-selling isn't rare. According to the U.S. Department of Commerce, in 1993, 29.4 percent of all single-family-home sales and transfers were conducted by the owner. (Although the real estate industry argues that the total drops to 10 percent if you subtract sales between family members.)

And the savings can be substantial. Say you sell your house for $140,000. The average agent's commission is 6 percent, so the approximate cost of using an agent is $8,400.

While selling your own home can be an excellent idea, it can have pitfalls, and it is important to educate yourself. This article will provide a basic outline of what readers said they did to sell their homes, but we can't cover the whole topic in this limited space.

So the first step is reading one or more of the many books on the subject. The one most highly recommended by readers is *How to Sell Your Home in the '90s* by Carolyn Janik (Viking Penguin, 1991). Also recommended were *Sell Your Own Home* by Warren Boroson, and *For Sale by Owner* by Louis Gilmore (Simon & Schuster, 1989). These, and others, should be at your library or available through interlibrary loan.

The next step is to ask around for a local lawyer who specializes in real estate. Make contact and tell him or her your plans. (Usually, this first consultation is free.) Some readers have never used an attorney, relying instead on advice from their bank or other sources, but most felt that having an attorney on your side is crucial to avoid mistakes. The attorney can guide you through the whole sales process.

Now, you need an appraisal. You can pay $200 to $400 for a professional one, but many readers got one free from their local real estate agents. To avoid an ethics violation, "be up front about the fact that you plan to sell it yourself, but point out that you would consider their company in case you are unable to sell it," said Linda Courtney of Worthington, Massachusetts. One plan that made sense to me is to get five such appraisals and use the middle one to price your house. You can also attend open houses and review recent property sales information at your county recorder's office.

The next step is to spruce up your property. Eliminate clutter, paint with neutral shades, buy potted plants for your porch, mow the lawn twice a week if necessary, and clean, clean, clean.

The next step is marketing, and it is here that the advantages of FSBO really shine. As a reader from Salt Lake City, Utah, put it, "Realtors don't care which houses in particular they sell, as long as houses are sold. They will spread their resources and energy over as many houses as possible and let market forces do the rest. An owner-seller cares about selling her house in particular. She can concentrate resources and energy on it."

Readers' marketing strategies include:

- Make an excellent, handmade sign that includes your phone number (and "By Appointment Only" if you don't want random visits). Put them up on your street and, if possible, on any heavily traveled streets nearby. Attach a small box to hold flyers.
- Print a flyer to hand to people who tour the house, and to put in the box on your sign. Many readers sent copies of their flyers, and some were absolutely gorgeous. Nancy Tague of Baker, Louisiana, produced the best one I saw. It was printed on eye-catching orange paper and included, along with the usual nuts-and-bolts information, the house's history, a complete floor plan, photographs of the front, back, and sides, a description of nearby amenities and attractions,

and a month-by-month breakdown of gas, electric, water, and sewer bills.

• Put out the word. A surprising number of readers sold their homes through word of mouth. Rebecca Gumina of Rocky River, Ohio, said that through this strategy she got visits from the doughnut shop manager's brother, church members, relatives of neighbors, and her daughter's soccer coach.

• Advertise creatively. Along with an ad in the newspaper, advertise in unusual places and publications. Sharon Jonah of Highland, Michigan, sold her home through an ad in the local hospital's employee newsletter. "Any major employer within a few miles of the house is an ideal place to find potential buyers," she wrote.

• Have an open house. Sunday afternoons are best.

• Try to sell in the spring or summer, if possible.

For any of these marketing strategies to work, people need to be able to reach you. If you are not home for much of the day, you'll need to have an answering machine to field calls. Change your outgoing message so that it mentions that you are, indeed, the people who are selling a house.

Prepare for the fact that up to half the calls you'll get will be from realtors trying to get your listing. They may also say they've got the "perfect buyer" for you. But be aware: If you sign a contract and the realtor doesn't provide this buyer, you'll have to pay him a fee even if you attract a buyer on your own later.

Arrange visits at a time that's convenient for you. For safety, arrange to have a companion with you during house tours. Have a stack of purchase agreements (available from any title company or office-supply store) on hand in case anyone makes an offer.

When people visit, point out nice features that they might otherwise miss, but generally leave them alone; you want to give them the chance to mentally arrange their furniture in your living room.

Avoid verbal dickering. If someone asks, "Would you take . . . ," you should always answer, "I'll consider any offer that I receive in writing," and hand them a purchase agreement to take.

Any formal offer should be accompanied by a check to demonstrate seriousness; $1,000 is a good number. The check isn't cashed; it's held by the title company or closing attorney and usually voided at closing. You should also ask for some evidence, such as a loan preapproval, to indicate that the buyer can come up with the money.

Most potential buyers expect a counteroffer. Many readers said they appreciated not having a realtor as a go-between in this process. As with the original offer, the counteroffer should be made in writing.

The closing itself is generally handled by the title company or an attorney.

Again, I emphasize that this is just a general overview. You may approach the whole process differently.

There is, in fact, a new kind of owner-selling that seems to be catching on. The book *How to Sell Your Home in Five Days* by William G. Effros (Workman Publishing, $14.95) outlines a method to attract many potential buyers quickly and get them bidding

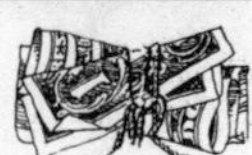

against each other for your home in that short period. To anyone who has spent six months trying to keep a house spotless for showings, Effros's five-day plan may have real appeal. Effros says he's sold 100 homes this way, always at market value or above. Effros successfully demonstrated his method for CNN. As it happens, I was interviewed by the same CNN journalist who did his piece, and he agreed, to his amazement, that the method did work.

All of the above is not to say that readers had no negative comments. Among the ten readers who had failed FSBO experiences, one said she got tired of giving tours to people who were "not serious." Another felt that prospective buyers were reluctant to talk business with owners.

But the vast majority of the general comments were positive, and informative. For example:

• "I am a former real estate salesman," wrote Richard Bachler of Peoria, Arizona. "We were taught that 'laymen' can't possibly sell their own homes without professional help. Hogwash!"

• "Over the last 12 years, we have bought and sold six homes: three with the help of a real estate agent, three we sold ourselves. Let me tell you, the houses we sold ourselves went much more smoothly than the houses we listed with an agent," contributed Erin Tolli of St. George, Utah.

• "Brokers will say, 'Buyers will discount the price because they know you aren't paying a commission.' The truth is, if you have a saleable house, you will get market value," wrote Ann Crowley of Beverly, Massachusetts.

• "My only caveat would be that owners must realize that it takes more effort than just sticking a 'For Sale' sign out on the front yard," cautioned a reader from Colorado Springs, Colorado. "Professional realtors are correct when they say that people who do just this are likely to fail."

• "We hired a retired real estate agent on a consulting basis," wrote Jenny Beatty of Monkton, Maryland. "This cost less than $200 and was invaluable."

• And, finally, a comment from Kathy Lloyd and Drake Barton of Clancy, Montana, points out that the benefits of owner-selling are not just financial: "An advantage of FSBO is that it promotes self-sufficiency, and sidesteps those who would try to convince us we can't handle our own affairs."

LOOK FOR FRUIT LOOPHOLES

When I was a kid, the local supermarket always had a bin full of imperfect produce, such as brown bananas and grapes that had become separated from their bunches.

But as more and more of the big chain supermarkets strive for an upscale image, less-than-perfect foods have become difficult to find—they just seem to vanish.

Or do they?

Gloria Whitelaw of Wilmington, North Carolina, struck up a conversation with the produce manager at her local store. He told her to come in on Tuesdays, Thursdays, and Saturday mornings and she could have all of the overripe produce she wanted.

"So, every other day I've been

coming home with literally bushels of peaches, tomatoes, green beans, bananas, limes, apples, kiwi fruit, mushrooms, etc.," she writes. "He charges me a dollar or two for a cart full. We've never eaten so well, and I am stocking the freezer and pantry."

To see if Gloria's experience has widespread applicability, I had one of my staffers visit seven supermarkets in and around his hometown. In each, he casually sidled up to the produce manager and asked what happens to overripe fruits and vegetables.

At two of the upscale supermarkets, the PMs informed him that all overripe produce goes immediately to the local food bank.

At another, equally upscale place, the PM told him that it's strict company policy that all dated produce gets thrown out. "We used to give it to a pig farmer, but he stopped coming," he said.

At another relatively posh market, the PM directed him to a wheeled cart full of 11¢-per-pound spotted bananas in an obscure corner of the produce section. As my staffer loaded up (he eventually peeled and froze them), the PM informed him that this cart appeared irregularly, and that there were no private backroom deals made.

At a considerably lower-scale market, the PM told him that "we order carefully, so there's no waste." At another market of a similar economic stratum, the PM was only mildly encouraging. "We may have something, but it would be very rare," he said. "I'll keep you in mind."

My intrepid staffer was about to give up when he decided to swing by the lowest-scale market in his area. Here, he hit the jackpot. The PM informed him that she had private arrangements with several individuals to buy large quantities of outdated produce. While she did not offer the kind of prices cited by Gloria, she did say that she generally sold the stuff for less than half of its usual retail price.

As my staffer reflected on his survey, he realized that the important factor here was probably not so much upscale versus downscale as it was chain versus independent. Chain supermarkets, even those with as few as three stores, generally have cast-in-stone policies against backroom deals of any kind. One-of-a-kind mom-and-pop stores, while free to set up creative side deals, are often too small to have any produce section at all. So the optimum place to get a backroom deal is a store that is similar to the last store my staffer visited—large enough to have a good-sized produce section but not part of a chain.

Finally, Laura Smith of Maple Valley, Washington, points out that she's found a similar phenomenon in meat sections. "Your friendly butcher makes his hamburger out of the roasts and steaks that he didn't sell after they're a few days old," she writes. "See if you can make a deal with him to buy them at hamburger prices. Also, chicken and turkey parts are generally tossed after a few days; if you can get him to sell them to you, go for it."

So, next time you go to the market, strike up a conversation. You may be pleasantly surprised.

SCRATCH 'N' SPIFF

Dear Amy,

If your glasses have plastic lenses and are scratched, try spraying them with Lemon Pledge, spreading it gently over both sides of each lens, and then wiping with a soft cloth. The furniture polish fills in some of the scratches and improves your vision without the purchase of new glasses.

—Anita Puzon
Poulsbo, Washington

GOT TWO COVERED

Dear Amy,

My husband and I receive full family health insurance coverage from both of our jobs. My employer will refund a portion of the premium that they would pay if the employee can show that he or she is covered by the spouse's insurance.

—Julie Doerr
Watsonville, California

BIG BUCK SAVINGS

Dear Amy,

Every year, deer are hunted and killed, taken to processing plants, and not even picked up by the hunter! It is illegal in many states to sell deer meat, so the plant processor sells the deer for the butchering fee alone, which in this area is around 40 cents a pound. Venison can be eaten alone, mixed half and half with beef hamburger, or ground with beef fat to make a less lean ground beef. If you don't care for the flavor, you can disguise it in chili, stews, and casseroles.

—Cathy White
Idabel, Oregon

TAKE A LAPSE

Dear Amy,

To reduce the cost of membership in a warehouse club, we intentionally allow our membership to lapse each year, renewing it several months after it has expired. So, for example, if we allow three months to elapse before renewing, in effect we reduce the cost of membership by 25 percent. Naturally, we time our purchases to maximize the time period between membership renewals.

—Patrick Kearney
Shippenville, Pennsylvania

ODD ADVICE

Dear Amy,

In "Get a Piece of the Auction," (see page 68), you mention making a mental note of the top dollar you'd pay. My husband and I attend several auctions and have noticed most people's "top dollar" is even money. Example: If the bid is $700, and your "top dollar" bid is $725, you are likely to get it. This concept works well for sealed bids, too. We got an answering machine for a sealed bid of $10.28. The only other bid was for $10 even.

—Judy J. Nelson
Gilmore City, Iowa

BUYS IN THE 'HOOD

Thought I'd pass along my greatest yard-sale find, which happened just yesterday. At my very first stop in a wealthy Mobile neighborhood, I purchased eight complete six-piece place settings plus serving dishes, cream and sugar bowls, etc. of brand-new Mikasa china for $20. I asked the owner why she was selling it and she told me they buy new china about once a year and she was tired of that color. I stopped at a department store later that day and priced the china. It sold for $130 a place setting. I am still in shock. With all of the other china she included in the set, it was about a $1,400 value.

—Jeanetta Seay
Chatom, Alabama

SOAP CRAYONS

Take one cup of laundry soap and add 30 to 40 drops of food coloring. Add water by teaspoonfuls until soap becomes liquid. Stir well. Pack soap into ice cube tray. Set in a sunny, dry place for two days. Crayons will become hard and great for writing in the sink or tub.

—Julie T. Offutt
Louisville, Tennessee

OLDER BUT MISER

The high school in my town allows any adult resident to attend classes with the kids free of charge, as long as there is room in the class. I took a class in pottery. I had a lot of fun and made some pieces that I used for Christmas presents.

—Linda Bodnar
Windsor, Connecticut

HELP FOR WEARY WIPERS

Dear Amy,

My thrifty husband has a way of making our windshield wipers last for "one more rainy season." He lightly sands the edge of the brittle rubber with sandpaper, and once again they're like new!

—Kathleen Balge
New Berlin, Wisconsin

AVOID THE TRAPEZOID

Dear Amy,

Regarding your reconstruction of a "mutant" pillow ruined by washing (see page 38), next time you wash a pillow, take the time to "tie" it with yarn, running the yarn through both the inner casing and fill, just as if you were tying a quilt. This keeps the polyester from shifting. Then clip the yarn when you are done.

—Jessica Ayers
Cassopolis, Michigan

WOW KNOW-HOW

Once when I inventoried my supply of kids' clothes before yard-sale season, I had then nine-year-old Jamie try on a pair of respectable-looking boots. She agreed that they would be satisfactory for the following winter. However, six months later she informed me that she now wanted green L. L. Bean–style boots like most of her classmates had. She also decided that the boots she had previously approved were slightly too big for her.

Although I felt no parental obligation to satisfy her change of tastes, I did want her to have boots that fit properly. So before we headed to a retail shoe store, I suggested we hit our church's thrift shop. It offers clothing at yard-sale prices; however, the selection of footwear is so poor that I guessed I'd have a better chance of converting Donald Trump to frugality than I did of finding suitable boots for her there. But as we browsed, Jamie plucked a pair of plum-colored L. L. Bean–style boots from the shelf and exclaimed, "I want these kind of boots . . . only green!" Amazingly, these boots were exactly Jamie's size, in great condition, and cost just 25¢. Although she wasn't interested in the boots, I bought them anyway.

Once home, I attempted to "sell" these boots to my disinterested daughter. "Look, these boots are almost exactly what you want. Do you think I should spend $25 to buy new boots for you?" My daughter's response was revealing: "Mmmooommm! I didn't say *'new,'* I said *'green'*!"

By her own admission, the only difference between the boot alternatives was the color. So I offered my counterlogic: "Okay, plum-colored boots cost 25¢ and green boots cost $25. Are green boots a hundred times better than plum-colored ones?" She admitted they weren't and quite contentedly wore the plum-colored boots for the rest of the winter.

This story provides an example of a crucial tightwad test for value: examining the ratio of satisfaction-to-price between two or more alternatives. Put another way, it's important to examine the "cost per wow," or CPW, when making purchase decisions. The point should always be to get the most wow for the smallest expenditure of money.

The concept applies to nearly every purchase. Suppose you have the choice of a $600 camping vacation or a $6,000 luxury cruise. You

evaluate how much you would enjoy each vacation on the 1-to-10 wow scale. The camping trip would rate 5 wows, and the cruise would rate 10 wows. This means the camping trip would have a $120 CPW as compared to the $600 CPW of the cruise. Although you would enjoy the cruise twice as much, you would get only a fifth of the value. If you go camping, you'll have funds in reserve to purchase other things that are also relatively low-cost per wow. So you wind up with 40, 50, or even 60 wows for the same $6,000 that would have yielded 10 wows if spent on the cruise.

Mastering this value test requires a somewhat different thought process than many people use. Most people will buy the more expensive alternative if they 1) like it more, and 2) can afford it. These two criteria don't include the question of whether they receive sufficient value for the money they spend. And it's not always enough to go further and vaguely consider if the purchase was "worth the money." Using the 1-to-10 wow scale enables you to make more precise decisions.

I also use the 1-to-10 wow scale as one of many ways to determine how important financial and/or time-usage decisions are to other family members, especially with kids whose feelings are hard to read. Some kids express themselves in a way that leads you to believe all of their wants are a 10, while others lead you to believe every desire is a 1. By asking them to place a number on their wants in conjunction with asking them other questions such as "Would you pay for half of it yourself?," I can determine how important the want is to the child and make decisions accordingly.

For example, over the past years I've often felt that our family was devoting too much time to Scouting activities. (At one point there were about 12 commitments during a two-week period.) I was unsure if the children were enjoying it enough to warrant the hassle of hurry-up dinners and ferrying them around. When I asked them, I learned that Scouting is an 8 for them, so we decided to stick with it. Had I learned it was a 3, I would have suggested the kids drop out.

Here are some other pairs of options where I concede the expensive alternative may be nicer but it fails my personal CPW test:

- In-theater movies versus a $1 rented tape at home.
- Restaurant versus home-cooked meals.
- Retail merchandise versus good-but-not-perfect yard-sale stuff.
- Cable TV versus broadcast TV.
- A new car versus continuing to drive a five-year-old one.
- A kid's haircut at a salon versus one at home.
- First-class versus coach airline travel.
- Real maple syrup versus homemade "maple" syrup.
- A magazine subscription versus old freebies from the library.
- New CDs versus yard-sale purchased LPs.

However, there *are* some cases where more expensive options do pass the 1-to-10 wow-scale test.

- Given my family's size, my home is several times better than a house that might have cost half as much.
- Given the needs of our business, a $1,800 new computer is

more than twice as good as a $900 used one.

- Given my tastes and the fact that it could remain in the family for generations, a $200 antique empire bureau from an estate auction is more than four times better than a beat-up $50 yard-sale find.

Two final points. No one can dictate, or even guess, what wows another person—it's best simply to ask directly. And sometimes, with time, our feelings about wows can change. I asked Jamie about the effect of not wearing green boots all winter. She said that once she had the plum-colored boots she began to notice a lot of other girls had plum-colored boots as well.

POWER YARD-SALING

Articles I've written in which I refer to yard sales have prompted letters from newsletter readers. A few doubted that I was finding clothing as cheap as I claimed (from free to $1 per item). They hadn't seen *any* clothes that cheap at yard sales. Others, noting that I said I went to more than 200 yard sales per summer, questioned the payback on my time and gasoline.

So I thought it might be useful to discuss my yard-sale techniques. Finding good deals requires going to a lot of yard sales because the merchandise is unpredictable. But to ensure a high payback, I use certain strategies to save time and gas.

In my area, yard sales are held for up to three consecutive days, generally from Friday to Sunday. I've experimented with going on various days and have been most successful on Saturdays. This allows me to hit some sales on the first day (good stuff goes early) and some on the last day (leftovers go cheap).

On Friday, I pick up the newspaper from Lewiston/Auburn, the metropolitan area of about 30,000 where I go to yard sales. The classifieds list from 50 to 100 sales. The ads are arranged by town but are otherwise listed randomly, and so are hard to work from on yard-sale day. In addition, I'm unfamiliar with most of this area's complex sprawl of streets.

So on Friday night I get out my city map. Using a pencil, I circle the street names and write in the street number(s) next to the circles. By doing this I can easily see where the yard sales are clustered and how to drive the most efficient route possible. Although I bring the newspaper with me, I seldom refer to it during the yard-sale day. Since I rarely go with another adult and must navigate as well as drive, I can easily fold the map small enough to reveal one section at a time, and can hold it with my thumb pointing to the next sale. Before I yard-sale again, I will erase all my markings. One map will last through the summer.

I always take our 1983 Plymouth Horizon as opposed to our Chevy Suburban; the Horizon uses less gas and is easier to park and turn. It's also our least valuable car, and so the best candidate to subject to the stop-and-start rigors of yard-saling. In the last several years, I had to return with our Suburban just once, to pick up a free-for-the-hauling bureau.

Yard sales start between 7 and 9 A.M. I plan to arrive at the first sale by 9, unless I know that many yard sales at the beginning of my circuit are open earlier. So-called

early birds arrive before the advertised time hoping to get the good deals. The rudest may even stop in the day before the sale or at 6 A.M. I prefer to go to more yard sales to offset my politeness disadvantage. On a few occasions when I've accidentally arrived early, I've been turned away, or found that all the merchandise wasn't unpacked yet and my preplanned route didn't allow me to return at a later time. It's true that a lot of the good stuff, particularly furniture, goes early, but proprietors are less likely to negotiate in the early morning, whereas they'll announce "Make any offer" later in the day.

Your route will depend on geography as well as the type of stuff for which you are looking. New suburban developments generally offer more stuff for kids, but have only '70s Sears-style household decor items. Older neighborhoods tend to yield interesting near-antique junk. Affluent areas may consistently offer neatly displayed name-brand clothes—with higher, nonnegotiable prices. Moderate-income neighborhoods seem to have more jumbled piles of clothes for 10¢ to 25¢ per item, and these have yielded good-looking clothes.

Aside from my map, I bring:

- A measuring tape and my kids' clothing inventory (as discussed on page 6.)
- Snacks and a Thermos with a cold drink. If I'm traveling with a child, I make sure these are especially appealing snacks.
- Paper bags and a blanket to hide finds with gift potential.
- A pocketful of coins and dollar bills, because I can make purchases faster if I have the correct change.

• A lightweight jacket and other clothing that will accommodate unpredicted cold or hot weather.

Although I have never been this organized, I've also thought I should bring a large selection of working batteries to test suspicious electronic stuff.

Though I travel faster alone, I often take one child at a time. It's a way for me to do one-to-one quality time. I also want my kids to get used to yard-sale prices, so they experience sticker-shock in retail stores. Each child must swear to keep mum if I find a gift for a sibling.

If you have to bring toddlers along and you want an early start, try this: Dress them in sweatsuits for bed the night before. Pack a portable breakfast. In the morning, put the groggy kids in the car without changing their clothes. Give them a breakfast once they're fully awake.

Although some people will simply pass by "boring-looking" yard sales, I stop anyway since I've already invested time locating the sale. I've learned that *any* sale can yield surprise finds.

The one type of yard sale I avoid is the perpetual yard sale—those that appear to be permanently set up in garages. Because these people are more interested in making money than in getting rid of stuff, the prices are higher and less negotiable. In addition, the merchandise has already been picked over. I keep a list of addresses of the suspect garage sales so I won't waste time going there again. Similarly, flea markets have become a sort of communal perpetual yard sale. They offer so few good deals that I seldom stop at one.

Once I arrive at a yard sale, I don't dawdle. I look very quickly at every single item. If I don't find anything I want, I can complete a single yard-sale stop within 60 seconds. But if the merchandise looks more promising, I'll look more carefully. I poke through every "free box" item by item. These have yielded such things as a rechargeable battery, an unopened bar of soap, an air mattress, old sneakers with new laces, a handful of Legos, measuring spoons, and a bag of Band-Aids. One box was full of girls' tights and socks; I carted away the entire box.

When it comes to *buying* stuff, I usually negotiate unless the merchandise is already so cheap that negotiating would seem rude. There are several techniques you can use. If I am the only buyer at the sale, I may refrain from actually picking up the item (which would indicate a greater degree of commitment). Approach the proprietor and ask, "Would you take $5 for the garment bag over there?" Depending on the original price, my offer could be 10 percent to 50 percent off. If she says "No," it's my choice to pay her price, negotiate further, or walk away. If the item is marked much too high for a yard sale, I always walk away, rationalizing that I'm doing my part to keep yard-sale prices low.

If a child wants to buy something, I have him negotiate as well. Proprietors rarely turn down a child, and some give items to kids for free. If my child is shy, I'll conegotiate by saying, "My son would like to buy that telescope over there. Would you take $1 for it?"

Is power yard-saling worth the time and gas? This can be easily figured by comparing yard-saling to department-store shopping. If I

spent five hours going to yard sales, I subtract the one hour I might have spent doing the same shopping in retail stores. If I used $2 worth of gas to go to yard sales, I subtract the 50¢ I might have spent in gas to make a special trip to the retail stores. If the stuff I brought home from my yard-sale day might have cost $75.00 retail, I subtract the $10.00 I spent at the yard sales as well as the $1.50 extra used for gasoline. So, in theory, I spent four hours extra to shop at yard sales and saved $63.50. In this case, my tax-free hourly wage would be $15.88.

People who aren't shopping for children and who already have all the household stuff they need probably won't do this well. I always do this calculation and know my hourly wage is rarely below $10, and often it's much higher. Jim actually does better because he buys tools.

An article about yard sales would be incomplete without pointing out the sheer fun and thrill of the hunt. And when I return home, my children all gather around to see if I brought them anything—a "new" shirt, a 10¢ jar of beads, or maybe some trinket from a free box. Bringing them something regularly reinforces the concept that good things come from yard sales.

FREQUENT-BUYER MILES

Fritzi Griffis of Tucson, Arizona, writes, "In your first book I noticed a newsletter reader's comment: 'Why would anyone pay a fee for a Visa card?' Well, we do, $50 a year, and so far it has paid for itself and more." Fritzi says she uses one of the many "affinity" credit cards that give you one frequent-flyer mile for every dollar you charge.

I have an aversion to affinity cards. The deals are complex and constantly changing, and I've always figured that the payoff, if any, is probably too small to warrant tedious calculating and comparing. But enough people have written extolling the virtues of credit cards that are linked to frequent-flyer miles that I decided to study this further.

Here's the deal: Generally, you have to accumulate 25,000 frequent-flyer miles to get one free round-trip ticket anywhere in the continental United States. In her postcard, Fritzi states that in 1994, by using her affinity card, she earned 11,987 miles. In other words, her $50 fee put her about halfway to the goal of a ticket that could cost as much as $700 (that's about the upper limit for purchased flights that have the same kind of restrictions that frequent-flyers must obey). So it does look like a good deal.

But the catch is that she had to rack up $11,987 in credit card purchases in that year. Fritzi explains that her husband is a consulting engineer who travels often, and he uses the credit card to cover business expenses.

This unique circumstance—the ability to use the card for business costs—can, clearly, make these

cards worthwhile despite their high fees ($50 is about the cheapest fee you'll find, and they range up to $100 annually). But if you're frugal and use your credit cards strictly for personal business, you need to do some analyzing:

First, decide where you would like to travel and learn the lowest price on round-trip airfare there. Then dig out your credit card statements from last year and total up the dollar amount spent during the year. If you could have used the card more—say, for groceries or gasoline—add on your estimated annual expenditures for those categories. What you're trying to calculate is the maximum amount of your normal purchases that you could make annually with the credit card.

Suppose you come up with a total of $5,000. Divide 25,000 by that figure and you discover that you'd have to pay 5 years' worth of $50 fees to earn one airline ticket. So if the ticket you want costs more than $250 and you would probably buy it anyway, the card could be a good deal.

But before you plunge ahead, I would add several cautions:

1. Obviously these calculations assume you'll pay off your balance each month. Affinity cards generally charge high interest rates. Carrying a balance will make them considerably more expensive.

2. One study revealed that people spend 23 percent more when they use credit cards instead of cash. Be sure you have the self-control to spend no more with the card than you would with cash.

3. Be aware that the airlines can change the rules; they can boost the required miles and/or the annual fee.

4. Airlines "black out" popular travel dates and restrict seating for frequent flyers. Make sure you can fly when you need to.

The bottom line is to do the math. Griffis has, and continues to do so. "I think this has been well worth the $50," she says, "but you can be sure we will continue to evaluate this investment more than once a year, since we also have a free Visa through our credit union."

REVIVAL BY REMOVAL

Sometimes what makes an item of clothing look secondhand is not what it lacks, but what it has. Simple clothes seldom look dated—it's the faddy add-ons that give them away. When you understand this you realize that updating these clothes can be as simple as "taking it off."

Often secondhand clothes are missing the belts, and the empty belt-loops are a dead giveaway. I simply remove these. Recently I carefully removed the loops on a pair of girl's slacks because my daughter Jamie never wears belts.

I have successfully removed the fancy embroidery stitching from the "designer pockets" on '70s jeans by carefully picking it off from the inside with an X-Acto knife. If the pants are faded, I test a small area to see if the design will show after the stitches are removed.

I was given a dress I liked except for a large lacy collar. Using a small pair of scissors, I cut off every bit of visible lace at the neckline seam. I always get compliments on this dress.

Although more sewing skills are

required, you can update a big, pointy, circa-1970 shirt collar if the collar is made with two sections of fabric. By removing the outer section you leave behind a "Chinese-style" collar.

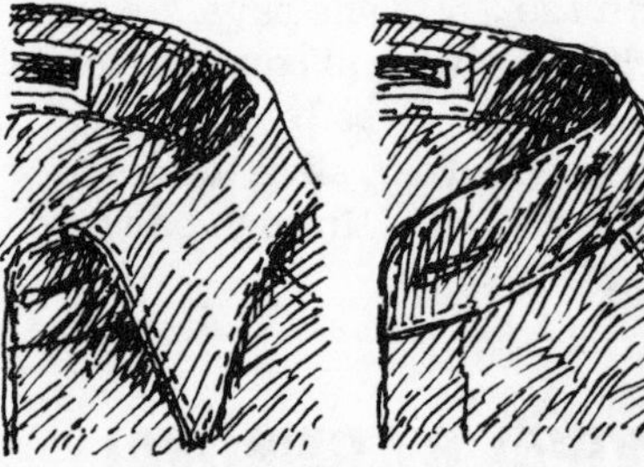

My daughter Laura had a jersey with two sets of three decorative gold buttons. One of the buttons was lost. I simply removed all the buttons.

I bought a 25¢ sweatshirt for Jamie that had beads and sequins sewn onto the front. These began to come off and were annoying her. So one night I carefully removed all of this adornment.

Other excesses like epaulets, Davy Crockett fringe on suede jackets, pom-poms, and the like can also be easily removed.

SUSPEND THRIFT

Dear Amy,

Some insurance companies allow you to suspend the collision and liability portions of your auto insurance if your car is not in use, even if just for a week. While on vacation this year, we suspended coverage on both cars and saved $65. Just ask your company if they have this feature.

—Karen Collier
Southington, Connecticut

DEALS FROM THE DEAN

Dear Amy,

A real find for us has been the Purdue University Surplus and Salvage Barn. Whenever they update equipment or furniture, the old stuff is taken there to be sold. We have gotten solid oak library chairs for $10, dorm armchairs with oak frames and cushioned backs for $5 each, and metal cabinets that normally sell for well over $100 for $30. They also sell unclaimed items from the lost and found. These usually include good ten-speed bikes that students leave behind at the end of the year. Other tightwads who live near universities might check to see if this is available to them.

—Jo Holmes
West Lafayette, Indiana

PARSIMONIOUS PAGES

Dear Amy,

I keep a tightwad journal in my organizer. Each day I enter even the most minor frugal triumph: an aluminum can found in the park, grape jelly discovered dirt cheap, avoiding using the car by biking for errands, etc. When I need a "pick-me-up" I reread a few months of my journal. It really helps!

—Denise Yribarren
Mesa, Arizona

STOCK-UP MARKET

Dear Amy,

Our lot is too shady for gardening, but I get fruits and vegetables for canning another way. There is a farmers' market downtown on Tuesdays, Thursdays, and Saturdays. I wait until almost closing time to go. I then go to the booths that have the best prices and offer to take a bushel or two for about half the price they are asking. I figure they can't hold the food much longer, and they really don't want to pack it up again, so they usually agree.

—Susan Arkles
Jackson, Michigan

WASTE-FREE PASTRY

Dear Amy,

When baking an apple pie, there is no reason to waste anything. I use the extra dough to make mini–cinnamon rolls; and I make snacks from the peels by coating them in oil, sprinkling cinnamon and sugar on top, and baking at 250 degrees for an hour or more.

—Marilyn Bruggema
El Cajon, California

HOSE SPRAY CAN YOU SEE

Dear Amy,

We have no water (truck delivers), so living in the desert, I really conserve and watch the H_2O! For drip irrigation of plants, garden, or whatever, I take an old garden hose, measure where I want the water to drip out and make slits in those places. But the water will spray all over, so the key is to take used soda cans and cut a hole in each end wide enough for the hose to go through. Then slide the cans over the hose to cover the slits. The water squirts into the can and slowly drips out just where you want it.

—Monica Thomas
Yucca Valley, California

AA-OKAY

Dear Amy,

Our local photo center sells used AA batteries for 10¢ each. They come out of the "all in one" disposable cameras and last as long as new batteries.

—Denise Cox
Callahan, Florida

THRICE AND EASY

Dear Amy,

A home perm kit is supposed to provide just one perm, but I get three perms out of a kit. My hair is short and thin, so I need only one third of the solution each time. I have been doing this for three years, and it works great.

—Grace Hallas
St. Johnsbury, Vermont

100-YARD-SALE DASH

Dear Amy,

Our homeowners' association (which includes about 80 percent of the city) has a ban on garage sales, except on the first Saturday in May and the first Saturday in October. On these two days, people come by busloads to the "Mill Creek Garage Sale Saturday." This has advantages to both buyers and sellers: 1) No advertising is necessary for individual sellers. 2) Sellers get more foot traffic because whole neighborhoods are having sales on the same day. 3) Buyers can garage-sale shop more efficiently because of the large number of homes joining in the "garage sale fever."

—Kimiko Rhoten
Mill Creek, Washington

INTERIOR DECLARATION

Dear Amy,

After renting a one-bedroom apartment, I spread the word among my coworkers that I would take *anything* for free. I've received a single bed (my couch), a wooden coffee table (my desk), a glass coffee table (my TV stand), a loaned TV, a small dining room table with four chairs, a double bed, an armchair, a bookshelf, two lamps, two plants, two end tables, one TV table, six bottled-water crates, one trunk, numerous plant cuttings, one coffee maker, one automatic can opener, one roll-around vacuum, one spice rack, food, dishes, hangers, clothes, and a framed painting. It's amazing! I now have a furnished apartment and it cost me *nothing*! Ask and you shall receive, and receive, and receive.

—Sherri M. Felton
Germantown, Maryland

GUIDE AND PEEK

Dear Amy,

I briefly borrow my neighbor's TV magazine each Sunday. I just write down the few programs I am interested in and a brief description so I can record them on the VCR. Then I return the magazine to her, saving either the cost of the Sunday paper ($1.25) or *TV Guide* (which is 80¢ at the grocery store).

—Naomi A. Fowler
Ringgold, Georgia

(It goes without saying that this reader seeks opportunities to return this favor. FZ)

THE MARCH OF A DIFFERENT DREAMER

Fifteen years ago, while freelancing in a Boston design studio, I became friends with Nancy, another graphic designer. At that point, our lives seemed similar: We lived in the same city, had the same occupation, and we both married in the early '80s.

Nancy and I stayed in touch and managed to see each other every few years. Each time we met, I marveled at the different roads we had taken. About the time my third or fourth child was born, Nancy was still pondering whether she would *ever* have a child. When I told her Jim and I were saving for a New England farmhouse in which we hoped to live for the rest of our lives, she shuddered—she couldn't imagine living in the same place forever. Just as I was feeling disenchanted with graphic design, Nancy's career flourished. The job that had been an empty experience for me was meaningful for her.

I last saw Nancy about four years ago. We again compared notes on how different our lives were. Nancy had decided not to have children. Feeling pressure to take yet another "grown-up" step in life, she and her husband had been shopping for a house. After months of indecision, she realized she didn't want to own a house either. She was content with their small apartment, which enabled them to have a streamlined, uncomplicated life. She went on to confide that she really wanted to save for a one-year trip around the world with her husband. She told me they had been squirreling away money but had not made huge lifestyle changes; for example, they still sometimes ate in restaurants.

The conversation then turned to my odd career direction, and, as many people do at a similar point in conversations with me, she described herself as "not frugal" in an apologetic tone. She felt this way not only because her goals were different, but also because she used fewer frugal strategies than Jim and I did. I leaned toward her and said, "But what you just told me five minutes ago is the essence of frugality."

My point was that although our goals were vastly different, we had both stripped away the expectations of others and had decided to generate surplus income to pursue our dreams. Jim and I had less disposable income, so we had needed to use every strategy possible. Nancy and her husband both had good-paying careers and no children, so they would need to use

fewer strategies to accomplish their goal.

Neither did I think it "spendthrift" of her to spend a good chunk of her life savings on this one temporary pleasure. Replacing their savings would be easy since their ability to generate more income was high and their personal expenses would be few. And since both of them couldn't imagine their lives without working, spending money wouldn't result in a painful tradeoff of having to work to replace the money.

There's a reason why I have chosen to relate this story. On my book tours I occasionally bump up against two reactions that concern me. The gentler response comes from those who, like Nancy, apologize for not being frugal. This response is strange coming from people who clearly have adequate resources for all their needs. The second response is a criticism. During a radio interview, the editor of a competing thrift newsletter called in and accused me of being a "thrift terrorist," because the ideas I publish "aren't really appropriate for Middle America."

Both of these responses are based on the same incorrect assumption: that all people should be frugal in the same way, regardless of their circumstances. Everyone's goals, resources, talents, values, and "frugal comfort zones" are different, and there are many legitimate ways to be frugal.

Further, it's incorrect to assume that certain frugal ideas are appropriate for upper-class Americans, others for the middle class, and yet others for low-income Americans. If I've learned *anything* in six years of publishing, it's that no two people agree on what is and isn't an acceptable idea. For instance, in some parts of the country, furnishing a home with curbside finds is socially acceptable only for the lowest-income groups. Yet this practice is considered to be "chic" in New York City by people of all income groups.

My readers fall into a variety of categories. I support all of these choices:

- Some have ample economic resources and modest goals. These readers may choose to use a more limited range of frugal ideas.
- Some have modest resources and are facing desperate circumstances such as unemployment, house foreclosures, and/or bankruptcy. For these people few ideas would be "too extreme," and it would be shortsighted of me to withhold ideas that might not be acceptable to everyone in "Middle America." I want to provide them with the "black-belt" techniques their situation demands.
- Some readers have ample resources and still want to use the black-belt strategies. It's perfectly legitimate to find hard-core frugality a worthwhile lifestyle for noneconomic reasons, such as enjoying the challenge, preserving the environment, or passing on frugal skills to kids.

In other words, I'm an easygoing person. Most people spend money in ways that I wouldn't, but the only time I think of people as "spendthrifts" is when:

- They have spending habits that are making them or their families unhappy, or may make them unhappy in the future, *and* they complain rather than making the lifestyle changes required to improve their lot in life.
- They have wasteful spending

habits yet they carry no health insurance, declare bankruptcy, or fail to pay child support.

In short, it's my job to provide the range of strategies from which you can choose. It's not my job to determine which or how many frugal strategies you should use, or what to apply your surplus toward. Those are *your* choices.

Nancy did take her yearlong trip around the world, returning in the fall of 1995. Interestingly, she wrote me to say that the experience made her more frugal, as she and her husband had been forced to adhere to a tight budget to avoid having to return early. Not only does frugality vary from person to person, but we can adjust it individually day to day—that's one of the wonderful things about it.

KEEP YOUR PORTIONS IN PROPORTION

Unless you've been living in a cave, you've seen that the old "Basic Four Food Groups" nutritional recommendations have been scuttled. The new recommendations are found in the USDA's "Food Guide Pyramid."

The notable aspect of this pyramid from the tightwad perspective is that, with the exception of the pyramid's peak (fats, sweets, and oils), the more you are supposed to eat from a category of food, the cheaper those foods tend to be. The following costs are based on the tightwaddiest alternatives from the various groups:

- Bread, grains, rice, and pasta cost from 15¢ to 50¢ a pound, or about 2¢ for a slice of homemade bread.
- Vegetables cost from 20¢ to $1 a pound, or about 5¢ for a 1-carrot serving.
- Fruits cost from 30¢ to $1 a pound, or about 10¢ for a 1-banana serving.
- Milk costs from $1.40 to over $2.00 per gallon, or about 9¢ per 1-cup serving; cheese costs about $1.60 a pound, or about 20¢ per 2-ounce serving.

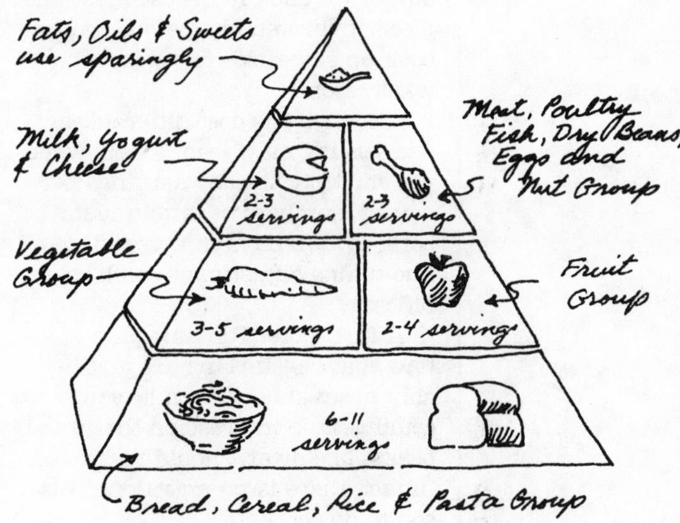

- Meats, dried beans, and peanut butter cost from 50¢ to several dollars per pound. At $1 a pound, meat costs 25¢ per 4-ounce serving.

It has been said to me, "I don't understand. I eat the same foods and pay the same prices as you; why is my grocery bill higher than yours?" The reason may be because there's a third variable: the proportion of foods from different groups that are consumed.

A common health-and-budget mistake people make is to serve a big slab of meat accompanied by tiny dollops of vegetables and rice. Others make choices that aren't

unhealthy but are needlessly costly: Dieters often eat endless salads and restrict their consumption of grains, and parents with young children often allow unlimited consumption of juice or fruit.

In my home we tend to hit these USDA minimum numbers on average. If a child has had juice and two servings of fruit in a given day and asks for more, I'll suggest he eat popcorn or a muffin instead. At dinner we usually prepare just one piece of chicken per person, but we cook up extra rice for those who want seconds.

Although the cost differences per serving may seem small, when you multiply that by servings per day, by numbers of family members, by 365 days in a year, this fine-tuning adjustment can be significant.

A final note: The new plan has a flaw that vegetarians are justifiably upset about. From it, you could get the impression that dried beans, like meat, should be limited. In fact, there is no nutritional reason to do so.

SHIFT AND SAVE

Many parents who have "done the math" have come to a startling realization: When child-care and transportation expenses are subtracted from take-home pay, their "good" jobs actually pay very little.

Cherise Harper, a graphic artist from Middletown, Pennsylvania, came up with a solution that works well for her. After her first child was born in 1993, she persuaded her boss to allow her to work three 12-hour shifts each week instead of the usual five 8-hour shifts.

"In the last two years, there have been no 'cons' to this schedule," she writes. "I pay less in child-care and travel expenses and have more quality time with my daughter." The benefits to her employer were longer office hours three days a week, computers that were not as tied up during the day, and the ability to have "rush" jobs completed at night without having to pay overtime. If a 12-hour day seems too long, another possibility is four 10-hour days per week.

Cherise believes many employers would be open to reasonable agreements such as this to keep reliable, responsible workers, and statistics from the U.S. Labor Department bear out her claim. The number of full-time workers with flexible schedules was 12.1 million in 1991, up from 9.1 million in 1985—all part of a general movement toward offering more "family friendly" work hours.

Cherise writes that the key is presenting the idea in the right light; you should point out that it's beneficial to the employer as well as the employee. She adds, "Sometimes the most difficult part of changing your schedule is asking!"

DIAPER DO'S AND DON'TS

In my book *The Tightwad Gazette,* I wrote about the savings (at least $7 a week) and the minimal labor (about 30 minutes a week) involved in using cloth diapers. Since then, several readers have offered additional information or asked questions that I didn't originally address. What follows is based on reader input, my ten years of experience, and information from Gerber, a leading maker of cloth diapers.

WHAT TYPE OF CLOTH DIAPER TO BUY

I used standard "prefolded" diapers. These have layers stitched together, with extra material in the middle. After washing and drying I piled them in a stack. If you're really lazy you could store them loose in a laundry basket. I also found that nylon pants last longer than plastic pants.

Rose Ann Kirsch of Springview, Nebraska, asked, "What do you think of preformed diapers with Velcro and elasticized legs?"

There is a variety of new diapering systems with different price tags. Some readers have said that contoured cloth diapers with Velcro wraps make cloth diapering easier, as no pins are needed. Some prefolded diapers also have Velcro fasteners. I never used these because they cost more and I was skeptical about how well they would work.

Catherine Washburn of Baltimore, Maryland, confirmed my suspicions. She bought contoured flannel diapers and Velcro wraps but found it was "a big mistake!" The wraps cost $11 to $15 each, compared to $1 a pair for new nylon pants. Since you'll need several sets of wraps or pants as the baby grows, this can add up to a big difference. She also discovered that the wraps leaked much more quickly than the nylon pants.

Another drawback: Her son learned how to remove the wraps at 11 months of age. In comparison, none of my six kids ever undid a pin or was hurt by a pin that came unfastened. And in ten years of diapering, we poked a baby just twice. If you put your hand between the diaper and the baby, you can't poke the baby. If you rub the pin along your scalp, it picks up natural oils that let you push the pin easily through the diaper.

Catherine found she disliked contoured diapers' lack of versatility. In contrast, a prefolded diaper can accommodate a child of any size if you vary the folding, as shown on page 130. A single folded-in-half diaper will accommodate a tiny infant. Two of the same diapers can be used for a toddler.

Catherine has since returned to prefolded diapers, pins, and nylon taffeta diaper pants.

HOW TO ACQUIRE CLOTH DIAPERS

Many people don't buy cloth diapers because they are put off by the "high" initial cost. But even if you bought 50 new diapers (about a five-day supply) at $1 each, they would pay for themselves in seven weeks. And there are ways to get diapers cheaply or for free:

• While you're pregnant, let family and friends know that you plan to use cloth diapers on your baby. With luck, you'll get diapers and paraphernalia as shower gifts instead of $20 baby outfits that

will fit for two weeks. Also "put out the word," as you may know parents who have diapers they no longer need.

• Deborah Collier of Fairview, North Carolina, buys "discard" diapers from diaper services. These companies sell diapers that are a little stained or slightly frayed for "rags"; however, Deborah picked out 50 acceptable ones for 40¢ each. Laura Boynton of Bellingham, Washington, bought used diapers by the pound from a commercial laundry.

• Look for diaper stuff at yard sales. I found a shopping bag of diapers for $1, and nylon pants at a children's consignment shop for 25¢ each.

HOW TO WASH CLOTH DIAPERS

Christina Stone of Ann Arbor, Michigan, wanted directions on washing diapers, and asked specifically, "Do you rinse the messes in the toilet?"

Elizabeth Case of Belfair, Washington, hunted through parenting magazines and baby books and "couldn't find answers to even basic questions about cleaning diapers."

It's hard to track down laundering guidelines because systems vary depending on several factors. For instance, during our "diaper years" we lived in five different houses. The varying proximities of the changing area (i.e., bed or top of freezer), bathroom(s), and laundry room dictated my systems. Individual "squeam" levels also vary widely. Nevertheless, offering some guidelines would be useful.

Elizabeth quizzed other moms and came up with a regimen that works well. The following washing system is based on both Elizabeth's and my experience, and on recommendations from Gerber.

1. Choose a diaper pail. Any 5-gallon bucket will work, but it should have a lid that can close tightly. Though it's rare, a toddler can drown in a bucket of water just as he can in a toilet, believe it or

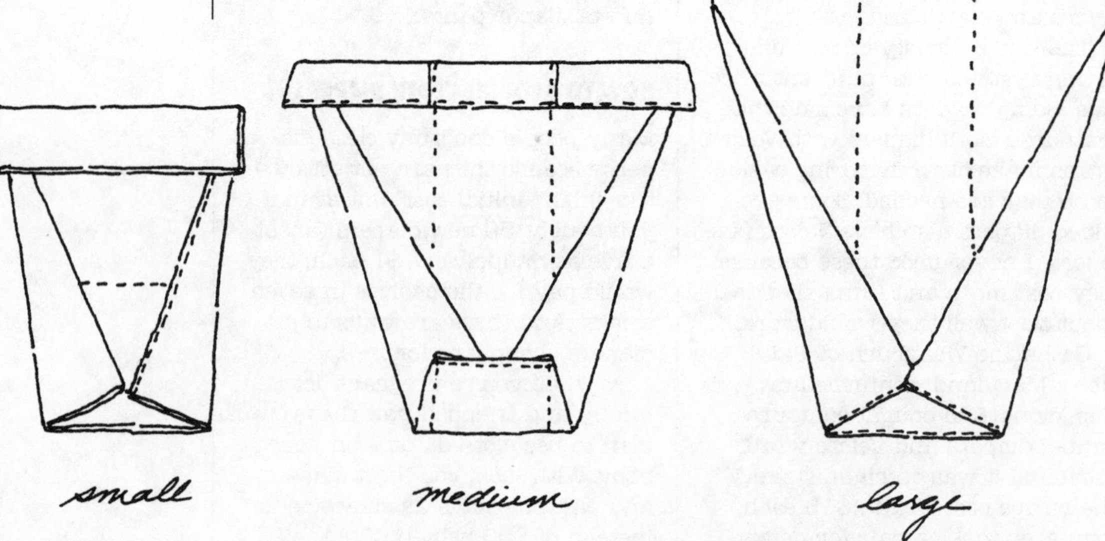

not. I always used 2 buckets so that I could collect enough diapers to make a full laundry load.

2. Fill the pail three quarters full with water. To control odors you can add ¼ cup of borax, but this is optional.

3. Put wet-but-not-soiled diapers and nylon pants directly into the pail to soak.

4a. Remove as much of the solid material from soiled diapers as possible. Some of it will just fall off the diaper into the toilet. Many parents remove solid material by holding the top edge of the diaper firmly, dipping it in the toilet, and flushing. You can also soak soiled diapers in a separate bucket for a few hours to make "sticky" solids fall off easily with a little swishing or rubbing. Once the solids are removed, transfer these diapers to the regular soak bucket. Dump the water from the "soiled" bucket at the end of each day. Wash your hands after handling diapers.

4b. If having to swish soiled diapers is all that's keeping you from using cloth diapers, you might try a compromise strategy: disposable diaper liners. These let you remove solids more easily, though you must still remove the material from the liner because it isn't flushable. I know several cloth-diaper moms who like liners, but I dislike the expense and disposal aspects.

5. When the pail becomes full after one or two days, tote it to the washing machine and pour it all in, including the yucky soak water. Set the machine on "spin" to spin out the soak water.

6. When the machine is through spinning, add your regular amount of detergent. Avoid detergent with bleach or softeners that can irritate the baby's skin. Wash diapers on a regular-length, medium-load, hot-water cycle. Dry on a line or in a dryer.

7. Rinse out the diaper pail in the bathtub. Refill with water.

HOW TO PROLONG CLOTH-DIAPER LIFE

Rose Ann also asked, "Do you have any ideas on how to prolong the life of cloth diapers? My first son is not yet two and he's got some pretty ragged ones."

According to Gerber, using bleach, or detergent with bleach or softeners, will prematurely wear out your diapers. Although bleach is a disinfectant, you can also kill germs with white vinegar or borax added to the wash, heat (hot water, hot dryer), or sunlight (air-drying).

Nylon pants age prematurely in a hot dryer, so air-dry them. An extremely hot dryer will also prematurely wear the diapers.

Regardless of how you care for them, diapers will wear out. As the stitching in the prefolded diapers comes apart, these diapers will "tangle" inside-out in the dryer and can be difficult to make right again. I periodically resewed these seams and around any ragged edges. Each diaper required only a few seconds (and a few feet of odd-colored thread) to repair, but this extended the life for many months. If I was diapering with two diapers, I often used a still-absorbent-but-too-ragged-to-pin diaper on the inside and a good diaper on the outside.

ALES BY COMPARISON

Angela Spicer of Davisburg, Michigan, asked, "Can you tell me if it's cheaper to make your own beer at home?"

Her inquiry led us to our files, where we found a letter from Joan Harris of Albuquerque, New Mexico. She wrote, "We have found that home brewing doesn't provide us with the cheapest possible beer, but for the price of a cheap beer and a little effort we get premium quality beer. Plus it's a fun hobby."

For some precise numbers, I spoke with Karen Barela, president of the American Home Brewer's Association in Boulder, Colorado, and Tim Tardif, owner of Beverage World in the nearby town of Lewiston, Maine. He sells both home-brewing supplies and a wide range of bottled beers.

First, you need equipment. For $27.50, Tardif sells a basic home-brewing kit that consists of a bottle capper, a sanitizing agent, an instruction book, a hydrometer, a plastic bucket for brewing, and an air lock. Another onetime expense is non-twist-top bottles, which cost $2 for 48 at a redemption center. Caps cost 2¢ each.

But Barela points out that an industrious scrounger could assemble his own better, cheaper system. She says plastic fermentation buckets can be difficult to sanitize, and the best choice is a 5-gallon glass bottle such as is used for a water cooler; these can often be found used. She says plain bleach is as good a sanitizing agent as the stuff sold specifically for that purpose. A $2 air lock and a $12 bottle capper can fill out your kit. She says a hydrometer, which measures alcohol content, is optional.

Tardif says a home brewer can make a batch of "basic beer" (similar to Budweiser or Miller) that yields 48 bottles for about $14.50, which equals $1.81 per six-pack. To make a beer that approximates the taste of the most expensive imports requires more expensive ingredients. The cost works out to $3.31 per six-pack. For the purpose of comparison, the bottled beers Tardif sells range from $2.56 to $14.65 for a six-pack of 12-ounce bottles.

Depending upon the process you use, it might take you three to five hours of hands-on time to brew and bottle a typical batch. At this point, I could calculate a theoretical hourly wage for you; however, since beer is a luxury item, and there are variables in costs, making such a claim would be iffy. It's fairer to say that beer-making is a low-cost hobby.

Barela says "almost anyone" can make beer, it is simply a matter of following a recipe. You can get a set of basic beer-making instructions for free from the American Home Brewer's Association, P.O. Box 1679, Boulder, CO 80306. You can also request information on the home-brewing club that's nearest to you. There are over 500 nationwide. Barela said the best book on the subject is *The*

New Complete Joy of Home Brewing by Charlie Papazian (Avon, 1991), which is widely available.

Incidentally, home brewing was federally legalized in 1978. You can make 100 gallons per adult per household, or a maximum of 200 gallons per household per year.

FIX-ITS FROM READERS

Fix-it solutions are unique to circumstance. Each involves an item in need of repair combined with a specific resource. For instance:

The rubber-glove fix. Lynn Wright of East Greenwich, Rhode Island, repairs holes in rubber gloves by cutting a small piece from the cuff end, turning the glove inside out, and using "super glue" to patch the small piece over the hole. The glove must be dry. She says it never leaks in that spot again.

The waterbed fix. Carol Everett of Meadville, Pennsylvania, had a hole in her waterbed. She applied a 1½-inch square of Shoe Goo over the dried hole-area and let it dry uncovered.

The clothes-dryer-door fix. Robin Jackson of Lafayette, Georgia, wrote that her dryer's door no longer stayed closed and a replacement latch would have cost $70. Instead, her husband screwed on a latch from an old screen door. It works great.

The overstuffed-chair fix. Sharon Carr of Brookesmith, Texas, stopped the stuffing hemorrhaging out of the arm of her overstuffed chair with an iron-on patch. Then she tacked place mats of complementary colors on the worn spots on the arms. "The chair actually looks dressier than before," she says.

The on/off-switch fix. When the switch on her TV wasn't working properly, Cathy McSweeney of Plano, Texas, sprayed it with Cleaner Degreaser, a $4.99 product sold at Radio Shack for cleaning electronics. She saved herself a $40.00 repair charge.

The cheese-cutter fix. Mel Hanson of Milwaukie, Oregon, says that if the wire on your cheese cutter breaks, you can replace it with guitar wire. Ask your guitar-playing friend to save a correct-thickness wire for you.

The sneaker-lace fix. Pam Lenza of Staten Island, New York, says when the plastic tip comes off laces, you can repair it with trans-

parent tape (not "magic" tape, which isn't sticky enough). Simply wind it around the end of the lace several times.

The sofa-cushion fix. Edna Musso of De Bary, Florida, suggested that if you absolutely ruin a sofa cushion on a sofa that backs up to a wall, you can remove the upholstery from the back to use in making a new cushion cover. Replace the fabric on the back with something compatible.

The wooden-knob fix. When the screw no longer holds in a wooden knob, such as on a bureau drawer, Linda Corssmit of Greenwood Village, Colorado, suggests fixing it with a wooden match. Coat the match with white glue, insert it in the knob hole, and break it off flush. Replace the screw and let dry. *(FZ note: I tried this and it worked.)*

The high-chair fix. Dabney Nunley of Phoenix, Arizona, lists these steps to replace the torn vinyl covering on the back and seat of a high chair. First, remove the screws that hold the back and seat to the metal frame. Cut three pieces from a vinyl tablecloth—if you use a rectangular cloth, you can be left with a usable square cloth. Cover the bottom with one piece, wrapping it around and securing the edges to the seat's underside with hot glue. Use two pieces on the back (one to cover the cushion, the second to make the back look finished). Reattach to chair.

The scorched-Formica fix. Instead of replacing the whole countertop, Betty Garman of Lititz, Pennsylvania, points out that a carpenter (or you, if you are experienced in Formica work) can carefully cut out the damaged section and replace it with a piece of butcher block.

The silverware-drainer fix. Julie Dennis of Portland, Oregon, says if the bottom of your dishwasher's silverware drainer has broken out, use a long embroidery needle to thread dental floss in a crisscross pattern across the bottom.

The eyeglasses fix. If your eyeglasses or sunglasses keep coming unscrewed at the arm hinges, screw tightly and apply a thin coat of clear nail polish. Once it dries, they won't become loose again, says Linda Mientkiewicz of Waterford, Pennsylvania.

The cat-scratching-post fix. Theresa M. Lemire of Iowa City, Iowa, says you can recover a deteriorating scratching post by removing the old carpeting and winding the post tightly with sisal twine.

The sagging-headliner fix. Use upholstery twist pins to reattach the cloth liner that covers the interior of a car's roof, suggest Don and Gail van den Berg of Waxhaw, North Carolina.

The crock fix. Fill the crack in a crock with melted beeswax, says Laurie Bingham of Pittsfield, Maine. This is for crocks that hold items at room temperature; it's not for Crock-Pots.

The nicked-appliance fix. Marcia Lanphear of Collegedale, Tennessee, says you can touch up white kitchen appliances with

white correction fluid. She says it is durable and matches well.

The scratched-woodwork fix. Fill in with a crayon and buff away excess with a cloth, suggests Dawn McFadden of Calhoun, Georgia.

The vacuum-cleaner fixes. This one is from my own experience: When the cord-retracting spool inside our vacuum cleaner broke and stopped retracting, Jim snipped off all but about 6 inches of the cord and added a new male plug. We now use the vacuum cleaner with a heavy-duty extension cord, which has an advantage: it's longer than the original cord, so we can vacuum farther without moving the cord.

This one is from one of my staffers: When the connection between two metal sections of his vacuum cleaner's hose became worn and too loose to stay together, he put a metal, screw-adjustable pipe clamp around the female end. By carefully tightening the screw, he made the female end small enough to get a good friction fit.

WOOL-AID

Dear Amy,

I have a safe, easy way to liven up yard-sale wool sweaters. Kool-Aid (and generic equivalents) will dye wool to a variety of brilliant colors. Wash and rinse the sweater in room-temperature water, using dish soap. Fill a big pot with room-temperature water. Add two or three packages of Kool-Aid (from the small packets that don't contain sugar). Wring out the sweater and add it to the pot. Slowly bring pot to simmer, simmer for 10 minutes and cool down. The water should be colorless. Rinse in water that is the same temperature as the sweater. The Kool-Aid is absolutely colorfast. I have been told that Kool-Aid also works to dye cotton, but the colors are not as intense as with wool.

—Elaine Brannen
Fairfield, Iowa

(Elaine sent samples that are quite lovely. At 10¢ a package for generic Kool-Aid versus $1.99 for Rit Dye, the savings are significant. FZ)

FAREWELL, TWO ARMS

Dear Amy,

Pullover bibs for small children can be made very inexpensively from used sweatshirts purchased secondhand. Leave the front, complete with its design, and trim off the sleeves and back. Finish the rough edge with a zigzag.

—Jeannette Paulson
Grand Rapids, Michigan

CHEAP CHOPS

Dear Amy,

If you live near a university, check to see if students produce or package food in any of their courses. I buy top-quality meat at discount prices at the Iowa State meat lab. When we lived near Penn State, we got great honey, cheese, and ice cream.

—Katherine Jackman
Ames, Iowa

ALMOST-FREE A-TO-Z

Dear Amy,

If you need encyclopedias, you should check with your local library first. Our library buys a new set each year and sells a five-year-old set each year. I was able to buy a five-year-old set for $20.

—Martha Bisacchi
Lake Village, Indiana

ROD AND ROLL

Dear Amy,

While painting my pantry recently, I needed an extension rod for the paint roller. I discovered that my broom handle unscrewed and fit the roller perfectly.

—Charlotte Baillargeon
Hinsdale, Massachusetts

NO-SHOWS AND UH-OHS

Dear Amy,

Our pizza place sells "mistake" or unclaimed pizzas at or below half price. We can buy a large pizza for $2 or $3. Usually during their busiest hours, like Saturday evenings, you can stop and pick up a cheap pizza.

—Corine Sandifer
Nashville, Tennessee

CORN-BROCCOLI CASSEROLE

This casserole does a wonderful job of absorbing our abundance of mystery-can corn. Yellow squash, zucchini, cauliflower, and a wide variety of other vegetables can be substituted for the broccoli with impressive results. This one-dish supper can be made in about 15 minutes of hands-on time if you are using preshredded cheese and frozen broccoli. If you use fresh broccoli, it should be steamed al dente first.

1 can corn, drained
1 can creamed corn
1½ cups shredded cheddar cheese
4 eggs, beaten
3 cups frozen broccoli, thawed and chopped into ½-inch chunks
1 small onion, minced
⅔ cup milk
1 sleeve saltines, crushed
2 tablespoons margarine, melted

Preheat oven to 350 degrees. Combine first seven ingredients and ¾ cup of saltine crumbs. Pour into 10½-inch metal-handled frying pan or large casserole dish. Combine remaining crumbs with margarine and use to top casserole. Bake uncovered for 40 minutes, or until firm. Serves eight.

CUBBIES CONQUER CHAOS

Betty Cotter of Wakefield, Rhode Island, saw a magazine photo of me posing before a set of "cubbies" that Jim built. She wrote to say it was a great idea and suggested that I mention it.

We built them because we had a huge problem with storage of coats, gloves, snow pants, boots, schoolbooks, backpacks, and lunch boxes. Multiply these by six kids and you get the picture.

We used a combination of scavenged and leftover lumber; Jim estimates they could be built with about $25 worth of new lumber. We recycled hooks we already had (a quirk of our pre-1900 house was that each closet bristled with dozens of coat hooks) and used leftover white paint.

I won't launch into construction details. I'll assume readers will modify the basic idea based on their skills and available space and materials. However, it's useful to discuss how we arrived at the measurements.

The total width of the unit was based on our available space—the distance from a corner to a window in our laundry/mud room. We divided this into six equal spaces of about 12 inches each.

Each cubbie has three levels: the bottom shelf for boots, the middle section for coats and snow pants, and the top section for books and lunch boxes.

The depth of the cubbies was determined by the length of a teenager's boot—about 12 inches deep. The height of the middle section was determined by the placement of the coat hook: It had to be low enough for a small child to reach and high enough to hang snow pants or a long coat of an older child, so the hook is 42 inches above the floor. The top section had to be tall enough to accommodate a standard 8-inch-tall lunch box. Add an inch or two here and there, and the total height is 57 inches.

Aside from neatening up our lives, the cubbies proved to be a time-saver. We spend less time looking for misplaced schoolbooks and winter gear.

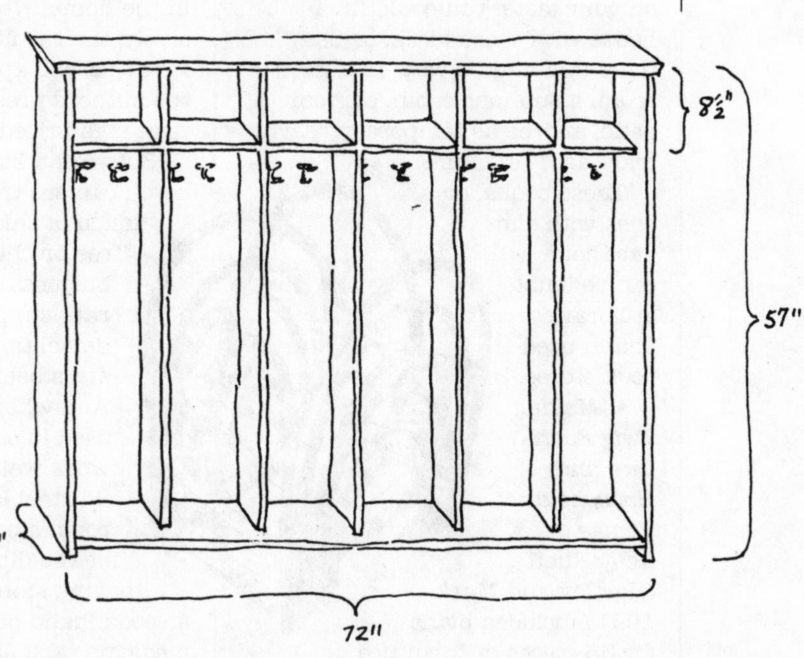

STICKS AND STONES MAY GRACE MY HOME

When it comes to finding low-cost furniture and household accessories, most tightwads have already discovered yard sales, flea markets, and auctions. These sources generally offer items suited for those with mainstream tastes and modest-to-average budgets.

If you have adventurous tastes or a thinner wallet, there are other alternatives. The following four books explore untraditional furnishings and accessories made from free or low-cost stuff.

Many of the ideas are whimsical or weird, depending on your point of view. For example, it takes a unique turn of mind to attach a wooden sled to your kitchen's ceiling and hang saucepans from its slats, as suggested in *Found Objects.* Depending on your taste, you could fill a house with these ideas, or use them in a limited way: in a kid's room, a summer cabin, on your patio, and/or as temporary "early marriage" furniture.

These books, or ones with similar themes, can be found at libraries and in used-book stores.

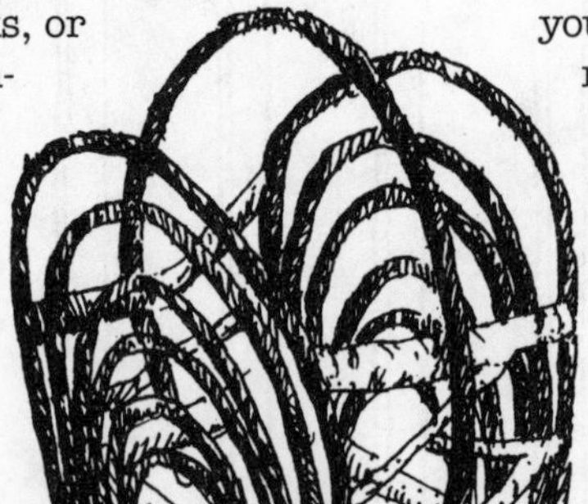

- *Making Twig Furniture and Household Things* by Abby Ruoff (Hartley and Marks, 1991) includes plans for 35 pieces of furniture and household objects ranging from a love seat to a small twig-and-bark basket. But beyond the individual project plans, this book's value is in telling the beginner all about finding, cutting, storing, bending, and assembling twigs into useful objects.

A houseful of twig furniture—or even a single, large piece—might be too much for a contemporary decor, but any home could be complemented by small pieces such as twig planters, picture frames, or a magazine rack.

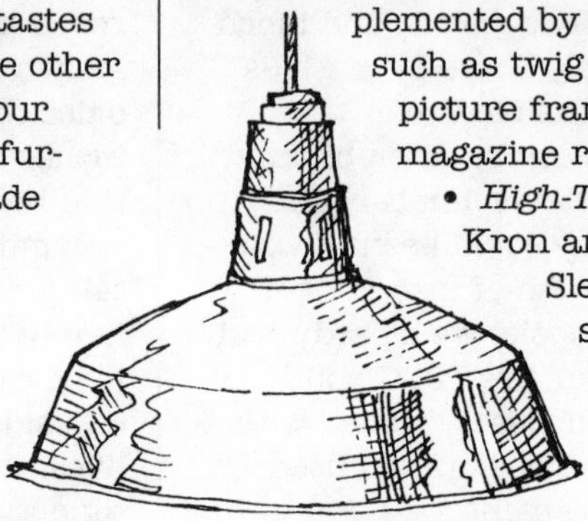

- *High-Tech* by Joan Kron and Suzanne Slesin (Clarkson Potter, 1978) is as far away from twig furniture as decorating gets. The style uses industrial hardware, furniture, and materials in the home. When used exclusively, the result is a cold, uncozy look that will appeal to few. And the authors presume you will buy new, high-priced stuff.

But with a little imagination, you can see the frugal angle: much of this stuff is available free or cheap at going-out-of-business auctions, restaurant-supply stores, demolition sites, or Dumpsters behind businesses. And when the items are used in a limited way, they work well. Examples include old steel lockers for kids'-room storage, a factory light for the dining room, piled-up paving stones for an end table, a secondhand bakery pie-case for a medicine cabinet, hung-on-the-wall

bicycle baskets for vegetable storage, a wallpaper hanger's table for a desk, geological survey maps for art, and stainless-steel hospital dressing jars for kitchen canisters.

• *Found Objects: A Style and Source Book* by Joseph Ruggiero (Clarkson Potter, 1981). "Found objects" are anything you can get for free, and so they encompass natural items, industrial discards, and everything in between. This book celebrates the beauty of these items and shows you how to work them into your home. Some of the odder ideas will make you chuckle and/or scratch your head, such as an oil drum converted into a chair. You may also be amused to note just how lovely a bowl of rocks looks on a $1,000 coffee table.

But the basic concept of decorating with found objects is quite valid. The book depicts how you can use a weathered clam basket for a magazine holder, a gnarled tree trunk topped with glass for an end table, new-but-vintage-looking can labels and seed packets for framed art, a wooden nursery flat for a lap table, and a terra-cotta chimney-flue liner as an umbrella stand.

• *Nomadic Furniture* by James Hennessey and Victor Papanek (Pantheon, 1973). This was popular in the groovy '70s and some of the "modern" ideas look dated today. And a few ideas, like the kids' cardboard car seat, don't meet current safety standards. But many of the ideas will work in '90s homes.

The premise is that this stuff is lightweight, recyclable, and/or easy to take apart and move, but much of it also happens to be cheap or free. Examples include the cut-from-one-sheet-of-plywood desk, a basic cardboard-cube structure that supports up to 400 pounds, a chair made from an old mattress, a bureau made from scrap wood and plastic tubs, and a simple three-legged collapsible table made with tied-together dowels or broomsticks.

Unlike the previous books, this one stresses innovation rather than choice of materials. Therefore, when looking through it, consider possible cross-over ideas with the other books. For example, the three-legged table could be a very stylish permanent end table if made with birch-twig legs and neatly tied jute.

Although these books are diverse in style, the common lesson is that if you can accept the unconventional, you'll save money when furnishing your home.

NO MORE CULTURE SHOCK

Though the steps required to make yogurt are fairly simple, success has eluded some of the finest frugal cooks that I know. Their attempts, and mine, have too often yielded (at worst) failed batches or (at best) yogurt that's runnier than store-bought. Other batches were too tart or had an odd texture. And it bugged me to keep buying store-bought yogurt for starter, particularly when the success of the homemade batches was so inconsistent.

But the economic advantage of homemade yogurt is clear. Here in Maine, a quart of milk costs from 35¢ (from powdered milk) to 52¢ (from a $2.09-per-gallon jug), while a quart of store-brand yogurt costs $1.39. Even factoring in other ingredients, homemade yogurt costs less than half as much as store-bought. A two-quart batch can be made with 15 minutes of hands-on time, which makes the hourly wage over $7. And homemade yogurt can be made less tart than store-bought.

So I decided, once and for all, to solve this yogurt mystery. I started by comparing all the yogurt-making articles and recipes I could find. These 25 sources suggested a boggling array of ingredients, proportions, preparation methods, batch sizes, and troubleshooting tips, and many declared themselves to be magic "never-fail" recipes.

To compare them, I made up a big chart that breaks down these variables, and I converted the recipes to uniform measurements and batch sizes.

Then, over two months, staffers and I tested the different variables by making two separate batches at a time but altering one variable in a batch. To ensure our findings weren't anecdotal, we also interviewed Edward Yaghoubian, director of dairy food research for the National Dairy Board. Here's what I learned:

THE STARTER

Yogurt begins with "starter"—plain store-bought yogurt with the words "Live Cultures" on the container's label. Yogurts that were heat-treated after incubation have dead cultures and won't work as starter.

Dannon is a well-known brand with live cultures. Although recipes may specify its use as the starter, Yaghoubian said no one brand is better than another.

You can have a continuous supply of cheap starter by "chain yogurting." Use starter from a previous batch that's less than five days old. Subsequent batches may become increasingly runny. Yaghoubian said that's because over time, other microorganisms enter the yogurt and start to overwhelm the yogurt cultures. Most sources say you can chain-yogurt up to four times.

Eventually you'll need fresh starter. To avoid purchasing store-bought yogurt for starter every few weeks, I checked out other options.

I investigated dried yogurt starter sold in health food stores. Since this has an unlimited shelf life, I wondered if it would be cheaper than buying a 45¢, 1-cup container of yogurt. But I found that dried starter costs 65¢ per quart of yogurt.

Then I tried an option I'd read about: freezing commercial yogurt

in ice-cube trays, storing the cubes in a Ziploc bag, and thawing for use. Each cube equals about 2 tablespoons. I found that previously frozen starter works as well as never-frozen starter.

Most recipes call for from 2 to 4 tablespoons of starter per quart of milk. We compared using 2 versus 4 tablespoons and found the resulting yogurt was identical. The smaller amount is the obvious tightwad choice. Two tablespoons of store-bought yogurt cost 5¢.

Some sources say tart starter results in tart yogurt. Yaghoubian disputes this, emphasizing that the most critical variable is incubation time. However, in our comparison test, the tart starter did produce a tarter yogurt.

By buying starter yogurt at the cheapest unit price (usually quarts), freezing it in cubes, and chain-yogurting, the starter cost can be as low as 1¢ per quart.

THE MILK

The recipes called for milk in many forms: whole, low-fat, skim, instant powdered, noninstant powdered, evaporated, or some combination.

Yaghoubian said any of these will work, but milk with a high concentration of milk solids yields a thicker yogurt that is more similar to store-bought. You can achieve this by adding ½ cup of powdered milk to a quart of liquid milk.

Some recipes said using *non*instant powdered milk was the "trick": either using it exclusively or for the added ½ cup of powder. (For details on this product, see *The Tightwad Gazette II.*) Yaghoubian said there is nothing special about noninstant powder that would yield better yogurt. It's about twice as dense as instant powder, so adding the same half-cup will make a thicker yogurt. But

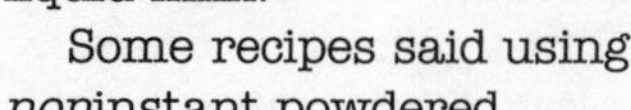

when we added the same weight of each to two batches, the resulting thickness was the same. In some of my experiments, the taste was the same; in a few cases the instant seemed to make a tarter yogurt.

PREPARATION METHODS

Most recipes require heating the milk to 180 degrees, then letting it cool to about 115 degrees. The most sophisticated equipment you'll need, then, is a candy thermometer. (Test yours for accuracy by measuring boiling water; it should read 212 degrees.) Yaghoubian said preheating kills off microorganisms that might compete with the culture, and it breaks down the milk proteins, which leads to a tighter curd and a better yogurt.

Interestingly, some sources said that not boiling the milk was critical, whereas others, like my *Fannie Farmer Cookbook*, said the milk should be boiled for one minute. In my boiling/nonboiling comparison tests, the result was the same.

The most tedious aspect of yogurt-making is watching the thermometer as you wait for up to an hour for the milk to cool. But you don't have to stand over your stove the entire time. You can:

- Time how long it takes for your milk to cool. When making subsequent batches, set your timer to ding a few minutes before that period has elapsed.
- Make yogurt when you'll be doing other small tasks in the kitchen. Each time you complete a task, recheck the thermometer.
- Make your yogurt an hour before you go to bed. Take the cooling milk with you into the living room while you watch TV.

After the milk drops to 115 degrees, whisk a half-cup of the warm milk with the starter. Then add this mixture to the pot of warm milk and whisk again. Undermixing can result in a failed batch, so mix well. Despite common belief, vigorous mixing won't kill starter.

INCUBATION METHODS

The milk-yogurt mixture should incubate *undisturbed* at a constant temperature of about 115 degrees for 4 to 12 hours. The longer the incubation period, the tarter the yogurt will be.

You can use any container, such as a pan or bowl. I use quart-sized canning jars with lids. I use a jar to measure out my quart of milk before heating it, and the tall quart jars use little space in the refrigerator.

There are two basic forms of incubation: insulation-only, or providing an outside heat-source.

Insulation-only methods include putting mixture directly in a Thermos or a specially made insulated container for yogurt-making, or wrapping jars in a towel and placing them in a small cooler, or wrapping jars in a quilt.

Yaghoubian said that providing a constant, correct temperature is crucial. And as my friends and I recall the failed batches we've made over the years, we suspect they resulted from using an insulation-only method or an outside heat-source that was insufficient. So, I recommend a method that provides constant, reliable heat from an outside source. You can:

- Place jars in a pan of water, cover with a towel, and place near a warm radiator.

• Place in a gas oven near the pilot light.

• Preheat electric oven to lowest setting. Turn the oven off, turn the oven light on, and place yogurt in the oven overnight, as suggested by Nancy Jensen of Logan, Utah.

• Place the jars on a heating pad set to "low" and cover them with a towel, as suggested by Ann Stephens of Pittsburg, California. I've been using this method, with a large inverted soup pot over the top for extra measure.

If you're having failures, experiment with different methods of incubation before you change other variables. A staffer had been getting batch after batch of runny yogurt using her yard-sale purchased yogurt maker. When she switched to the heating-pad method, which had a 100 percent success rate in all our testing, she made her first successful batch of thick yogurt.

THE FZ PREFERRED METHOD

For quick reference, here's a recipe that consistently produces a quart of thick yogurt:

Before making yogurt, put 2 tablespoons or a frozen cube of starter in a small glass, cup, or bowl, and allow to warm to room temperature.

Put a quart of milk in a large saucepan. Blend in ½ cup of milk powder. Heat the milk to 180 degrees and cool it to 115 degrees. Add a small amount of this warm milk to the cup of starter, whisk, add this mixture to the saucepan of milk, and whisk again. Pour this into a quart jar, screw on a lid, place on a heating pad set on "low," cover with a towel, and cover that with a large soup pot. Incubate for eight hours.

You can make double and triple batches; but to efficiently chain-yogurt and to avoid old, tart-tasting yogurt (yogurt grows slightly tarter each day in the refrigerator), don't make more than your family will eat in five days.

Several sources pointed out that you can make "yogurt cheese" by lining a colander with cloth, plopping in the yogurt, and draining (in fridge) overnight.

And remember that all failed and too-tart yogurt can be used to make popsicles and in cooking.

IN CONCLUSION

Through all of this, I've concluded that the reason there are so many recipes and theories out there is that everyone's situation is unique. If you don't succeed using the guidelines above, experiment as we did.

This investigation has changed our diet. Due to the expense, we had given up on buying store-bought yogurt years ago. Now yogurt has become a regular part of our diet again.

WHAT TO DO WITH . . .

Scorched ironing-board cover. Make potholders and oven mitts from unscorched parts. (Karina Millet, Greenville, Ohio)

Bread tabs. Make ties that allow balloons to be reused. Slit a tab, put the twisted end of an inflated balloon in the slit, wrap it around the tab once, and put the end in the slit again. (Maureen Melton, Lucas, Texas)

A plastic audio-cassette case. Use as a windshield scraper. Take apart and insert fingers in the clear "pocket" part for good grip. (Helen Darinsig, Port Carbon, Pennsylvania)

Leftover flat root beer and other soda. Use to make gelatin. Combine 2 cups with 1 packet or tablespoon of gelatin granules. (Joan Ayers, Elkton, Maryland)

Dead umbrellas. Use the fabric to repair snowsuits and nylon jackets. (Carolyn Hoppe, Little Rock, Arkansas)

Styrofoam cups. Use to make party-favor hats. Place cups upside down on a cookie sheet. Place in a warm oven until the edges curl up and outward. Decorate with ribbon and tiny flowers. (Name withheld by request)

Dad's old T-shirt. Use to make superhero cape. Slit up the front, leaving the neck intact. Depending on the desired effect, the child can put his arms through the sleeves or not. (Vicky Grist, Buxton, North Carolina)

A refrigerator magnet. Place over keyhole on car door to prevent it from freezing. If already frozen, heat key with match or lighter. (Meg Winfield, Columbia, Maryland)

A milk jug. Make a disposable dish for a dog who chews dishes. Cut the jug off below the handle. (Marilyn MacLachlan, Morganton, North Carolina)

Dental floss. Use to resew ripped stitching in loafers and sneakers. [FZ has used this tip.] (Fran Hulette, Lawrence-ville, New Jersey)

Old chain belt. Make a paper-towel dispenser by fastening it to wall with cup hooks. (Barb Carlson, Randolph, Vermont)

WATTS AND WAIT

Dear Amy,

We have been using the "time of use" program offered by Wisconsin Electric for a few months now, and recommend it highly. When we began the program, the electric company gave us a wired-in type of timer for the water heater and paid an electrician to install it. They also provided an appliance timer for no extra charge.

—Christine Henkel
Oak Creek, Wisconsin

(These programs, which offer reductions during nonpeak hours of up to half off the normal rate, are becoming common at utilities around the country. It's worth a call to your utility company. FZ)

A NEW WRINKLE

Dear Amy,

To increase my chances of winning local prize drawings in stores, I fold my tickets several times in interesting ways to make them more susceptible to being drawn. So far I have won a bag of groceries, a $10 gift certificate, a large Christmas stocking, and a small propane bottle.

—Teresa Busse
Klawock, Alaska

SPHERE, ROVER

Dear Amy,

I can't bring myself to buy new tennis balls for our dog to play with. I went to the local racquet club and asked if they had any old tennis balls that my dog could have. They showed me bins and bins of "dead" balls that had lost their bouncy newness and said, "Take all you want."

—Linda Bukvic
Williamsburg, Ohio

LOW-PRESSURE TACTIC

Dear Amy,

Air is the main cause of freezer burn. Here's a way to almost completely remove the air from food to be frozen in Ziploc bags. Place food in bag and almost seal the bag up completely. Place a straw in the corner and suck all of the air out of the baggie. Then, while still sucking, remove the straw and quickly seal the last section. Then place the baggie in the freezer.

—Christine Sunda
Centreville, Virginia

BOYS TO WOMEN

Dear Amy,

I was having a hard time parting with the money for some new winter boots. Out of desperation, I tried the boys department. I found the same style, and it fit my wider foot nicely—at half the price of the women's version.

—Michele Giesen
Boulder, Colorado

DIPLOMAS AT A DISCOUNT

We've all seen the terrifying statistics. The annual cost of tuition and room and board at the average private college has now passed $16,000. Public schools run around $8,000.

To compound the problem, college costs have increased at more than twice the rate of inflation since 1982 (9 percent versus 4.4 percent). At this rate, costs for a child born in 1995 would be $75,000 annually for the average private school, and $38,000 for public school.

Articles written on the subject generally conclude that you should invest large chunks of cash in mutual funds starting from the year the child is born. At this point, with a sinking feeling, you turn to the comics page.

Don't get me wrong. I feel that saving for a child's education is crucial, and I do not want to let anyone "off the hook" about this basic parental responsibility. And the invest-early-and-often-in-mutual-funds strategy does make sense.

But, as with every other financial decision in life, it pays to think more creatively.

Each of the following options requires careful consideration. Though we have called and confirmed the accuracy of addresses and telephone numbers, I can't vouch for the quality of the services offered. Like any other major money-saving ideas, you need to do research to see if one or more of these fit your needs.

Go to a free college. Readers have sent us information about two tuition-free colleges: College of the Ozarks, Point Lookout, MO 65726, (417) 334-6411; and Berea College, College Post Office 2344, Berea, KY 40404, (606) 986-9341. Both are highly rated academically, but have, as you might expect, fairly restrictive entrance requirements. An admissions director at College of the Ozarks told us that if a student qualifies for a Pell Grant, he or she has virtually a 100 percent chance of acceptance; otherwise, only about 1 in 20 appli-

cants gets in. And Berea College requires that 80 percent of the student body come from the Appalachian region.

Parents work at college. Parents who are employed by colleges often get reduced or even free tuition for their children. This can make it worthwhile to take a pay cut to land a campus position. Marcy Werner of Coral Gables, Florida, writes, "My husband teaches at the University of Miami and we all go free. The same applies to families of secretaries and office workers. Some schools even have reciprocal arrangements with other colleges."

Students work at college. There are many jobs that students themselves can do. Tanya Christman Kuntz of Grand Forks, North Dakota, highly recommends the position of dormitory resident advisor. At the University of North Dakota it pays $192 per month plus free room and board.

Students work outside college. More than 900 schools offer "co-op education" courses, in which formal study alternates with real-world, career-related work. It can tack an extra year or so on your college experience, but the work phase can pay up to $7,000 annually.

Do "distance learning." It's estimated that 100 American colleges and universities offer degrees entirely by "distance learning." This includes instruction by satellite, cable, audio cassette, video cassette, mail, computer conferencing, fax, and/or electronic mail. Tuition tends to be low, and you avoid the huge expense of moving to a distant college. Written tests are monitored by "proctors," sometimes at local high schools.

Reportedly, the best book on the subject is *College Degrees by Mail* by John Bear, Ten Speed Press, (510) 559-1600. Other books include *The Independent Study Catalog* and *The Electronic University*, both from Peterson's Guides, (800) 338-3282.

Mind Extension: The Education Network is a 24-hour cable network that offers degrees such as a BA from Maryland University College or even an MBA from Colorado State University. Videotapes are also available by mail. Call (800) 777-MIND for details.

For free booklets such as *Is Home Study for You?* and a directory of home-study-accredited schools, contact the National Home Study Council, 1601 18th Street NW, Suite 2, Washington, D.C. 20009, (202) 234-5100.

Go to a junior college. Roughly half the students entering college today go to junior colleges, which generally have far lower tuitions. It's become increasingly popular to go to a junior college for the first two years and then transfer to a four-year school for baccalaureate and graduate degrees. Be sure to thoroughly research transferability of credits before you enroll.

Go to a college with a high quality-per-dollar rating. Each year, *U.S. News & World Report, Money Guide* magazine, and *Lovejoy's College Guide* (all available through interlibrary loan) rate America's best college buys.

Get financial aid. There are two general categories of aid: outright gifts and cheap loans. These come from federal and state governments, private industry, and fraternal and religious organizations.

Because this is such a huge subject, it pays to read one or more books about it. The consensus among our readers and the financial-aid officials we interviewed is that the best books are published by Octameron Press, P.O. Box 2748, Alexandria, VA 22301, (703) 836-5480. Write them for a free brochure.

Octameron's flagship publication is *Don't Miss Out: The Ambitious Student's Guide to Financial Aid* by Robert and Anna Leider. We read a copy of the 1995–96 version and were very impressed. It's comprehensive (did you know there are generous scholarships available for former golf caddies?) and makes this confusing subject quite understandable. At $7 plus $2 shipping and handling, it's an excellent investment.

Over 1,200 colleges offer academic scholarships to students who have a B average and SAT scores of 900 and above. Most of these awards aren't based on financial need. Octameron's *The A's and B's of Academic Scholarships,* edited by Debra L. Wexler, lists 100,000 scholarships available at these schools.

Two more comprehensive books are *Cash for College: The Ultimate Guide to College Scholarships* by Cynthia Ruiz McKee and Phillip C. McKee Jr. (Hearst Books) and *The Scholarship Book* by Daniel J. Cassidy (Prentice Hall).

Go off-hours or off-season. Many colleges reduce tuition rates for evening, weekend, and summer classes.

Be a smart high-school senior. Many high schools now offer advanced-placement courses that allow students to enter college with several hours of tuition-free credit. Some colleges offer free on-campus classes for high-school seniors.

Go for three years. Popular in Europe, three-year baccalaureate degrees are catching on in the United States. For example, at Albertus Magnus, a liberal-arts college in New Haven, Connecticut, 80 percent of the freshmen signed up for a three-year bachelor's-degree program. It cost 17 percent less than the four-year program.

Take an equivalency test. ACT/PEP (American College Testing/Proficiency Examination Program) tests are offered by over 800 colleges and universities. They cost from $45 to $140 and are worth from three to eight semester credits per test. You can take them through your school registrar's office, or contact ACT/PEP directly at P.O. Box 4014, Iowa City, IA 52243, (319) 337-1363.

The CLEP (College Level Examination Placement) tests are similar. Call (609) 771-7240 for information, or call College Board Publications at (800) 323-7155 to order *The College Board Guide to the CLEP Examinations.*

Many colleges also offer "challenge" exams, in which you take the final examination for a particular course and get credit for it if you pass.

Do the military thing. Go through the four-year ROTC (Reserve Officer Training Corps) program and in your junior and senior years you'll receive $100 a month. The Montgomery GI Bill pays veterans up to $400 per month for 36 months. To qualify, soldiers, sailors, or airmen must contribute up to $1,200 into a special fund while they are enlisted. For more information, call (800) USA-ARMY.

Do the early-tuition-payment thing. Many states offer prepaid tuition plans—you pay at today's tuition rates and the state ensures it will be sufficient for the date your child enters a state university. Make sure you can get a refund if your child wins scholarships or goes to school out of state. The admissions office at your school of choice will have details.

Carefully match the student with the school. A newsletter reader from Boulder, Colorado, offers an important point: "If your child is unhappy because of an inappropriate situation, the costs in poor grades and making arrangements to transfer will outweigh the tuition you saved."

Peggy Beals of Marshfield, Massachusetts, puts it even more forcefully. "People who would never buy a lottery ticket or put their money in stocks and bonds without a careful study of track records will blow thousands to get their darlings into the most prestigious college that will accept them."

Peggy recommends a year or two in the workforce learning about "reality," or a couple of years in junior college, before spending the big bucks on expensive colleges. "It takes tough love to be firm with these youngsters as they devour college catalogs and dream of some faraway school, dorm life, beer parties, and no parental killjoys nagging them. Being realistic hurts parental pride, but it is kinder in the long run for everyone involved."

BRAIDERS OF THE LOST ART

Like quilting, rug braiding is an old craft that was developed to use up leftover material or to recycle old garments. And like quilts, braided rugs have become expensive; a kit to make a 3-foot-by-5-foot rug costs about $100, and buying a hand-braided rug this size might cost $300. But if you make a rug the way our grandmothers did, it can cost very little.

I spoke with three area braiders: hobbyist Donna Tretola, rug-braiding teacher Nancy Young, and professional braider Anna Smith. I also read several articles.

Space limitations prevent me from covering more than the basics. A library book would be useful for detailed information. I was told the best book on the subject is *The Braided Rug Book* by Norma M. Sturges. It's available from Lark Books at (800) 284-3388.

Ideally, braided rugs are made only of wool fabric. Unlike other fabrics, it's extremely durable, naturally repels dirt, is heavy enough to lie flat, and yet remains soft. Sources of wool include plaid skirts, winter coats, shirts, uniforms, and mill ends. White fabrics can be dyed to achieve hard-to-find colors. Since pure wool comes in a limited range of colors, many braiders also use 80 percent blends.

First, machine-wash any recycled garments; it doesn't matter if they shrink. Cut or tear the wool into strips. As there is a fair amount of waste in each garment, it saves space to do this in advance. Roll the wool into balls for storage.

The optimum width to cut strips is about 2 inches. Cut thicker wools into narrower strips and thinner wools into wider ones. Hand-baste or machine-sew them end-to-end to make longer strips.

Fold the strips with raw edges inside: narrow strips into quarters, wide strips into sixths. Test before cutting to ensure that the final

folded strips are uniform in thickness.

Experienced braiders fold as they braid. Beginners may prefer to baste or press the strips closed. Some braiders use Braid-Aids, small, metal devices that fold the strips as they are fed through. But they cost $7 each, you need three, and they don't work well with used fabric, as the joining seams get caught in them.

Braid the folded strips and join the braids in a circular pattern to form the rug. Originally, braids were hand-sewn together, but in the 1940s a faster and stronger technique was developed: lacing through the braids, not the fabric, with a blunt needle or a Braidkin, a flat, curved tool that costs about $1.50.

"Hit-or-miss" rugs are easiest for beginners, and the most economical, since you don't need a specific quantity of certain colors. For the most pleasing effect, stick with a small range of colors, such as blues and greens. Rugs with planned designs are more challenging. You need to braid a little and lace a little to anticipate color changes. Change colors by adding new-colored strips, staggered one at a time. Depending on the colors and your preferences, you might add one new color per 6 inches of braid, or one new color per row.

Finish the rug by tapering the strips, braiding them to a point, and sewing this on.

As for economy, braided rugs are extremely cheap. Over the years, Donna has spent $20 on her hobby, has made 15 rugs, and has enough material left over to fill two large trunks and a huge basket. Once people learned that she braids rugs, they began to *give* her their wool castoffs, and she was given thread by a relative. Nancy buys unsaleable garments by the pound from thrift shops. A 3-foot-by-5-foot oval rug might require from five to seven full-length winter coats, or 9 pounds of strips.

The biggest expense is the thread to lace the braids together. Although some articles suggested using carpet-and-button thread, twine, or kite string, my sources said these won't hold up for more than five years. A stronger but more expensive thread is six-ply linen (or three-ply for small rugs). A 3-foot-by-5-foot rug requires 225 yards (or 4 ounces) of six-ply thread. Mail-ordered, this quantity costs $12. Anna uses waxed six-ply linen/nylon, purchased in quantity from a local discount source. Her thread-cost is $3 for a rug this size. Nancy uses beeswaxed Nytex, purchased through a shoemaker.

Ask local braiders for their sources of low-cost thread.

Aside from ovals, braided rugs can also be round or heart-shaped. Rectangular rugs can be made by sewing together parallel lengths of braid and leaving the ends ragged. This shape would complement contemporary decor.

These three braiders agreed that a 3-foot-by-5-foot oval rug might require a total of 50 to 60 hours of work, or about 2 hours per night for one month, done while watching TV or visiting.

It might seem that braiding rugs saves a small amount of money for the time spent, particularly when compared to purchasing machine-made versions. But hand-braided rugs are more durable; they can last 35 years in highly trafficked areas and indefinitely elsewhere. Two rugs in the entryway of Donna's home were ten years old and looked almost new.

Also, hand-braided rugs are much more attractive and can be made in subtler designs and to match any color scheme. They can be made larger or smaller as needed. They are easily repaired. If you lack fabric to finish your rug, you can still use it until you find more. And unlike other types of rugs, braided rugs have two usable sides: an everyday side and a "company" side.

Rug braiding interests me because over the last ten years I haven't found any rugs I've liked at yard sales. From now on, I'm going to save all of our old wool garments, and maybe I'll make one of those rectangular rugs for our living room someday.

FREEZER FIGURES

Gricelda Chavez of Upland, California, writes, "My husband and I are looking to buy a freezer. What size do you recommend for a family of four? Is upright better than horizontal?"

Freezers are sized by the cubic foot. We have eight people in our family, and we own a 23-cubic-foot Kenmore freezer, the largest of the standard sizes. Because we have an 8,000-plus-square-foot garden, we fill it right to the brim at the end of summer, but even at its lowest it's at least half full. We can a lot of foods specifically because we don't have room in our freezer.

On the other hand, friends of ours, a couple with one eight-year-old son, have a 14-cubic-foot freezer. They freeze some produce from their 600-square-foot suburban garden, and also freeze garden surplus from friends (us) and bulk-purchased meats. Their freezer has never been more than two thirds full, and they concede they could probably get by with a somewhat smaller model.

So a good general rule is to buy a freezer with about 3 cubic feet per person in your household; less if you don't garden, more if you garden intensively or have a neighbor who hunts moose.

As for the upright-versus-chest question, the 1995 edition of *The Consumer Guide to Home Energy Savings* says the typical annual energy cost for a 15-cubic-foot chest is $35; for the same-sized upright it's $44 (based on the national average of about 8 cents per kilowatt-hour).

When it comes to which brand to buy, go for the best price. One effect of efficiency standards that were imposed in 1993 is that there are no longer significant differences in efficiency between brands of new freezers of comparable sizes.

When freezer shopping, be sure to buy a manual-defrost model. These consume 35 percent to 40 percent less energy than automatic defrost versions. Auto-defrost freezers also tend to dry foods and cause freezer burn.

Due to large advances in freezer efficiency in recent years, this is one of the few areas in which I recommend you buy new rather than used.

OWN TO RENT

Sandy Croslow of Vincennes, Indiana, wrote to us about the success she and her husband have enjoyed as live-in landlords. "This can be a wonderful way to buy a first home," she wrote. Because the Croslows are also CPAs, we called Sandy for details.

They moved to Vincennes in 1987, in debt "up to our ears" from a business failure. They researched the rental market and found there was a shortage of housing for college students. Then they "ran the numbers" (both realtors and CPAs can do this for clients), calculating all factors, including the mortgage payment, property taxes, rents, utilities, and depreciation.

Ultimately, they put $3,000 down on a $50,000, four-apartment Victorian home (housing is cheap in the Midwest). Rent from the other three apartments equaled $875 and their mortgage payment was just $500. This allowed them to save for their "dream home," a single-family dwelling on ½ acre where they moved last year. They still own the Victorian and operate their CPA firm from it.

Sandy says banks favor live-in landlords. They typically ask 10 percent down from live-in landlords versus 20 percent down from absentee landlords.

She says a key to success is carefully screening tenants. "In my experience, the only people who get into trouble doing this are those who are so desperate to rent that they'll take the first person who comes along."

CHECK THE CEREAL NUMBERS

Mary Ellen Wobbecke of Cleveland Heights, Ohio, sent me two curious articles, each addressing the rising cost of cold cereals.

The first made these points:

- Of the 150 cold cereals the reporter surveyed, the average retail price was about $4 a pound. (Compare that to the retail price of cereal's raw ingredients: Rice, oats, wheat flour, cornmeal, and *sugar* cost from 15¢ to 40¢ a pound.)
- It's estimated that 15¢ of material and 15¢ of labor go into a $3 box of cereal.
- A 1992 survey of advertisers showed that 67 percent of a cereal's price is spent on marketing.
- Despite the above, in 1994, cold-cereal retail sales in this country exceeded $8 billion, a 5.7 percent increase from 1993.

A bizarre reaction to spiraling cereal prices was detailed in the second article. Congressmen Sam Gejdenson of Connecticut and Charles Schumer of New York have asked Attorney General Janet Reno to launch an antitrust investigation of the biggest cold-cereal producers. Representative Schumer, who confesses he can gobble a whole box of cereal for dinner, told the Associated Press that high cereal prices make his "blood boil."

This struck me as strange. If name-brand cereal is too expensive, why should the government get involved? Why don't consumers *stop buying it*?

Speculating that the congressmen had overlooked this obvious solution, I called Scott Kovarovics, legislative assistant to Representative Gejdenson. He shot down my idea. Cold cereal, he essentially said, is a necessity.

"Look at modern lifestyles. People don't have time to make pancakes or waffles, bacon and eggs. It isn't something you can just give up, it's something more and more people have come to tremendously depend upon," he said.

He added that generics aren't the whole solution. "You have to have time to search high and low for the generics, squint at prices, make the calculations. People just don't have time to do that."

Kovarovics said they suspect name-brand companies of colluding to keep generics off the shelves. However, they know of just one case that might support this theory. His office's main concern seems to be simply that the cost of this "necessity" is too high.

My reaction:

- If the name-brands are colluding to keep generics off the shelves, it's worthwhile to investigate that.
- But it's silly to say people don't have time to comparison shop. Unit pricing is now the norm in most stores, thereby making squinting and calculating obsolete.
- And I don't believe cold cereal is a necessity for busy Americans. Even if they lack time on hectic weekdays, they can make and freeze muffins, pancakes, and waffles on weekends and microwave them later in the week. A huge batch of granola requires ten minutes of hands-on preparation.

In our house, we eat cold cereal less than once a week, and it's always either a $1-per-18-ounce box of store-brand, on-sale, stockpiled cornflakes, or homemade granola. And if I had to eliminate any breakfast that we generally have, cornflakes would be the first to go. Two hours later, I'm always hungry again.

FIRST-CLASS IDEA

Dear Amy,

When mailing in camera film in the provided envelopes, it states on the envelope that you need two stamps. But that doesn't mean you need two first-class stamps. You need one plus a 23¢ stamp. You save 9¢.

—Margie Walter
Munising, Michigan

(This applies to all first-class mail. Up to one ounce is 32¢. Each additional ounce or fraction of an ounce is 23¢. For example, postage on a 2½ ounce letter is 78¢. FZ)

TANK USED

Dear Amy,

During some recent plumbing problems with the toilet, the fixture itself actually broke. A new toilet would have cost a minimum of $75, but our local plumber sold us a used one for $30. It was in perfect condition, clean, and worked properly. The previous owners got rid of it simply because they wanted a fancy $300 toilet. The plumber went on to explain that plumbing shops often have these used toilets and that people simply need to ask.

—Jan Kingston
Beaverton, Oregon

GLOVE CONNECTION

Dear Amy,

I wear rubber gloves when I wash dishes. I'm right-handed and the right glove is usually the one that gets a hole first. Instead of throwing away both gloves, I save the left ones for my left-handed friend, who saves the right ones for me.

—Cathy Sylar
Kelseyville, California

SPOUTING WISDOM

Dear Amy,

You can make a wonderful lid with a pouring spout from any canning jar. Take an empty, round salt box and, using the lid from the canning jar as a guide, cut out a circle from the top of the salt box. Place this new lid onto the top of the canning jar, screw on the ring, and you have a pouring spout on your jar. I use mine for dried parsley, basil, and my own cinnamon-sugar mix.

—Ellie Pett
Elmhurst, Illinois

CHEAP DATES

Dear Amy,

Never buy a calendar. You can always get one free from a bank, just for the asking.

—Nancy Graham
Keokuk, Iowa

SHE THAWED IT THROUGH

Dear Amy,

There is a new product called Miracle Thaw that advertises you can greatly reduce the amount of time needed for thawing frozen foods without using the microwave. Then I read an article in the local newspaper that said all this item consisted of was a sheet of aluminum with a Teflon coating. I decided to try a test with my good, heavy, anodized aluminum pans. Much to my surprise, the ice cube in the pan melted in less than a minute at room temperature while the control ice cube just sat there. Now, I thaw things faster with my aluminum pan (I still use the microwave in an emergency) and saved myself the $19.95 plus shipping and handling.

—Jill Armstrong
Houston, Texas

(If you don't have an aluminum pan, any heavy steel or cast-iron pan will also speed thawing. These metal items act as heat exchangers, quickly equalizing temperatures between the cold items and the warm room. FZ)

RESCUING LOST SOLES

Dear Amy,

I found a pair of shoes in perfect condition in an unlikely spot: the local shoe-repair shop. The owner was selling shoes that had not been claimed in over a year. There was quite a large collection.

—Kathleen Layman
Whittier, California

TASTY TATERS

Dear Amy,

Here is a homemade recipe to replace those expensive "shake and bake" potato recipes that are becoming so popular:

1 cup flour
1 cup cracker crumbs
1 tablespoon salt
1½ teaspoons sugar
2 teaspoons Italian seasoning (combination of basil, oregano, and garlic powder)
1 tablespoon oil

Mix and store in refrigerator. Put a small amount in a plastic bag. Shake together with potatoes cut into ½-inch to 1-inch chunks. Put ¼ cup oil in baking sheet or cast-iron skillet. Bake coated potato pieces in skillet at 350 degrees for 30 minutes or until they brown.

—Terry Zimmer
Courtland, Virginia

CLEAN-SLATE RATE

Dear Amy,

In 1990 my son had an at-fault auto accident. For the next three years he had to pay surcharges on his policy. Last fall at renewal time, his insurance company tried to charge him again. He sent a check for $10 to the local motor vehicles department and received a copy of the last three years of his driving record. When it arrived, sure enough, he had a clean record and his insurance company immediately lowered the premium $300 a year.

—Mrs. William Laurent
Mountainside, New Jersey

CARD TRICK

Dear Amy,

If you want to make your own cards, don't buy card stock. I priced it at $13.00 a pack! The stationery store clerk suggested 8-inch-by-5-inch unlined index cards; a pack of 100 costs $1.85! They are made of the same card stock. Fold them in half, decorate any way you like, and you have wonderful, sturdy cards.

—Kimberly Mendoza
Rockledge, Florida

MUTUAL MOOCHING

A couple of years ago we solicited older readers of the newsletter for recollections of the Great Depression. Their tales of hardship and deprivation were memorable. Most moving were the stories of how neighbors came through for each other. Cooperation was often the key to their survival.

As I read, I couldn't help but reflect on how much times have changed. Today, suburban neighbors seldom cooperate and help each other. In fact, they often don't know each other. Generally, each house is a self-contained unit. On a street of 20 homes with 20 families, there are 20 weed-whackers, 20 gas barbecues, and 20 *Lion King* videos, though each of these is used only a few hours per year.

But cooperation can work as well in the 1990s as it did in the 1930s. Once, I asked a fellow who helped Vietnamese refugees get established in this country how they became so successful so quickly. After all, most arrived here with no money and couldn't even speak English. He said that, aside from their frugal diets, their key to success was cooperation. They shared virtually everything, even housing and cars, and pooled the money they saved to start businesses.

I suspect a major factor in our transition to a more solitary, uncooperative culture is the breakdown of communities. Our society has become more transient, and we don't invest in short-term relationships. And because every family has an entertainment center rivaling the technology of NASA, we don't leave our homes long enough to chat with our neighbors across

the fence. Mass production has made goods more affordable, and so while sharing is economically beneficial, it's not a necessity. And we are a less patient bunch of people; we want to be able to use that router immediately when the whim hits us, rather than waiting for our neighbor to return home so we can borrow his or get ours back from him.

We're all aware of this trend away from cooperation, and we all complain about it. But what should we *do* about it? The key is recognizing that when cooperation doesn't occur naturally, we have to *cultivate* it.

First, *offer* goods and services to others. Start by asking such things as, "I'm going to the bakery thrift shop, can I pick up something for you?" Whenever we moved into a new area, I would scope out my new neighbors in this way. Some were cool to these offers, whereas others immediately understood that this is how the game is played and accepted.

Second, if a new neighbor offers you a favor, accept it when feasible. When my offers were consistently and curtly turned down, I stopped offering. I became aware that if someone made me an offer I couldn't accept, I should at least say, "No, thank you, but let's stay in touch. Maybe I can do something for you sometime."

Once the first exchange occurs, the relationship can proceed to surprising levels of trust and benefit. But this can occur only if both parties abide by certain rules of engagement:

- Start by offering something small and "safe," such as surplus from your garden. Offering larger or more valuable goods and services in the beginning intimidates people; they don't want to feel deeply indebted to a stranger.
- Reciprocation is crucial. If you've accepted a favor or two, actively look for ways to return them. You might even say, "You've been so helpful. Let me know if I can do something for you."
- If you borrow something, return it in the same condition it was in when you received it—or better. Clean it, fill the tank, sharpen it, and so on. If damage occurs, always make good on it by replacing or repairing it.
- If you offer a service, do it well. Offer to do only those things that you're good at. The fact that you're doing it for free doesn't excuse lateness or sloppiness.
- If someone turns down several offers, stop offering. Some people are simply uncomfortable with accepting favors of any kind.
- Be patient when reciprocation doesn't occur; don't keep a scorecard. In many cases, you might never look for reciprocation, such

as when you do favors for an elderly person.

• But if someone accepts many of your offers and *never* reciprocates, even when it seems appropriate (you babysit her kids but she is always "unavailable" when you need a sitter), consider redirecting your favors to those who understand that cooperation is a two-way street.

Cooperation can take place at many levels, and these levels tend to correspond to the level of friendship.

The most basic and common level is to mutually *offer* small goods or services. This level occurs between new neighbors and acquaintances. It can be useful, but the financial impact tends to be small.

Mutual mooching starts when either party feels free to *ask*, politely, for small favors from the other, such as asking a friend to pick up milk for you when she goes to the store. You might precede your request by saying, "If it's inconvenient, please feel free to say no." Or you might wait until you've performed a large favor (helped paint their house) before you ask for a small favor (borrowing a tool). This level usually occurs between friends and family members. It's far more efficient, because it's hard to guess and make offers that fit a friend's needs.

At the next level, either party feels complete freedom to *ask* for even large favors. This generally occurs only between black-belt tightwad friends who have a very open understanding of the economic benefits they both enjoy from the relationship. When a friend asked if I had a spare bicycle for his seven-year-old, I was delighted. It meant that our friendship had progressed to where we could ask each other for a wide variety of useful goods and services.

At this level, the concept of shared ownership is introduced. For example, we pooled resources with two other families to buy staging for house painting.

The ultimate level is the one those Vietnamese immigrants enjoy—shared ownership of even large, expensive items such as houses. This is unfamiliar to many Americans, who have a long-standing tradition of independence and privacy. But I do know of two small families who purchased a home together and had a successful, harmonious life for many years. And, in any case, a sharing arrangement like this seems *very* sensible for the growing number of single-parent families. For instance, two (or more) single mothers could share a household. If they worked different shifts, they could also eliminate child-care costs.

Cooperation-and-friendship is a chicken-and-egg thing. Often cooperation comes out of friendships. But cooperation can also be a way to initiate and build friendships.

CLEAN AND LEAN

Ground beef is a tightwad mainstay. We seldom eat it in the form of hamburgers, but we frequently add it to casseroles and other dishes. It's convenient to cook, tastes good, and can be purchased on sale for as little as 89¢ a pound.

Unfortunately, the cheapest

ground beef tends to have the highest proportion of fat. So I was interested in a handout from the Minnesota Beef Council sent to me by Linda Erdahl of Proctor, Minnesota. It explains an easy method to greatly reduce ground beef's fat content:

The first step is browning the beef over medium heat. If the recipe calls for them, you can also add onion or garlic at this time. Then use a slotted spoon to place the beef "crumbles" on a large plate lined with three layers of paper towel. Blot the top of the beef with a paper towel. Let sit one minute, blotting with an additional paper towel. (Apparently due to fears of contamination, the Beef Council advises you to use paper towels that are white and nonrecycled. This seems overcautious to me, but use your own judgment.)

Then place the beef in a strainer or colander and pour about 1 quart of hot tap water over it, stirring while the water pours. Drain for five minutes and use in recipe.

The fat reduction accomplished by this method is impressive. A 3-ounce cooked portion of 70-percent-lean ground beef has 18 grams of fat when fried in the form of a patty. But the same portion, fried into crumbles and then blotted and rinsed, has just 6.1 grams of fat.

The Beef Council reports that less than 10 percent of the meat's protein, iron, vitamin B_{12}, and zinc are lost in this process.

Remember that it doesn't take much ground beef to make a satisfying addition to a casserole. We find that one pound of uncooked ground beef—which cooks down to considerably less than a pound—is about the right amount for a family of eight.

Since you can never have too many recipes that use browned and crumbled ground beef, I thought I would share a Rice-A-Roni-style concoction of Jim's that our family enjoys.

1 pound ground beef
1 medium onion, chopped
1 cup rice
8 ounces spaghetti, broken into 1-inch pieces
4 tablespoons margarine*
4 cups broth, or water and bouillon
salt and pepper

Brown beef and onion in a large skillet. Drain (and rinse if desired). Brown rice and spaghetti in margarine. Add in beef, onion, rice, and broth. Cover and simmer for 20 minutes, or until rice and spaghetti are fully cooked. Season with salt and pepper.

*You can use no-stick spray and reduce the margarine, or substitute olive oil.

DISCOUNTS FROM DIXIE?

About 60 percent of the furniture made in the United States is made in North Carolina. Because of this, hundreds of outlet stores cluster around Hickory, North Carolina. Many people travel long distances to shop there and there are even packaged shopping tours. The outlets also take phone orders and ship to customers nationwide. The average saving, it's claimed, is about 50 percent.

You've probably heard of this before. It's been touted in many major-city newspaper articles, in save-money books, and on *Oprah* when Kate Gladchun, author of *The Fine Furniture and Furnishings Discount Shopping Guide,* appeared as a guest.

I had never pursued this because new furniture holds little interest for me. Secondhand furniture (including some antiques) usually costs less and holds it value better than even wholesale-priced new furniture.

But sometimes new furniture is the best option, such as when I decided to replace our creaky hodgepodge of dining room chairs. I've never found eight secondhand matching chairs I've liked. I even called a restaurant supplier and learned that sturdy commercial chairs, even used, cost $100 each. And antique chairs wouldn't survive six kids.

So in July of 1995, when I visited relatives in North Carolina, I tested the strategy as I looked for chairs. For many reasons, I narrowed my search to casual-looking "thumb-back" chairs with a woven seat.

To compare prices, you should first shop locally and collect manufacturers' names and model numbers. Then you need to find North Carolina outlets (manufacturers don't sell directly to individuals) that carry those items. To find the outlets, you can order Gladchun's book, or call the Chamber of Commerce in Hickory. I got more accurate and complete information by calling the manufacturers directly. I got their numbers through directory assistance.

Before leaving, I did phone research and shopped extensively in Maine. During my trip, I visited the Hickory Furniture Mart, a 12-acre complex of outlets. I also went to the Mart's clearance center and a dozen other stores in Hickory and surrounding cities.

My conclusion: The North Carolina furniture-buying strategy isn't all it's cracked up to be.

Why? First, this strategy may pose an ethical dilemma. Many people might feel it's unfair to view merchandise and collect buying information from local merchants. After all, the merchants aren't reimbursed for providing essential elements of long-distance shopping. In an interview, Gladchun told me that if people are uncomfortable doing this, outlets will send customers photocopies of catalog pages. But few people would feel confident buying furniture based only on viewing photocopies. Although you can return shipped furniture, you're out the shipping fee and must also pay up to a 30 percent "restocking" fee.

Further, most of the North Carolina outlets carry only high-priced name-brand furniture: Lexington, Drexel-Heritage, Henredon, and so on. So even the discount prices may still be too high for average pocketbooks. Even the clearance

center's prices seemed steep; it sold no chairs for under $100.

In addition, when shopping for under-$100 chairs, I found that *no* price tags contained model numbers, and few even listed the maker's name. Store owners in North Carolina and Maine were evasive when I asked for this information. Two gave me false information.

I finally acquired manufacturer names and numbers for two different thumb-back chairs, called many stores for prices, and found that the lowest prices from North Carolina weren't impressive. A Maine store's sale price for an unfinished thumb-back was $59, versus the North Carolina shipped price of $64. A Maine Pier One Imports store would order the other, finished thumb-back for $66, versus the North Carolina shipped price of $64. Interestingly, Pier One Imports told me that if they stocked this chair, the retail price would be $89. They can offer better deals on ordered furniture, while prices on stocked furniture must reflect in-store overhead. I realized then that while in this latter case I would save $16 on eight chairs ordered from North Carolina (not factoring in my phone bill), this was only because a North Carolina store was willing to make a better deal. Each store has identical chair costs and shipping costs. In theory, a Maine store should be able to give me the same deal.

thumb-back Chair

As we needed to take our trailer anyway, I hoped to buy in North Carolina to save the shipping costs. But I could find no North Carolina stores that stocked the chairs that I wanted—all had to be ordered and shipped to me. I could have brought the chairs home myself only if I had given the stores several weeks' notice.

The few under-$100 stocked chairs I could find in the North Carolina outlets cost the same or more than I could have paid at home. For example, a made-in-Thailand white-and-clear-finish Windsor chair sold for $60 in North Carolina. This same iffy-quality chair sells in discount department stores nationwide for as little as $29.

Although I didn't comparison-shop larger, more expensive types of furniture, the *Columbus* (Ohio) *Dispatch* did and found similar patterns; local sale-priced furniture often cost less than shipped North Carolina furniture.

On a separate note, shipping charges varied depending on stores' policies. Chairs, which are compact and lightweight, cost about $5 to ship to Maine through UPS. Some stores ship only through trucking services and this can cost $15 per chair.

Though I wasn't impressed, I can't say this strategy never works for anyone. If you like and can afford new, expensive furniture, and what you want never goes on sale, you might find North Carolina shopping worthwhile.

Gladchun's book can be ordered by sending $19.95 to Resources, Inc., P.O. Box 973, Bloomfield Hills, MI 48303-3440.

DISCOUNTS FROM DIXIE? UPDATE

A few months after the previous article ran in the newsletter, we took delivery of ten chairs made by a North Carolina firm, and we are delighted with the deal we made.

Here's how we did it. After we decided on the brand we wanted, my staffer Pam said she would ask her husband, who owns a building-supply store, if he could order the chairs we wanted directly from the North Carolina manufacturer. Her husband simply called and placed an order. The shipped price to him was $50 per chair. He resold them to us for $55 each. Ordered through Maine's Pier One store, they would have cost us $66 each. The normal retail price is $89.

This seems like a good place to plug a good company. My chairs are the Homestead model made by Builtright Chair Company, P.O. Drawer 1609, Statesville, NC 28687, (704) 873-6541. This company makes casual hardwood dining room chairs (Builtright calls them "kitchen chairs"), rockers, and barstools.

Based on my extensive search, I believe these may be the best hardwood chairs available for the money. Builtright chairs have a unique, tension-fit frame construction that requires no glues, pins, or nails and virtually never loosens up. I have Builtright chairs that have seen daily use for 15 years and are still perfectly solid. The chair I bought has a natural sea-grass seat that resists stains and can be easily cleaned.

Another unique feature is that the seat of each chair is a separate screw-on unit. These are well made and far superior to those I've seen by other companies. Builtright sells replacement seats for about $10. The company has been around for 55 years, so it will probably still be in business when you need to replace your old seats.

Builtright also sells much cheaper chairs than the ones I bought. Their slat-seat "Carolina" chair sells for $35 retail, and they say—quite sincerely, I believe—that it is the best chair for the money sold anywhere in the world.

If you're in the market for chairs, write Builtright for the name of the store nearest you that stocks their chairs. If there's no such retailer nearby, you can engineer a deal through a retailer (one that could conceivably sell furniture, such as a furniture, hardware, or department store) just as we did. Builtright will mail you a flyer that illustrates their line of chairs.

A REASONABLE REGISTRY

For a tightwad, it's frustrating to be asked to buy wedding gifts through a registry at an overpriced department store. So I was pleased to receive a letter from Angela Henson of Southgate, Kentucky, about a refreshingly practical solution.

She says she didn't want to subject her wedding's guests to the expense of a traditional registry, but people kept asking her mother what she wanted.

"So my mother finally had me make a list of everything I could think of that I needed," Angela writes. "Because my household items included one set of old dishrags and a Papa Smurf glass, I

deduced that I needed everything. I wrote down everything from buckets and brooms to cookware to towels. The only thing I requested in a specific pattern was Corelle dishes in Morning Blue.

Angela says that whenever a guest asked what to buy, her mother simply pulled out the list. The person would look it over and decide what he or she wanted to buy, and her mother would check off the item.

"People kept telling her how sensible I was, and how wonderful it was to be able to

pick an item and shop for it wherever they chose instead of being forced into shopping for expensive items at expensive stores.

"The list was extremely successful. I got everything I needed, and then some. The most wonderful thing about this is after seven and a half years of marriage and two beautiful daughters, I still use all of these wedding gifts daily. I haven't yet had a need for china, and can't really see a need for it in the near future!"

SUITE DEALS

There are several ways to save on hotel-room rates. You can sometimes negotiate a good deal directly with the hotel. Or you can have your travel agent dig up a hotel that's having a special.

But one of the newer and more interesting ways to save is to book your room through a hotel discounter. Valerie Smith of Chicago, Illinois, sent me a *Chicago Tribune* article about these organizations, which have expanded dramatically in the last few years. They buy hotel rooms in bulk, cheap, and pass the savings on to customers. The *Tribune*'s independent survey found room rates averaged 30 percent below the regular rate.

Discounters include:

RMC Travel Centre; books rooms for hotels in over 100 American cities: (800) 782-2674.

Quikbook; serves 21 cities: (800) 789-9887.

Hotel Reservations Network; serves 20 cities: (800) 964-6835.

Accommodations Express; serves ten cities: (800) 444-7666.

Central Reservation Service; serves Miami, New York, Orlando, San Francisco: (800) 950-0232.

We received information from Quikbook and RMC Travel Centre that listed the regular rates and their discount rates for various hotels. To learn if the discounts were real, we called 15 hotels and asked them for their room rates. We found that when calling expensive hotels, the discounts were significant. But when we called economy hotels, we were told their regular rates were much less than the discounter stated; their regular rate was about the same as the discounter's rate.

Wendy Galfund, marketing director for Quikbook, said that happens "occasionally" because discounters can't keep up with all of the low-rate specials offered by moderately priced hotels.

I called a local travel agent to discuss hotel discounters with her. She said they seem legitimate and she had actually dealt with some. But she added that to be on the safe side, she would work only with those discounters that allow you to pay the hotel directly. Quikbook, which claims to be one of the largest discounters, is among the services that operate this way. Other services require you to pay the discounter in advance.

One often-asked question is: Will I be given a room in the basement? The discounters with whom we spoke said the rooms they book are as good as the ones the hotel books directly with its customers. "The hotels know that if they give our customers bad rooms, we can drop our affiliation with them," said Galfund. She said that since discounters fill rooms that would otherwise go empty, hotels don't dare threaten their relationship with discounters.

Hotel discounters may be like coupons. The one that gives you the biggest "discount" may not be the one that gives you the lowest price, and other hotels that don't work with discounters may offer better deals. So if you consider using a discounter, verify the regular room rate with the hotel and compare the price offered with that of other hotels in the area.

THIS ARTICLE WILL KEEP YOU IN STITCHES

Twenty years ago, my grandmother gave me the sewing notions that had belonged to my late great-aunt. Since then I have acquired a second thread inheritance. Because my sewing is limited to crafts and clothing repair, these spools have been sufficient all my adult life.

But I've been trapped in a time warp. The wooden spools have stamped-on prices of 15¢ to 50¢. You can imagine my sticker shock when I found that a spool now costs $2.50. Yet I've seen bins of thread selling for prices that harked back to my old spools' stickers.

So I decided to unravel the thread mystery. I interviewed David Coffin, associate editor of *Threads* magazine, and Lois Hathaway, a local quilter.

Thread varies tremendously in price depending on quality. Department-store 2/$1 spools are usually poor-quality 100 percent polyester and generally should be avoided. This thread can literally melt when ironed.

Some people economize by using large cones of "serger" thread for regular sewing. At $1.25 for 3,000 yards, this seems like an amazing deal compared to those 400-yard/$2.50 spools. But serger thread is much thinner than regular thread, as a serger uses several strands at a time, so it probably won't hold up to any real stress.

There are different types of quality thread. Silk and 100-percent cotton are the best but cost the most. Cotton-covered polyester and 100-percent polyester cost less but can serve well if you know what to look for. Although there's a

lot to be said about the type of thread needed for certain applications, quality mostly boils down to a question of smoothness. Even to the naked eye, cheap thread is fuzzy and irregular and will cause poor stitches. Matching the thread to the needle size is also important. Consequently, if your machine seems to be sewing poorly, try a different thread before you take it into the shop.

Instead of buying poor-quality thread, economize in other ways:

- Stock up during sales. Ask to be put on your fabric shop's mailing list so you'll be notified of upcoming sales. With luck, you'll get thread at half price, or about .3¢ per yard.
- Look for thread at yard sales. Make sure the quality and thickness suit your needs.
- Use up low-quality thread in less-critical applications, such as hand-stitching a hem.
- Revive old thread. Cotton can dry out with age, become brittle, and break easily. *Threads* contends it can be remoisturized by placing it in your refrigerator's vegetable bin.
- Remember that exact color-matching is critical only for top-stitching. Otherwise, you can use a thread with the same color value (lightness or darkness); a neutral gray blends with many colors.
- Buy large cones of thread in a few basic colors. If you can't find them locally, they can be mail-ordered from Home-Sew, P.O. Box 4099, Bethlehem, PA 18018, (610) 867-3833 (a free catalog is available on request). A 6,000-yard spool of Coats & Clark cotton-covered polyester thread costs $13.35, or a little more than .2¢ per yard. In other words, compared to $2.50/400-yard spools, 400 yards of this thread costs 90¢.

Most people think large cones require a $10 adapter or stand to feed the thread to the machine. Smaller-sized cones can be simply placed in a wide-mouthed canning jar.

Jacqueline Cannizzo of Shaker Heights, Ohio, offered a simple solution for larger cones. Tape a plastic paint stirrer to a jar or can large enough to accommodate the cone. Place the cone inside and pull the thread through the top hole in the stirrer. Adjust the can's position to maintain proper tension on the thread.

A VIN-WIN SITUATION

Dear Amy,

My husband etched the car windows with the vehicle identification number (as explained on page 166), and we've told a number of people about it. We got a substantial discount on our car insurance for making the effort. Be prepared to plead your case when you call your insurance company headquarters. Don't give up at the first

"I never heard about this." Persist. Ask for the supervisor, then the supervisor's supervisor. Get their 800 number right away and call back on that number to save toll costs.

—Lou N. Overman
Manteo, North Carolina

COMBO COOLER

Dear Amy,

Instead of buying Snapple (or similar) drinks, I mix homemade iced tea with juice. Cheaper, delicious, and not so sweet.

—Dianne Meier
Des Moines, Washington

WASH AND WALK

Dear Amy,

I wash yard-sale shoes, even leather ones, in the washing machine, then let them air-dry, stuffed with newspapers. This has not ruined a pair of shoes for me yet, though I couldn't guarantee it couldn't happen.

—Katie Jackman
Ames, Iowa

CATS ON CAMPUS

Dear Amy,

If you live near a college of veterinary medicine, or a community college that teaches veterinary technicians, they may do routine vaccinations, dentistry, neutering, and spaying at very reasonable cost. The work is always done by a licensed veterinarian. If your animal is ill or needs surgery, try to have it referred there.

— Julie Pinochet
Lexington, Virginia

GET GRATIS GROUPER

Dear Amy,

We took a deep-sea cruise and there were 35–40 people from all over the States on the boat. We all could fish. After docking, many people left the boat with the main large ice chest filled with the day's catch. We were the last off the boat and were offered numerous wonderful fresh fish to take home. The captain said many customers leave without their fish because they are vacationing and can't bring their catch along with them. It was his practice to give away the unwanted fish to whomever wanted them. If you live near a harbor where boats run charters, it might be worth asking about.

—Deborah Chalk
Chimney Rock, North Carolina

BUDGET-TRIMMING IDEA

Dear Amy,

Our barber is a talented lady, and one day I asked her if she cut women's hair, too. She said, "Of course!" I reasoned that if a barber can do a good job with thinning, short men's hair, then he or she should be able to do equally well with trimming thick, long hair like mine. I was right. I've had all sorts of good cuts from her now at $8 each. The only thing she can't do are treatments that require a sink for washing hair, so on haircut day I wash my hair just before leaving the house and arrive at the shop still dripping. She trims it and can even blow-dry it.

—Elizabeth Case
Belfair, Washington

MARINADE AID

Dear Amy,

For an economical, tasty stew, buy a cheap grade of beef roast, cut it into small pieces, marinate these in pickle juice for three to four days in fridge, then simmer them with veggies until cooked. Very tasty, and a lot cheaper than buying "stew beef."

— Jerry Sass
North Anson, Maine

REVIVE YOUR SPIRITS

Dear Amy,

Turpentine and mineral-spirit thinners/cleaners can be reused if they are kept in a tightly closed jar and the particles are allowed to settle to the bottom. You can then pour off the top of the jar's contents through a cheesecloth into a clean jar to reuse the product.

—Maxel and Stacey Newberry
Ithaca, Michigan

SPRITZ AND SAVE

Dear Amy,

We found a way to make our charcoal last longer. After grilling, we spray the coals with water and leave them in the grill. By the next time of use, they have dried and are ready to use again. (Add more if needed.)

—Patti Layman
Cherry Valley, California

THE YOUNG AND THE DEBTLESS

"I am praying that you get a big response to your 'Generation X Supersaver' inquiry, because if everyone is like the people I am surrounded by, I feel we will be in dire straits in the next century," wrote Nancy Oberdorfer of Brooklyn, New York.

"Thank you for requesting letters from your twentysomething readers. I've often wondered if we are the only ones you have!" contributed Kim Hainsworth of Lomita, California.

I have good news for both of you: We received 103 responses to our newsletter request for letters from tightwads who are in their 20s. It was extremely heartening to read so many upbeat stories of success and hope from young sin-

gles and couples. While rampant consumerism and maxed-out credit cards have hit this generation harder than any other, clearly there are many brave souls who have escaped and are doing well.

It's important to focus on people in this generation because they are the least likely to take frugality seriously, yet, ironically, they receive the greatest benefit if they practice it. Even if you are not of this generation, chances are you know someone who is, and can pass this article along to him.

I know the advantage of early-adulthood frugality from personal experience. The fact that Jim and I saved $49,000 in seven years on our annual income of under $30,000 a year is widely known. But what's not so well known is that we squirreled away $20,000 of that during the first 18 months we were married. This "pre-kid" period in marriage is often squandered, but it's actually a golden opportunity because:

• A couple, or single person, is free to live in a small, cheap, "kid-unfriendly" apartment.

• With no child-care concerns, both husband and wife have maximum freedom to work and earn.

• The earlier that money is saved and invested—whether in a home, a chest freezer, a mutual fund, or any other investment—the greater the return. Once you get ahead, life becomes cheaper, and you tend to continually get even farther ahead. You earn interest instead of paying interest, and the spread between the two increases daily.

Most of the young people who wrote to me had grasped and exploited these concepts, and told of impressive financial accomplishments:

• On an income of $18,000 a year, Shenan Ott of Stafford, Virginia, and her husband saved $5,800 a year, and recently purchased a home.

• Though she has never earned over $15,000 a year, Melissa Hitsman of Orlando, Florida, had saved $32,000 by the time she reached age 30.

• John Wood of Aurora, Illinois, saved $20,000 in three years while working as a teenager at a grocery store.

• At 28 years old, on a $35,000 annual income, a North Carolina couple (who requested anonymity) have paid off their mortgage on an owner-built house appraised at $75,000. They own two cars and have a small amount in savings.

Given these fairly obvious advantages, why is Gen-X frugality uncommon? Our respondents offered their theories:

"We were raised in the first wave of the MTV culture. The pressures of the heavily marketed view of life are manifested everywhere," wrote a newsletter reader from Eugene, Oregon.

"We are a generation that, while young, was blared at, sold to, and assaulted with images of plenty."

"Everyone wants to live as they did before they left their parents' houses: cable TV, fancy foods, new cars, and many fancy electric devices," contributed Jennifer Palmer of St. Paul, Minnesota. "They don't understand/remember how their parents lived when they first began without those niceties."

Aside from these observations, note that in previous generations couples didn't marry until they "could afford to," i.e., until the man earned enough money to support a family on his income alone. With the advent of the woman in the workforce and easy credit, today's dual-income couples can create a false affluence. They live it up for a few years before having children, believing they can easily sustain the debt and workload after they have children. When the children come and a parent wants to stay home with them, they feel "trapped" and "betrayed" by society, though they are actually victims of their own miscalculation.

But now for the good news. Clearly, the virtue of thrift has been successfully communicated to at least a few of these young people. I was interested in their comments about *why* they were different from their peers. Day after day, the most common criticism I get is that "once they get out of the house, your kids will become major spendthrifts to compensate for their frugal childhoods." These respondents prove otherwise. They are frugal, they say, because they were raised that way.

"I was home-schooled from the age of 11 and did not attend junior high or high school, and so missed out on a lot of the 'commercialism imprinting' that I think happens to teenagers in school." (Name withheld by request, Orlando, Florida)

"I was raised by my grandparents and learned many of my thrifty traits from them." (Kim Hainsworth, Rancho Palos Verdes, California)

"Having grown up under the influence of the Masters of Frugality (Depression-era family members), I was eager to practice all I had learned when I married in 1985. The best gift my parents and grandparents ever gave me was advice: 'Waste not, want not'; 'A penny saved is a penny earned'; 'Well, when I was growing up. . . .' " (Melissa Yell, Hesperia, Michigan)

"My parents raised me to be frugal. I never knew any different." (Deborah Burton, Crown City, Ohio)

What specific strategies did the Gen-Xers use to achieve their enviable positions? They sent along hundreds of details about their lifestyles and, actually, there was very little that was unique about the savings strategies they listed. It proved a point I've made all along: There are very few strategies that are unique to seniors, singles, or any other subgroup of society. The basics of frugality—yard-saling, bulk buying, scratch cooking, negotiating, doing it yourself, writing down expenses, and so on—work for any group.

Finally, if you're a Gen-X tight-

wad but your financial accomplishments are less impressive than those I listed earlier in this article, don't despair. Those were some of the most amazing we found in over a hundred letters. As I read most of the letters, it occurred to me that if a reader's accomplishments seemed unremarkable, that's perfectly normal. As people who are just beginning adulthood, the results of frugality are not as evident at this stage as they will be in 10 to 15 years. Rest assured that by the time a Gen-X tightwad hits 40, the net-worth gap separating him or her from other 40-year-olds who have similar incomes will be unmistakable—and gratifying.

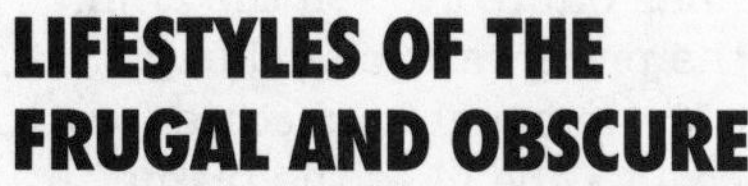

LIFESTYLES OF THE FRUGAL AND OBSCURE

During my second book tour I had the good fortune to stay with newsletter readers Marie and Mike Davies of St. Louis, Missouri, who own and operate a bed-and-breakfast called Lehmann House. It proved to be the most pleasant aspect of an otherwise grinding month for me.

The Davieses are thirtysomething parents of four young children. Both chemists, Marie left her job when she realized that after subtracting job-related expenses she netted $500 a month. She then investigated the bed-and-breakfast industry as a home-based business option.

Shortly thereafter, they purchased their 20-room, 7,500-square-foot brick Romanesque Revival fixer-upper/mansion on a historic city square. With their remaining limited funds, they renovated the foyer, library, and dining and living rooms enough to be presentable and completely renovated a few rooms to let out. The revenue from these rooms is being used to renovate more rooms.

As an old-house enthusiast, I was fascinated to stay in this house-in-transition and note how they were solving problems similar to ones I face in my home.

Although I could share many aspects of the Davieses' lives, of particular interest were the strategies they're using to furnish this vast home in the elegant style that is expected of bed-and-breakfasts. They have succeeded by using many strategies I've written about before, and a few that were new to me.

- Estate auctions. They've purchased furniture such as four oak dining room chairs for $100 and a burled-ash chest of drawers for $180. Once, when Mike didn't like the pair of

Eastlake chairs Marie bought for $25 each, they resold them for $100 each.

• Flea markets. Although they find that many items are over-priced, flea markets have been good sources of old photographs and other framable items for $1 each or less. They also buy old frames, and will pay $2 to $5 for framed art. Marie picks up china serving pieces for the dining room for as little as 50¢.

• Yard sales. These are also good sources of pictures, frames, and serving pieces. Marie buys coffee makers, sometimes just for the glass carafes, and juice pitchers for $1 to $3 (juice and coffee are available on small tables outside guest rooms). She buys old books for their library. When selling, Marie likes group yard sales, as she finds other participants will let her keep what they don't sell.

• Dumpster diving. Marie scouts nearby Dumpsters regularly, taking particular note of when people move. She found a mirror, originally attached to a dresser, which fit onto their sideboard. Mike was able to reassemble a maple rocker that he found in a pile of pieces. They've also found an antique steamer trunk, living room side chairs in need of reupholstering, pieces of marble for vanity tops, claw-foot tubs, lumber, and paint.

• Building suppliers. This source has provided useful temporary fixes. During my stay I peeked under a floor-length lacy tablecloth in my room and was amused to find not an elegant table but rather a table made from a fiberboard circle and dowels.

• Bartering. Marie has traded her sewing skills for an iron bed and a ceremonial kimono (which hangs on a guest-room wall). They traded an over-the-mantel mirror they couldn't use for a serpentine-front dresser and a hall runner, and they traded surplus building materials for a marble-topped foyer table.

• Helping people move. Marie has found that when she helps people move, she is conveniently poised to receive unwanted excess, which has included an antique upholstered side chair, a 6-foot pantry shelf, an antique treadle-table sewing machine, and general household items.

• Offering to buy. Marie often tells friends she would be willing to buy an item if the friend should ever think of parting with it. In some cases the owner, months later, has offered to sell the item, and the price was quite cheap. Once, Marie bought a picture for $5 because she liked the frame. Sometime later, a knowledgeable visitor mentioned that this rare, long, narrow picture was worth $150.

• Storing people's stuff. Marie stores large items for people if they let her use the items. Since the storage is free, the owners understand that any minor dings the item might suffer are a fair tradeoff. Marie is storing/using a baby grand piano, a sofa, an oak hall tree worth $1,000, a mahogany chest of drawers, a chandelier, and a refrigerator.

• Work for discounts. Marie works part-time for a renovator supplier. Aside from the wage, she gets an employee discount. This has enabled her to buy reproduction supplies, such as plumbing fixtures, for 10 percent over what her employer pays.

• Negotiate for discounts. Marie

told her paint store's owner that she was renovating a 20-room house and boldly asked for a contractor's discount. He agreed.

• Doing it themselves. Marie loves to sew and has made many accessories, including shower curtains, dust ruffles, Austrian shades, and curtains. People give her material, but she also buys yard-sale sheets and lace and discount fabric. Mike is generally handy and has done some light construction. Marie refinishes both woodwork and furniture. Mike bought a beveled-mat cutter, which enables him to do professional-looking framing when he puts together art and old frames.

As my weekend ended, I concluded that I'd had the rare experience of "meeting my match" in Zen-level, black-belt frugality, and had picked up a trick or two I plan to use in my home.

THE ANSWER FOR A GRIDDLE

When we visited my sister a few summers ago, Laurie made pancakes for breakfast. Upon observing the bottleneck created by making pancakes in a single pan for 13 people, Laurie commented that she did have a huge black-iron griddle, but she gave up on it because food always stuck to its surface. Like many people, she was unaware that her problem could easily be remedied by properly seasoning the pan.

Black-iron cookware (pans, popover pans, Dutch ovens, griddles, and so on) are excellent cooking utensils. If seasoned and well maintained, the cooking surface is almost nonstick, and so requires just a small amount of fat to prevent foods from sticking. But black iron must be treated differently from other types of cookware.

A new iron pan, which is gray, must be seasoned before use and will eventually darken to black. Used iron pans that have been poorly maintained, even rusty ones, can be revived through the same process.

If you're reviving an old pan you may want to remove excess crud and scaliness. It's normal for black iron to eventually develop a bumpy texture or buildup on the outside of the pan. Generally this should be left alone. However, an antique-dealer friend who specializes in black iron removes extreme buildup for aesthetic reasons. She places the pan in her oven at the self-cleaning temperature for two and a half hours. The heat makes the buildup flake off.

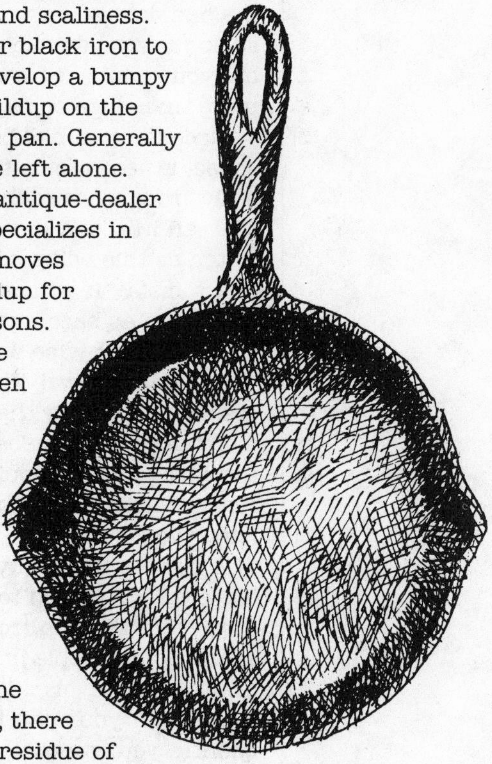

If you do the previous step, there will be a fine residue of rust on the pan. Similarly, a neglected pan may have rust. Remove this with fine steel wool and hot water. If you use soap, use mild hand soap, not strong dishwashing detergent. Rinse well.

From this point, new and in-need-of-reviving pans are seasoned in the same way. Coat the inside of the pan with vegetable oil or short-

ening and place in a 250-degree oven for 30 minutes. Remove the pan from the oven, wipe off the excess oil, and return it to the oven for another 30 minutes. Then turn the oven off and leave the pan in the oven overnight. You may need to repeat this step if seasoning a new pan.

This seasoning process draws the oil into the iron. As you cook, the pan will continue to absorb oil from the food, thereby replacing oil lost through use and washing. If the pan does seem to lose its nonstick quality, you can reseason it, but you shouldn't need to do this more than once or twice a year.

Once the pan has been seasoned, it needs to be treated differently from other cookware. Never soak an iron pan in hot, soapy water, as this will soak the oil out of the metal. If you cook a greasy food, such as bacon, you might be able to simply wipe out the pan with a paper towel. The remaining residue is good for the pan. Any food that sticks can be lightly scrubbed out. But avoid heavy scrubbing, which will remove oil from the surface.

If the humidity in your home is high, you may need to take steps to prevent the pan from rusting again. Some people immediately towel-dry their black iron after washing. If your pan is used infrequently, you can coat it lightly with oil before storing it.

When you're scouting black iron through secondhand sources, make it a habit to look for the maker's name. "Griswold" is *the* name in antique black iron. It's highly collectible; a piece of Griswold iron may have resale value beyond its yard-sale price.

SHOULD YOU GIVE IT A DRY?

Tracy Andrews of East Douglas, Massachusetts, wrote that while she enjoys her food dehydrator, she wonders about its economy. Her question: If you factor in the cost of purchasing fruit to dry, and the cost of buying and running the dehydrator, is it a worthwhile product?

I asked four dehydrator owners for their experiences and opinions, did a little reading, and interviewed Scott Reinhard, a spokesman for American Harvest, a leading maker of dehydrators.

Electric food dehydrators dry fruit, vegetables, meats, herbs, and flowers. The versions produced by American Harvest cost from about $29 for the 300-watt Snackmaster to $169 for the 1,000-watt Gardenmaster. They usually come with a couple of trays; additional trays cost extra.

Making "specialty foods" such as dried fruit, fruit leather, and beef jerky are among the most common uses, but these aren't generally money-savers. If you buy fresh bananas to make dried banana chips (to convert a cheap-to-buy food into an expensive-to-buy food) you're simply spending additional money on electricity to get the same food value. Avid backpackers are the only people who might save money doing this, as they have an ongoing need for lightweight fruits. But generally, unless you have a free or cheap fruit source (such as apple-orchard "drops"), this type of drying is purely recreational.

A more interesting question from the tightwad perspective is whether dehydrating homegrown

vegetables is a valid method of food preservation compared to canning or freezing.

Dehydrating does have advantages. Dried food is more compact. Eleven quarts of tomatoes, when dried, fit in the same space as a number 10 can. The storage of dried foods is simple: in paper bags in dry climates, in airtight glass jars in humid climates. Some sources contend that dried foods retain more vitamins than canned or frozen foods.

But disadvantages include:

• Dried vegetables have limited uses. Once reconstituted, they are generally suitable only for soup. To reconstitute some dried vegetables, such as green beans, you must pressure-cook them, or simmer them for up to four hours (thereby offsetting any nutritional gain from drying). Only a few vegetables, such as dried tomatoes, can be used in their dried form. Some people blenderize dried tomatoes into a powder and add this to soups. One how-to-dry book pointed out that some vegetables, such as carrots and onions, are so cheap to buy year-round that drying them may not be economical.

• The capital investment can be high, particularly for large-scale preservation. The Gardenmaster comes with four trays, and additional trays cost $12.50 each or $325.00 for 26 more trays. So this investment can cost up to $494.00. That's about the same as a new chest freezer, but freezers preserve a wider range of vegetables, as well as bulk-purchased meats, bread, and so on. The cost of canning equipment can be quite small. Our two pressure canners and hundreds of jars, all secondhand, cost under $50.00.

• The operating expense can be high. The Gardenmaster dehydrator requires ten hours to dry 30 trays of ⅜-inch-thick tomato slices. So, at 8¢ per kilowatt-hour, the energy would cost 80¢. I sliced up ten varying-sized garden tomatoes and measured their required drying area by laying them on a 1-square-foot area—the same size as a Gardenmaster tray. Then I crushed these and filled up quart canning jars. My ten tomatoes would fill three trays or two quart jars. So, you can can five tomatoes in a quart jar for 10¢ (for the lid and a little electricity). It also costs 10¢ to keep that five-tomato quart frozen. You can dry 100 tomatoes for 80¢ or five tomatoes for about 4¢. On the surface, then, the cost of drying seems lower. But Reinhard says the drying time is the same for 1 or 30 trays. So if you're drying 40 tomatoes (12 trays) or less at a time, it costs more than freezing and canning.

That's important, because few gardeners would have over 40 ripened tomatoes at once. Those who do might choose to use most of them to make ready-to-eat foods like spaghetti sauce, rather than rehydrating tomatoes to make sauce at later times.

A reader from Farmersburg, Indiana, has seen commercials for electric dehydrators and wonders if there are more economical methods. Solar drying is an ancient form of food preservation, predating electrical dehydrators by thousands of years. It was common until the invention of home canning and is still common in many parts of the world.

Herbs can be bundled and hung for air-drying. Some foods can be strung on thread for drying. Otherwise, food needs only to be laid out on a clean, smooth surface such as a cookie sheet or butcher paper. For better air circulation, you can make wood-framed racks of cheesecloth, nylon, or stainless-steel mesh (do not use Fiberglas, copper, galvanized steel, or aluminum). Put cheesecloth over foods that might attract bugs.

Library books and magazines such as *Mother Earth News* and *Organic Gardening* can provide plans for more complex solar-drying structures, such as boxes with many removable racks.

But solar drying has disadvantages. Sunlight destroys some vitamins. It works best in warm, dry climates because the drying might require several hot days.

Laura Vlaming of Gurnee, Illinois, asked for a recipe to make fruit leathers (or roll-ups). My mother makes them from her own blueberries. She simply purees fresh berries, puts the puree on a special fruit-leather tray, and dries it in her electric dehydrator. This makes excellent, hassle-free fruit leather. She stores the leather, rolled up, in plastic wrap.

You can also make fruit leather in the sun or in your oven. Tape plastic wrap onto a cookie sheet and spread the puree on it ⅛ inch thick. To sun dry, two or three hot dry days are required. (Bring the tray in at night.) When the leather is tacky, place it in a 120-degree oven for an hour, then cool and store. You can also dry fruit leather in your oven at 150 degrees for 6 to 12 hours, though a lot of electricity is needed.

In summary, an electrical food dehydrator may be fun to use, but it probably has too few cost-effective applications to justify a large initial investment. Solar drying might be a better option if you want just a few dried foods. If I found a dirt-cheap dehydrator at a yard sale, I might buy it. But even then I would use it only for free or cheap fruits and a few tomatoes.

DON'T MAKE A TRIPLE-PAY

The rent-to-own business has expanded dramatically in the last decade. It's grown from 2,000 to almost 7,000 stores nationwide.

But rent-to-own has another, more dubious distinction. According to a fascinating article in *Business and Society Review*, it's often a huge rip-off.

These stores rent TVs, stereos, furniture, appliances, and other items. If you pay the rent long enough, you get to keep the item. Sounds good. But the article states that rent-to-own customers routinely pay from two to four times as much as they would if they paid cash outright. As an example, it cites a 20-inch Zenith TV offered at a Roanoke, Virginia, rent-to-own store at $14.99 a week for 74 weeks, or $1,109.26. The same TV sold at Sears in the same city for $329.99, or less than a third of the rent-to-own price. If a customer put aside that same $15.00 a week, he could buy the TV at retail prices in 22 weeks.

COLD REMEDY

Dear Amy,

I get motion sickness when I fly, but I don't like taking medications that are costly and/or can make me sleepy. So I use plastic, refreezable ice cubes. I put them in an insulated lunch bag in my purse, and when it's takeoff or landing time I take a few out and hold them in my hands. It stops my nausea, and there are no side effects. I learned this trick from some flight nurses when I was being flown to a bigger hospital for a premature delivery. It really works. My husband and friends have tried it and it works for them, too. It works with other kinds of nausea as well.

—Cindy Warntjes
Boyden, Iowa

(I prefer to personally test out unusual tips such as this, but I decided to take Cindy's word for it instead of subjecting myself to "Egg Scrambler" amusement park rides. FZ)

À LA CARTON

Dear Amy,

I make egg-carton lunches. I simply fill the 12 spaces with small food items such as raisins, tiny cheese cubes, grapes, animal cookies, small crackers, etc. Each space does *not* need a different item; I double or triple up on favorites. I cover with a napkin and add a rubber band if we're traveling. We take these to the zoo, as car lunches, or just as a fun kid's lunch.

—Carolyn Marck
Seattle, Washington

(Bacteria can't survive on a dry surface, so be sure to use very dry egg cartons. FZ)

EVERLASTING BASKET

Dear Amy,

My husband, a fisheries biologist, came home with a "fish basket." It looks just like a round laundry basket, and that's exactly what I use it for. To give you an idea of its sturdiness, it holds 73 pounds of fish. I can almost guarantee that it will last a lifetime. I've had mine eight years and it

looks new. They do not fall apart like those ordinary, flimsy-plastic laundry baskets. He paid $10.25 for it at a commercial fish house.

—Laura McKenna
Greenville, North Carolina

PART SMART

Dear Amy,

I have a friend who did the most creative, tightwaddy thing that I have heard of in a long time. Her 1982 car was undrivable after an accident. She purchased another 1982 car of the same model. The first car was towed to her house, where she and her father removed and stored all of the usable parts. She now has hundreds of dollars worth of spare parts that fit her car, should she need them.

—Carolyn R. DeBliek
Indianapolis, Indiana

PACKAGE BENEFITS

Dear Amy,

I've found that people will pay double or triple the going garage-sale rate for a toy in its original box. A couple of years ago, I began pitching Christmas and birthday toy boxes into the attic. Toys the kids had outgrown were sold at my last garage sale in their original boxes, and you should have seen everyone snap up those toys! Those not in a box were passed up countless times.

—Marcia Noyes
Kingwood, Texas

AN ARTICLE OF INTEREST

If you're a new convert to frugality, you may be mired in credit card debt. Because credit cards such as Visa and MasterCard typically carry high interest rates, it's crucial to pay off these debts if possible. But if you can't do it immediately, you should at least lower your interest rate; this will allow you to pay it off more quickly.

An innovative way to do this comes from Joyce Bant of Hazelhurst, Wisconsin. She points out that credit-card-issuing companies are in stiff competition now and offer introductory interest rates as low as 5.9 percent if you switch your balance to their card. These rates are offered only for the first six months, but if you can't manage to pay off your balance by then, simply switch to another company that offers a card with a similarly low introductory rate.

How do you find these companies? Check your junk mail. A staffer says he receives at least three credit card solicitations a month. Read through them carefully and save the ones that offer *all* of the following:

- A low introductory interest rate.
- No annual fee, or an annual fee that is low enough that you'll still come out ahead due to the better interest rate.
- No other special restrictions that prevent you from using this plan to your advantage.

A SANER DRAINER

(Read the following with Andy Rooney inflection.) Have you ever noticed that the rubber trays that go under dish drainers are too darn narrow? Wet cups and glasses drip beyond the edge of the tray. Why is that, anyway? For years, we had a folded dish towel permanently positioned alongside the drain tray to catch these drips. And another thing: The drainer feet eventually make indentations in the tray; these indentations fill with water, and within a couple of years the water rots holes in the tray. Don't you hate that? (End of Andy Rooney inflection.)

Vexed by this situation, I told Jim about an expensive solution sent in by a reader, and without telling me, Jim had a sheet-metal shop custom-make a stainless steel drainer tray for (yikes!) $32. But after I got over the shock, I had to admit that I liked this idea.

Although the payback time is quite long (you can sometimes find replacement trays sold separately for $5, although the color might be different), I found I simply liked this drain tray better because it's wide enough to catch drips from cups and deep enough to have additional room to put a row of small cups behind the drainer.

If you like this idea, you'll have to measure your sink area carefully, as yours might be different from mine.

Our custom-made tray is 20 inches wide and 22 inches long. It has two metal pipes welded to the underside, a large one in the back, and a smaller one in the front, to give the tray a slight pitch (our sink unit is slightly higher than the adjoining counter section). Others might need just one small pipe or rod in the back. The tray has a ¼-inch lip that runs around three sides, and it tapers on its "sink side" because our sink isn't as wide as the tray.

Since we've had our tray we've noticed how common trayless drainers are at yard sales. Jim bought one recently. Then it occurred to me that our silverware holder was also too small for our needs. So I took the holder off this yard-sale drainer and now have two on the one in the kitchen.

These two modifications greatly ease our dishwasherless life.

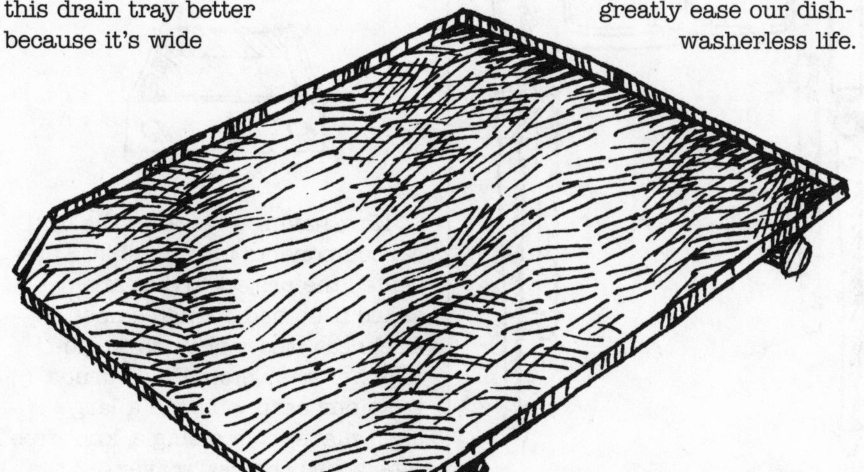

FUNDAMENTALS OF FURNITURE FUSION

Norm Abram, the head carpenter for the *This Old House* series, has his own show: *The New Yankee Workshop.* In each episode he demonstrates how to build a piece of reproduction furniture that he designed based on studying originals. I admire Norm for his skill and sense of design. But I also have to admire his workshop, crammed with every conceivable, expensive woodworking tool.

Although many people own (or can borrow) basic woodworking tools such as a table saw, drills, and clamps, they lack the tools and skills to turn a table leg or make a dovetailed drawer. Further, quality hardwood is so expensive it's usually cheaper to buy used furniture.

But years ago, I spotted an intriguing make-your-own-furniture method that does not require exotic tools. A magazine photo featured a blue-painted garden bench that was made from parts of unrestorable furniture. Since then, I've looked at junk furniture with a different eye.

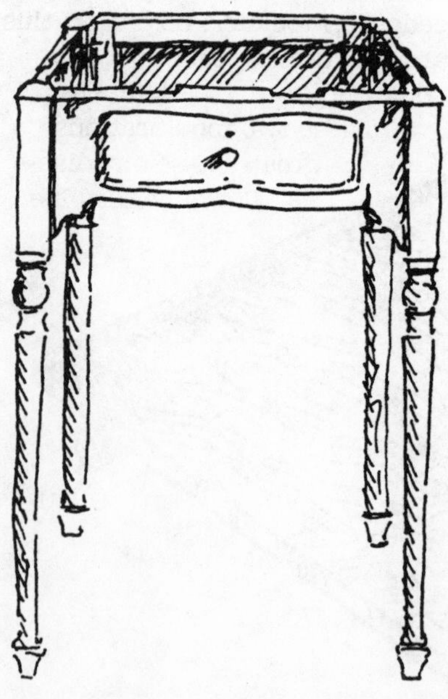

For instance, I spotted a junked sewing table donated to our church's thrift shop. It was missing both the tabletop and the machine. The sides of the table had buckled and broken veneer, and one side had a cutaway place that had accommodated a piece of the sewing machine. I didn't like the scalloped-cut sides or the fake-drawer/flip-out compartment. But the table did have four nicely turned legs and I could envision them as part of a smaller, Sheraton-style bedside table. I knew that the church deacons would simply cart the table to the dump, and so I asked and they let me have it for free.

A few months later I was at a sort-of flea market and found three small dovetailed drawers, complete with wooden knobs and broken veneer, for $3. I picked out the best drawer and offered $1 for it. The seller accepted.

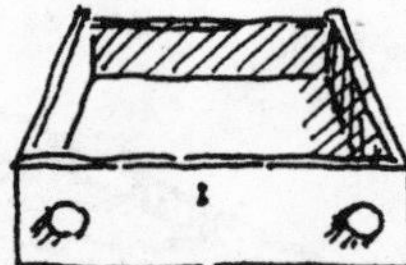

Now, having several of the critical components for my table, I presented the project to Jim and asked if he had enough same-thickness pieces of wood to glue together a tabletop. He returned from our barn loft with a large shelf made from a single, knot-free pine board (he had scavenged the

shelf for the metal folding brackets attached to its underside). He also found a hardwood, dark-stained table leaf that fit none of our tables, to make into new table sides.

Jim began by working on the drawer. He unscrewed the knobs and then used a heat gun to remove the veneer from the drawer's face. Then he sanded the remaining glue off the underlying wood surface.

He disassembled the table, which was primarily held together on the inside with metal brackets. We planned the overall size of the table based on the size of the drawer. It would be just wide enough so that the drawer would clear the inside brackets and just deep enough to accommodate the depth of the drawer.

Jim made new, straight-bottomed sides and a back from the table leaf. Using the old sides as a guide, he used his table saw to duplicate the edge-cut that fit into a groove in the table legs. He made a new face to fit around the

drawer front by gluing together four strips of wood. He made drawer rails and stoppers (so that the drawer didn't slide in too far).

Jim cut a tabletop from the scavenged shelf, making it large enough to overhang by an inch all the way around. Then he used his router to make a gently rounded edge.

Once all the elements were finished, he sanded them. The assembly of the table was simple. The sides and legs screwed together easily. He attached the top to the table using blocks on the inside screwed to the sides and to the top.

As you can imagine, at this point the table looked a bit hodgepodge due to the various types, stains, and finishes of the wood used. We solved this by duplicating a new style I've seen at furniture stores: combining paint with natural-finish woods. I left the knobs and top natural, and painted the remaining parts of my table an indigo blue, the dark-blue shade commonly found in Oriental carpets.

Our new table goes nicely with our country furnishings. The joy in such an effort is not just the finished project, but also in the process of making something attractive from items that would have wound up in the burn pile at the dump.

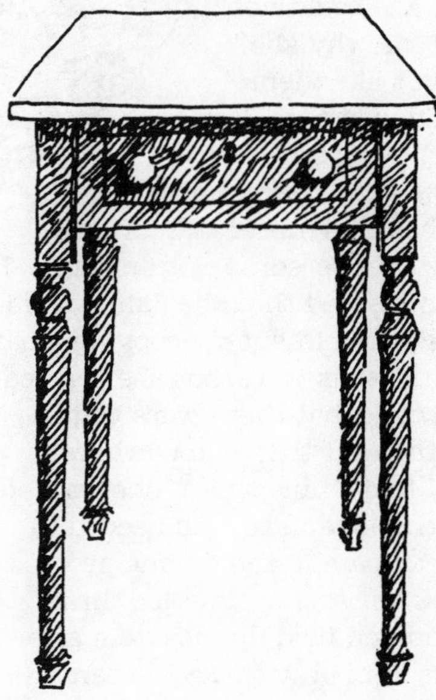

RETAIL REVELATION

For the 13 years during which I've been a frugal parent, I've heard one pessimistic prediction more often than any other: "Once your kids are teenagers, they won't wear secondhand clothes." But after watching the television series *My So-Called Life,* I concluded that, in the 1990s, teenager clothing demands can be met with two flannel shirts and a baggy pair of jeans.

Even so, I feel compelled to report the tiniest wrinkles in my frugal life, so readers will know we're "real." When Jamie was ten, I picked up subtle signals that she was dissatisfied. She would shrug—her polite way of saying No—at about half of the used clothing I brought home for her. The items were good-looking and similar to those worn by her peers, yet she could not tell me why she didn't like them.

It's not that Jamie was being too "picky." How she looks is important to her, and she is still forming her own personal clothing style. I was pleased that she didn't seem interested in simply copying what her friends wore, but she seemed to think that there were better clothes out there, somewhere.

I told Jamie that if she wanted clothes she liked, she needed to participate in the buying process. I took her to our church's thrift shop and held up nice item after nice item only to get the same shrugging response.

I then recalled a letter in my file from Jean McGrew of Coral Gables, Florida, who wrote that she made regular "scouting" trips to the mall with her daughter. Once her daughter showed her the styles she liked, Jean was able to watch for these things at secondhand sources. So I decided to try this with Jamie.

Jamie and I visited the major department stores in our area: Ames, Porteous, Sears, J. C. Penney, and Wal-Mart. We also visited T. J. Maxx, a discount store that carries unsold clothing from trendier stores, in faraway Portland, Maine.

Because neither of us had ever shopped the retail market for kids' clothes, we both were surprised to find the selection of clothes was fairly limited. We even checked with clerks to verify that this, indeed, was it. And, in an odd bit of tightwad serendipity, our maiden scouting trip occurred during a questionable fashion year. To me, the 1995 "fall collection" looked like *The Brady Bunch Goes to Colorado:* an abundance of faded denim combined with "retro" prints and busy stripes that evoked the childhood fashion memories I had tried to suppress.

Carefully guarding my reaction, I held up awful item after awful item and said, with the straightest face I could muster, "How about this, honey?" Jamie not only shrugged, but grimaced as well. And when she peeked at price tags she winced involuntarily.

Jamie didn't even like some of the fashions I felt were passable. She did like the simple jeans, the flared jean skirts, and the dark, solid-colored turtlenecks, but we commonly find these through secondhand sources for 25¢ to a dollar.

Our final stop was the Salvation Army, a store in which we rarely shop because the prices are higher than at other secondhand sources. Jamie picked out a flared stone-washed denim skirt with pastel-blue-and-pink flowered lace on the hem. It had a $2.99 blue price tag on a green-tag 50 percent-discount day. I could have returned and bought it on a blue-tag day, but I felt that buying the skirt on that day was a lesson at a bargain price.

I suspect that Jamie had believed there was a whole world of wonderful new clothes out there that I wasn't letting her see. Our excursion showed us both that although thrift shops have a higher percentage of ragged, weird clothes than department stores do, the percentage of clothing that appealed to Jamie was about the same in each kind of store.

After our trips, Jamie asked to look through the "ten-year-old girl" box of clothes in the attic again. This time she picked out a few items that she had passed over the first time.

I know, I know, this sounds a little too much like a *Leave It to Beaver* conclusion, but that's what actually happened.

REAL TIGHTWADS EAT QUICHE

My staffer Brad and I brainstormed article ideas by comparing the commonly served meals in our homes. The similarity ended when I listed quiche and he said his family never made it because it called for "so many eggs." He thought a quiche used 8 or more eggs and was surprised to learn that a 9-inch quiche is usually made with only three or four eggs, and that a quiche this size will serve at least four hungry adults.

It's true, however, that quiches can be very high in total fat. Aside from eggs, a recipe might also call for heavy cream, fatty cheese, and bacon. And don't forget the crust: A 9-inch pastry crust has 8 tablespoons of shortening, each tablespoon having 12 grams of fat. So one sixth of a quiche might have most of the fat you should eat for a day.

On the plus side, quiches are simple, elegant, and versatile. And because eggs provide a complete protein and contain all of the vitamins except C, quiche served with a high-vitamin-C food makes a very nutritious meal. Finally, depending upon the ingredients you choose, quiche can be reasonably frugal: A 9-inch one costs us an average of $1.25. We eat quiche about once a month, and make it only when our freezer contains a surplus of cooked rice, pastry scraps, or leftover vegetables.

So this article will have two parts: first, a "universal quiche" recipe, and second, how to work quiche into your life if you're trying to eat less saturated fat.

THE UNIVERSAL QUICHE

Crust. Use a standard pastry crust. Some recipes suggest prebaking this before filling to prevent sogginess. I don't. Instead, I prepare the crust, then prepare the various components of quiche, and then assemble the quiche all at once just before putting it on a lower shelf in my preheated oven. You can also make a rice crust using 2 cups of cooked rice, 1½ ounces of grated cheese, and one egg. Combine the ingredients, pat into a Pam-sprayed pie tin, and prebake at 425 for 15 minutes or until just firm.

Eggs. Use 3 or 4.

Cheese. Most recipes call for 1 to 2 cups (4 to 8 ounces) of a grated hard cheese. I use about 1 cup. You can use Swiss, cheddar, feta*, Monterey Jack, or Gruyère*. Or use from 2 tablespoons to ½ cup of Parmesan or Romano. Or use a combination of these. Some softer cheeses, such as mozzarella and American, will not set up well.

*Ha ha. Only if you have a free or cheap source of these items.

Milk or cream. Use 1 to 2 cups of milk, half and half, cream, evaporated milk, or powdered milk made with half the usual water. You may also use part sour cream, cottage cheese, or yogurt.

Filling. Use 1 to 2 cups of a combination of meats and/or vegetables. Meat possibilities include crisply fried and crumbled bacon, or pieces of crab*, lobster*, shrimp*, tuna, chicken, or ham. Use virtually any cooked or steamed vegetables, but squeeze out excess liquid. Don't be afraid to take risks. Once I made a sauerkraut quiche that was very tasty.

Seasoning. For a basic quiche, use up to 1 teaspoon of salt (bearing in mind the saltiness of the other ingredients), ¼ teaspoon pepper, and a dash of nutmeg. If you're a bit more adventurous, experiment with other seasonings such as chives, Tabasco, tarragon, dry mustard, Worcestershire sauce, cayenne pepper, sherry, parsley, paprika, dill, garlic, onion powder, lemon juice, basil, and/or oregano.

To make the quiche: Prepare the crust in a 9-inch pie plate. Grate cheese and prepare the filling ingredients (sauté, cook, chop, crumble, etc.). Beat eggs, milk, and seasonings together until just combined. Spread filling ingredients in crust, top this with grated cheese, and cover with egg/milk mixture. (If you've made too little egg/milk mixture, mix up slightly more. If you've made too much, toss the surplus in tomorrow morning's universal muffin recipe.) Bake for 10 minutes in an oven preheated to 425 degrees. Then turn the oven down to 350 degrees and bake for an additional 45 minutes, or until it's done. The quiche is done when it's golden brown and slightly puffed, and when a knife inserted comes out clean.

FAT REDUCTION STRATEGIES

- For filling, use vegetables and little or no meat.
- Reduce the total amount of eggs and cheese and increase the amount of filling. For instance, one Weight Watchers recipe uses just 2 eggs, 1½ ounces of cheese, 1 cup of cooked spinach, and ¾ cup of onion.
- Choose the nonfat milk options.
- Eat just one-eighth slice of quiche and serve it with low-fat foods such as soup, raw vegetables, and/or unbuttered bread.
- Choose the rice crust. Or use a pastry recipe that uses oil instead of shortening. Use (bulk-purchased) olive oil so that you at least use the right kind of fat.

REAL TIGHTWADS EAT QUICHE UPDATE

The previous article's exploration of the frugal advantages of quiche prompted a number of readers to point out that we neglected to mention "crustless" quiches. These generally have a cup of either flour or Bisquick (or a homemade Bisquick substitute, see page 193) added to the filling to stiffen it. If you are time-pressed or pastryphobic, this is a good alternative. Crustlessness can also help to lower the fat content, as a pastry crust has 96 grams of fat versus no grams for a cup of flour.

Judith Pratt of Hillsboro, New Hampshire, sent us this recipe:

1 cup plain yogurt (milk, cottage cheese, or other substitutions are possible here)
¼ cup water
2–3 eggs, slightly beaten
1 cup flour
½ cup grated cheese
¼ cup chopped, cooked meat
¼ cup chopped, cooked vegetables
Seasoning to taste

Preheat oven to 425 degrees. Mix all ingredients thoroughly. Pour into a greased 9-inch pie plate. Bake for 30 to 35 minutes or until set.

And Brenda Olson of Fremont, Michigan, sent along this recipe for a low-fat potato crust:

In a 9-inch pie pan, stir together 3 tablespoons vegetable oil with 3 cups of coarsely shredded raw potato. Or you can spray Pam in the bottom of a pie pan and omit the additional oil. Press the grated potato into a pie-crust shape. Bake at 425 degrees for 15 minutes or until just beginning to brown.

Remove from oven, add quiche filling, and bake.

Brenda says this is thicker than a pastry crust, so it is best to use just 2 or 3 eggs in the quiche. She adds that she often makes more than one crust at a time and freezes the extras after baking, which allows her to make quick meals in a pinch.

A MYSTERY DISSOLVED

In *The Tightwad Gazette II*, we ran a letter from a reader who had made an amazing discovery: Her dishes got just as clean when she used one tablespoon of detergent in her dishwasher instead of her customary six tablespoons.

That letter prompted Deann Polanco of Austin, Texas, to write to us about information in her new dishwasher's manual. It said: "The amount of detergent to use depends on the water hardness." Hardness is a measure of the concentration of minerals, primarily calcium and magnesium, in water.

Then it listed the following recommended measurements:

- Soft water, 0 to 3.5 grains per gallon, 1 tablespoon of detergent.
- Moderately hard water, 3.6 to 7 grains per gallon, 2 tablespoons of detergent.
- Hard water, 7.1 to 10.5 grains per gallon, fill cup.
- Very hard water, 10.6 grains and over, detergent alone may not be enough, water softener recommended.

Deann then called her water company and asked about hardness. She was told that water in her area ranges from 6 to 8 grains per gallon. "So, although I need more than the person who wrote the original letter, I need a lot less than I had been using, and it was so easy to get the water hardness information from our utility company." If you are on a well, you may be able to get hardness information from your cooperative extension agency.

I was curious about whether this tip also applies to the use of laundry detergent, so I called Jane Meyer, consumer affairs director for the Soap and Detergent Association in New York City. She said that, yes, the amount of laundry detergent needed also varies according to hardness. The recommended amounts listed on the box are for average water conditions. If your water is unusually soft or hard, you can vary the amount you use accordingly.

But she also noted that there are four other variables to consider: size of load, dirtiness of load, duration of agitation, and water temperature.

So when it comes to detergent, don't fall into the habit of simply filling the dishwasher cups or filling up and dumping the plastic scoop that comes with your laun-

dry detergent. Due to water hardness and other variables, each load of dishes or laundry is different. With a little research and experimentation, you should be able to adjust your detergent "dose" so that you always use the minimum amount that gets the job done properly.

ACQUIRE A POSITIVE RENTAL ATTITUDE

Surveys show that rental shops are used by only about 8 percent of the population. Yet a recent trip to a tool-rental shop reminded me of the surprising array of equipment available for rent.

For more information, I interviewed Charlie Marks, manager of Taylor Rental of Brunswick, Maine, one of the larger shops in this area. He said that you should call your local rental shop even if you don't know the name of the tool you need. Just describe the task you want to perform and the rental shop personnel will suggest tools. After a friend, equipped with only hand tools, spent an hour removing just 2 square feet of old vinyl flooring, he called his local rental store and asked, "Do you have a power tool that can handle this?" Sure enough, the store had a gadget called a "stripper." The $33-a-day tool saved about 80 hours of work.

Other items commonly rented by homeowners include stump grinders, pressure washers (to strip paint and remove mildew from siding), small-animal traps, pneumatic nailers, concrete drills and saws, hand trucks, pumps (for flooded cellars), generators (for power outages), and power edgers (to cut a slice in a lawn at the perfect depth for installing now-popular "invisible" dog fences).

If you are adventurous, rental places can lend you some serious equipment. For example, Marks has a $30,000 backhoe that rents for $200 a day. "We give you instruction. Everything we have can be operated by the average person," he says.

Marks says it is perfectly okay for several people to share one rental. "It happens all the time," he says. "One guy rents a chipper and it goes down the whole block."

And full-service rental places rent more than just tools. Taylor Rental, for example, rents beds, cribs, and high chairs, as well as odd items like karaoke machines and a "dunk tank" (which is used when, for example, students pay to throw a ball to dunk the principal).

Some other advantages of renting:

- It can save space. You might not want to have a cement mixer around forever.
- It can allow you to judge if a gadget is worth buying. We've wondered about how well paint sprayers work and have been researching the pros and cons; it might be useful to rent one to try for ourselves.
- It can help you postpone a major purchase while you're shopping for a hard-to-find item in the secondhand market. If you've been unable to locate a used utility trailer but need to move a piano today, try renting.

While renting is terrific for seldom-used items, you should still consider other options that may be even cheaper:

- Borrow whenever possible

(and allow others to borrow from you).

• If you will use a tool several times, it can be cheaper to buy. A Makita drywall screw gun costs $11.55 a day to rent and about $150 to buy, so if you'd use it for more than 13 days, you should buy it.

• You may be able to buy a tool secondhand, use it for the one occasion that you need it, and then resell it for the same price you paid.

DRIVE A BARGAIN

Dear Amy,

Make friends with several area car mechanics and used-parts dealers and let them know you are looking for an older, high-mileage car in good condition. We did this and bought a 90,000-mile 1986 Olds for $2,500. It is loaded and in great shape. As long as it lasts 18 months to 2 years and can be sold for $1,000 or more, we come out ahead. My goal is to pay $60 or less a month to own a car.

—Kenneth T. Podell
Glenside, Pennsylvania

HEAT BY THE SEAT

Dear Amy,

During the winter I like to keep the heat set as low as possible to save utility costs. I find when I work actively around the home I am comfortable with a lower temperature than when I work at my desk or read. Instead of turning the heat up, I place a heating pad turned on low behind my back whenever I sit for a time in a chair. I always wear a top and a sweater, which serves for a time as insulation. (Heating pads should not be used on infants or invalids.) I have saved a lot on heating bills.

— Judy Hedrick
Altadena, California

HECK OF A DECK

Dear Amy,

People have often accused me of not playing with a full deck, and I guess they are right. I cleaned out the drawer with playing cards the other day and found we have a whole lot of cards that don't make up a deck. I used to throw these out, but I had an idea: Why not combine all of them and use the deck for crazy eights only? We've played it a couple of nights in a row, and laughed so hard we almost cried. So what if the deck has only three queens? It has seven threes, which allows player 1 to play a three of spades and player 2 to play a three of spades on top of it, which we find awfully amusing.

—Melissa Hunter-Kilmer
Vienna, Virginia

CUT THE MUSTARD COSTS

Dear Amy,

My husband loves gourmet mustard, a holdover from our spendthrift days. Instead of buying those 3- to 10-ounce jars for $2 to $12, I have learned to make my own. I simply take ground mustard powder, purchased in bulk for $2.39 a pound. One-half pound makes a total of 32 ounces of prepared

mustard. You start by mixing the powder with water, wine, or beer to get the proper consistency; then you can add horseradish, honey, jam, pepper, herbs, spices, and/or coarsely ground mustard seeds to taste.

—Susanna C. Moulton
Chicago, Illinois

FANTASTIC PLASTIC

Dear Amy,

I sew, and have wanted a cutting mat for some time but was unwilling to pay the very high prices at most sewing-supply stores (from around $39 for a small one to $99 and up for larger ones). Then I came across fluorescent light panels at a hardware store. These are the large, translucent plastic rectangles that cover fluorescent tubes in fixtures and dropped ceilings. One side is hard and textured, but the other side is smooth and slightly pliable, like the pricey "self-healing" cutting mats. They are 4 feet by 2 feet, much larger than the sewing cutting mats, making them perfect for laying out most garment patterns. Best of all is the price: $2.97. I found mine at Home Depot, but they can be found at similar prices in any large hardware or home-supply stores.

—Laura C. Hartog
Oakland, California

TO COIN A FACE

Dear Amy,

A birthday gift for children ages five to ten: On colored paper, make a face. Use quarters, dimes, nickels, and pennies Scotch-taped on the paper. Do the outline in pennies, the smile in nickels, the nose with dimes and the eyes with quarters. Total cost is under $2. Wrap flat in a shirt box. This was a winner with our four boys.

—Marian Nordquist
Moscow, Idaho

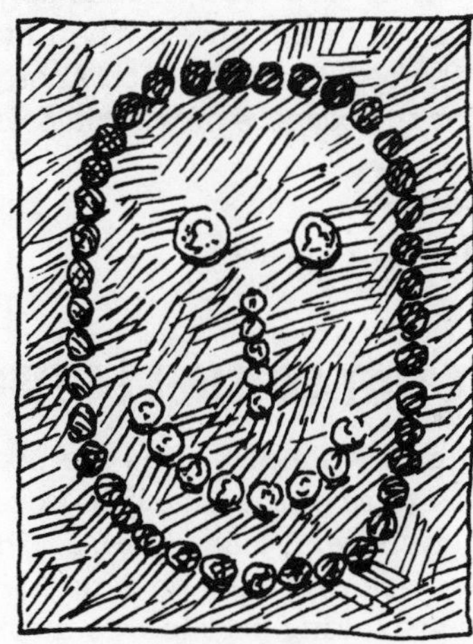

(This strikes me as a great in-a-pinch gift idea for those last-minute party invitations. FZ)

FILL OUT AND FILL UP

Dear Amy,

Send in those evaluation forms at restaurants and stores! I've sent them in critiquing restaurants (both positively and negatively) and received coupons for free meals. After sending in an evalua-

tion to our local juice bar, they asked me to be their mystery shopper. I get two free smoothies a week. I just have to send in quality-control forms every week.

—Susan Reese
Irvine, California

TOP-KNOT TIP

Dear Amy,

I can almost always find good used top sheets at garage sales, but not fitted sheets. I recently found a way to easily convert a top to a fitted sheet. Tie a knot in each corner of the top or flat sheet. When making the bed, just tuck each knot under the corners of the mattress.

—Joan Johnston
Milford, Michigan

THE NOT-SO-SIMPLE LIFE

"Voluntary simplicity" is the hot media topic of the moment. Dozens of newspapers, magazines, and TV shows are reporting on Americans who are taking part in this movement.

Voluntary simplicity is about scaling down—deliberately owning less and working less so that you can focus on what's really important to you, be it your spirituality, your family, or a social cause. And it isn't new. Throughout history, figures such as Christ, St. Francis of Assisi, Gandhi, Thoreau, and 1960s back-to-the-landers have advocated a life of fewer possessions. It was first called "voluntary poverty" but in this century gained its more palatable name.

Is it the same as tightwaddery? Tightwaddery can differ, as people may use it to acquire even more stuff for less money. But, in general, tightwaddery overlaps broadly with voluntary simplicity. Scaling down is a common theme in my newsletter, in my life, and, judging from my mail, in the lives of my readers.

Because of the obvious overlap, I received many calls during one particular media-blitz period. In one case I had a long conversation with a harried talk-show producer who was trying to ascertain if I'd be a good guest to appear with "simplicity authors."

But as the conversation progressed, I felt this possible appearance slipping away. I pointed out that living simply often means working less, and most people cannot do that unless they employ money-saving strategies, and these are not always simple. The producer seemed frustrated as she couldn't see how my not-so-simple strategies would fit into her show on simplicity. In a subsequent conversation with a simplicity author, I learned that she, too, felt people were often frustrated to learn that transitioning to a simple life might require some complex strategies.

Both she and I noticed that people seem to want simple, easy answers to complex problems. We've seen this before. In the 1980s, get-rich-quick gurus proliferated because they suggested wealth could be yours by (simply) adopting a new attitude about success and employing a few (simple) techniques. Similarly, new diet plans sold books as long as they offered new (and simple) strategies, like eating more grapefruit or drinking more water. But their simple solutions rarely worked.

(The sheer numbers of "Gutbuster" exercise gizmos at yard sales prove the point.)

Then *The Tightwad Gazette* came along in 1990. When I stated that, for example, it was possible to eat well for less money, I interested many people looking for simple answers. But some of these people seemed disappointed to learn that achieving a lower food bill requires not-so-simple lifestyle changes and learning new skills.

There are simple strategies out there, but many are so simplistic they're inherently flawed, such as: "Shop only in the perimeter of the store—the expensive foods are in the aisles." Unfortunately, so are the items needed to cook from scratch.

Even basically good strategies, when offered too simplistically, can be flawed, such as: "Buy in bulk." Unfortunately, the big sizes aren't always the cheapest.

Some simple strategies really do work, such as: "Buy cheaper cuts of meat." Unfortunately, even this may have a not-so-simple aspect of getting your family to agree to it.

Simple answers may help you save a little on your grocery bill but will not achieve the 50-percent savings that is common among my readership.

Required Reading for Living Simply

People are attracted to simple answers because they want to skip crucial steps that require brainwork. But real brainwork is required to become an excellent shopper and do-it-yourselfer.

Upon learning that frugality/voluntary simplicity often means learning new skills and working harder at certain tasks, people question, "Then what's so simple about 'voluntary simplicity'?"

The answer: People forget that working at a job isn't simple either. Particularly for parents, jobs create stress as employees try to meet the demands of a client or boss; these demands often compete with the immediate needs of the family. It's this competition that is complicated.

Frugality may not always be simple, but it's definitely more "family friendly." It might seem simpler to buy vegetables than to grow your own. But it isn't simple if you have to press a suit, put on makeup, drop the kids at a sitter, and commute 45 minutes to a job you dislike to earn money to buy vegetables. In contrast, an at-home parent who gardens may not be tending to his child continually, but if the child skins a knee, the weeding can wait. The frugal parent may not be working less, but he or she probably enjoys the work

more and isn't bound by a corporate schedule.

Learning to manage your money well may be the most important step on the path to a simpler life. Using simplistic strategies, even the good ones, won't provide enough financial leverage to allow you to give up a job. To gain an overall simpler life probably means doing some not-so-simple things.

I summed up my explanation to the TV producer this way: Remember when you learned to ride a bike? That wasn't so simple. In fact, if I had to explain in an interview how to ride, it would sound even more complicated. It would be easy to conclude that walking is simpler than biking. But walking is a much slower method of transportation than biking, so if you walk, everything else in your life must be compressed to compensate for the extra transportation time. So, if you put in the necessary time and effort to learn to ride, it will ultimately seem simple and simplify your life.

WHEN BIGGER ISN'T BETTER

A recent study by the Marketing Science Institute in Cambridge, Massachusetts, yielded information that tightwads should note: Large packages encourage consumers to increase the amount of a product they use.

A Harvard Business Review article sent to me by Ann Gilson of Port Angeles, Washington, reports that consumers who purchased large containers of Creamette spaghetti, M&M's, Diet Pepsi, Crisco Oil, or Mr. Clean ate more, drank more, and poured more than people who bought smaller containers of the same products. Wharton School marketing professor Brian Wansink said that's because consumers know they got the product for a lower unit cost and thus feel justified in using more.

His study also revealed that people use more of a product from a full container than from a half-empty one. As for products that recommend an amount to use, such as household cleaners, instructions are ignored 70 percent of the time.

Some people, understanding they use more if a product comes in a large package, avoid bulk packaging altogether. Others might "trick" themselves, by putting bulk-purchased items into smaller containers. But my advice is simply to be aware of the human tendency to overuse bulk-purchased items and modify your behavior accordingly. Understand that unit savings that come from bulk buying can easily be canceled by overconsumption.

On a similar note, John Kleinhenz of Dallas, Oregon, pointed out that consumers are often mistaken in thinking that the big sizes are always the cheapest. For example, he observed that a 4-pack of toilet paper cost 68¢. In the very next display, the exact same toilet paper, packaged in 12-packs cost $2.28. Three 4-packs would cost $2.04. He's found this with milk, toothpaste, and other items. Jim and I have noticed that five 5-pound bags of flour can cost less than one 25-pound bag of flour. These scenarios occur for both on-sale and regularly priced products.

MYSTIFIED BY HOMEMADE MIXES?

A newsletter reader from Cambridge, Massachusetts, has a few recipes that call for Bisquick and asked for a homemade version. Her request leads to the larger topic of the usefulness of homemade mixes. Recipes for these are commonly published in thrift books, women's magazines, and extension-service bulletins. So this article offers a "biscuit-baking mix," and some recipes for using it, but will also explain why I don't use homemade baking mixes.

To make homemade biscuit-baking mix: Combine 10 cups of flour, ⅓ cup of baking powder, and 1 tablespoon of salt. Mix this with 2 cups of shortening using a pastry blender, food processor, or two knives. Place in a sealed container. It will keep for one to six months at room temperature during cool, dry weather. Otherwise, refrigerate. Use as you would Bisquick. Some of the simpler examples:

Pancakes: Combine 2 cups of mix, 1 cup of milk, and 2 eggs.

Dumplings: Combine 2 cups of mix with ⅔ cup of milk.

Waffles: Combine 2 cups of mix, 2 tablespoons of vegetable oil, 1 egg, and 1⅓ cups of milk.

There are many varieties of homemade biscuit-baking mixes. A few call for oil instead of shortening. Some suggest the addition of 1⅓ cups of powdered milk. When using the mix, you add water instead of milk.

This homemade mix could be handy because some recipes do call for Bisquick, and because it would be convenient for camping.

But there are reasons why I don't use this or other homemade baking mixes. There are two basic types: universal mixes, such as the above biscuit-baking mix, and master mixes, which when combined with other ingredients make a variety of baked goods. Makes-one-thing mixes—and there are dozens of them—make just one thing or offer minor variations (such as a brownie mix that also makes peanut butter brownies). Each type has its disadvantages:

- The universal mixes don't save much time compared to using regular scratch recipes. For example, one master mix is a combination of seven ingredients. To use it to make yellow cake, you must combine five ingredients: the mix with four other ingredients (including sugar, an ingredient that is also in the original mix). But a scratch yellow cake recipe uses just eight ingredients. When making waffles with the biscuit-baking mix, you must add oil, thereby negating the time savings of adding shortening to the baking mix and saving you only the "work" of measuring salt and baking powder. Baking requires many steps, from recipe-reading to cleanup. These mixes may save you only a 30-second step in the process, but the rest of the steps are the same.

• Most universal mixes use shortening. But when I bake I prefer to use oil because it's healthier as well as easier to measure and combine.

• Like convenience foods, homemade mixes take up more space than staples alone. Your kitchen probably has several permanent containers of staples. If you use the ingredients in these containers to make several large containers of mixes, you could easily end up doubling the total amount of space required for baking supplies.

• The shelf life of the universal mixes and some makes-one-thing mixes is shorter than that of the uncombined ingredients. The baking powder, for example, loses some of its effectiveness over time when combined with other ingredients. Most of the makes-one-thing mixes are for desserts, which I usually prepare less than once a month, even with six kids. So some of these mixes might go bad before I would use them.

• Baking from scratch each time allows me to add varying types of whole grains, reduce fat, use up leftovers, and otherwise alter recipes. I never make plain white-flour-only pancakes, for instance. Although I could make up mixes using part whole grains, I would need a mix container for each type of whole grain that I commonly use.

• You may save more time, space, and/or electricity simply by preparing standard recipes in large batches and freezing the surplus. For example, rather than using a pastry mix each time I make a pie or quiche, it's quicker to make a triple batch of pastry and freeze the surplus.

If you disagree with me (it's allowed, really) and you like these mixes, look for Nancy Birnes's book *Cheaper and Better: Homemade Alternatives to Store-Bought Goods* at your library. She offers a "Biscuit Baking Mix" with 15 recipes, along with many makes-one-thing mixes.

Finally, you might want to add another recipe that calls for Bisquick to your repertoire. Kelley Reep of Gardener, North Carolina, sent this recipe for a delicious, easy dish.

PIZZA CASSEROLE

1 pound ground beef
2 14-ounce jars pizza sauce
3 cups mozzarella cheese, shredded
1½ cups Bisquick-type mix*
2½ cups milk
3 eggs

Cook and drain beef. Spoon beef into a 9-inch-by-13-inch baking dish. Top with pizza sauce and cheese. Combine Bisquick, milk, and eggs. Beat until smooth. Pour batter over casserole, covering evenly. Bake at 400 degrees for 30 to 35 minutes. Serves 8.

Kelley often stretches this by adding 1 cup of presoaked TVP (texturized vegetable protein; see *The Tightwad Gazette II*) along with the ground beef.

*If you don't want to mix up a big batch of biscuit-baking mix, you can make the required amount by combining 1¼ cups flour, 2 teaspoons baking powder, ½ teaspoon salt, and ¼ cup shortening or oil.

MAIL TO THE CHEAP

It's time once again to peruse some of the mail-order sources sent to us by readers.

Our research shows that these companies have at least the *potential* to save over local sources. Be sure to compare carefully, and take shipping and handling charges into account.

An asterisk (*) indicates that a company offers lower prices than a company I listed in my previous books.

APPLIANCE PARTS

Culinary Parts Unlimited
80 Berry Drive
Pacheco, CA 94553
(800) 543-7549

Parts for 35 brands of small appliances, including discontinued models up to 25 years old.

AUTOMOBILE/TRUCK PARTS AND ACCESSORIES

J. C. Whitney & Co.
P.O. Box 8410
Chicago, IL 60680
(312) 431-6102

Over 55,000 parts and accessories at low prices.

BIBLES

American Bible Society
P.O. Box 5656
Grand Central Station
New York, NY 10164
(800) 322-4253

Bibles available in hardcover for $7.00, paperback for $2.50.

BOOKS

New World Books
2 Cains Road
Suffern, NY 10901
(914) 354-2600

Up to 30 percent less than publisher's price on new books.

BULK FOODS, HERBS, AND SPICES

Glenn's Bulk Food Shoppe*
6411 West Morgan Avenue
Hutchinson, KS 67505
(316) 662-2875

Natural foods, including bulk pectin.

San Francisco Herb Co.*
250 14th Street
San Francisco, CA 94103
(800) 227-4530

Atlantic Spice Co.*
P.O. Box 205
North Truro, MA 02652
(800) 316-7965

A sister company to the San Francisco Herb Company, it offers the same prices and cheaper shipping to those east of the Mississippi.

CASSETTE TAPES

Roxan, Inc.
5425 Lockhurst Drive
Woodland Hills, CA 91367
(800) 228-5775

Blank video and audio cassettes.

CHECKS

Artistic Checks*
P.O. Box 1501
Elmira, NY 14902
(800) 224-7621

Discount mail-order checks.

CLOTHES

The Working Man
Antioch Wholesale
P.O. Box 140204
Nashville, TN 37214
(615) 883-1530

Used, reconditioned uniforms from rental companies.

Just My Size
P.O. Box 748
Rural Hall, NC 27098
(800) 522-9567

Large-sized women's clothes and lingerie.

DIAPERS

Dundee Direct
1440 North Expressway
Griffin, GA 30223
(800) 522-3388

Cloth diaper "seconds."

GREETING CARDS

The Current
The Current Building
Colorado Springs, CO 80941
(800) 525-7170

Half-priced greeting cards.

MUSICAL INSTRUMENTS

Elderly Instruments
1100 North Washington
P.O. Box 14249
Lansing, MI 48901
(517) 372-7890

New and used acoustic and electric instruments and supplies.

Musician's Friend
P.O.Box 4520
Medford, OR 97501
(800) 776-5173

New and used instruments and accessories.

SOFTWARE

HG Shareware
P.O. Box 515
Eagle Creek, OR 97022
(503) 637-3334

2,300 programs at 99¢ per disk.

"Shareware" often involves additional payments to the program's author.

Surplus Direct, Inc.
P.O. Box 2000
Hood River, OR 97031
(800) 753-7877

Sells older versions of commercial software at a discount.

Public Software Library
P.O. Box 35705
Houston, TX 77235
(713) 524-6394

VETERINARY SUPPLIES

Jeffers
P.O. Box 100
(353 West Inez Road)
Dothan, AL 36302
(800) 533-3377

Offers a complete line of pet, horse, and livestock supplies.

TAKER'S DOZEN

Dear Amy,

I am a commercial real estate photographer and I prefer to use 35mm film in 12-exposure rolls. I have discovered that when I load the film, I must make sure that the film is in the roller "teeth" or guide rail. When it is secure in both the top and bottom and it has one turn on the take-up roller, I close the back of the camera, advance the film one frame only, and click the shutter. Now I am ready to begin taking pictures, even though the film counter shows the dot *before* frame one! I always get one or two extra pictures per roll, but am charged for only 12 or 24, depending on the roll that I used.

—Jackie Steinberg
Saint Peters, Missouri

HEATER BEATER

Dear Amy,

Our electric company mailed us a chart showing the average cost of operating appliances. I noticed that a king-sized waterbed heater costs an average of $8.65 a month to operate. Three years ago, we put egg-crate foam on the waterbed, at a cost of $15. This allowed us to turn off the waterbed heater. Based on electric-company estimates, I am saving over $100 a year, and I recovered my investment in the first two months.

—Dabney Nunley
Phoenix, Arizona

SACK TACTIC

Dear Amy,

Lately I have seen paper lunch bags in pastel colors at K mart, 50 for under $1. I have used these as gift bags for smaller gifts in place of "real" same-sized gift bags that sell for $1 to $2. I wrap the gift in a piece of tissue paper, put it in the bag, fold down the top edges, punch two holes in the folded part, and tie a ribbon. The ribbon can be recycled or made from a spool of nicer ribbon bought at a fabric store on sale.

—Carol Harrison
Asheville, North Carolina

A COLOR-FOIL IDEA

Dear Amy,

Make foil-covered candy do triple duty. After Christmas, when the red, green, gold, and silver candy is heavily discounted, purchase what you need for New Year's Day (gold and/or silver), Valentine's Day (red), and St. Patrick's Day (green).

—Karen Jones
Lexington, Virginia

PAY NOW, SAVE LATER

Dear Amy,

Don't wait for self-employed persons to send a bill. I've found that most of them will charge less if offered payment at the time of job completion; or ahead of time, for that matter, if they can be trusted. I've talked to a plumber, a carpenter, and a construction worker, and all agreed this is true. I am self-employed as a tax preparer and have found this to be true in my business as well. If I have time to think about a bill, invariably it will be for more money. This is hard to prove, but I believe a considerable amount of money could be saved over a year using this strategy.

—Jean Doeden
Worthington, Minnesota

SAVE SOME BREAD

Dear Amy,

A money-saving technique I use because our household is only my husband and myself: When I buy bread, I put two slices at a time into fold-lock-type sandwich bags, put all the bags back into the wrapper, and freeze it. For toast or a sandwich I just remove what is needed at one time. It thaws in no time, and the remainder stays frozen without freezer burn. I found a store-brand box of 500 sandwich bags for 99¢ and have been reusing the bags for three years. I do bagels, muffins, and cake the same way.

—Frances Hohl
Pearl, Mississippi

SHOP AND SHAVE

Dear Amy,

When my husband expressed interest in a "foil" razor, I looked into it as a possible gift. My first stop was the mall razor store. The salesman helped me sort through the necessary features (cordless) and the unnecessary ones (bells and whistles) until I found a model that was suitable. The salesman sensed I was looking for a bargain and pointed out a rack in the back of the store that had the model I wanted for less than 50 percent of the retail price. He explained that the only difference was that it came in a blister pack instead of a gift box. Further, all their razors were 20 percent off. I did compare to discount stores, but no one came close to that price.

—Amy Butler
Alpharetta, Georgia

FOUR-WATTS FOR WHAT?

Dear Amy,

Four-watt bulbs, which can be used in night lights, are sold at Christmas time in big bins at 10¢ each without the packaging. Stock up then for the whole year. Even better, wait for the half-off after-Christmas sale. The normal sale price is two for 99¢.

—Wendy Howell
Camano Island, Washington

CHEAP SUITS

Dear Amy,

Casinos in Las Vegas, Atlantic City, and other places give away free used decks of cards. They are great gifts.

—Edgar Wunsch
Woodmere, New York

DEAR DESPERATE . . .

I have gotten several letters that start like this:

Dear Amy, *help!* I'm desperate!

The letters go on for several pages describing the writer's deep financial hole. Often, bankruptcy is looming.

These letters are hard to read. They are filled with genuine pain. They usually sum up with: "I know you're busy, but please write and tell me what to do."

With about one million Americans filing for bankruptcy annually, desperate financial circumstances are, sadly, becoming common. So I thought I would address the special concerns of those who are deep in debt. But often their past mistakes aren't easily fixable, so I also hope I can keep some people from winding up in similar straits. Here are the mistakes/factors that commonly create serious debt—and some ideas on how to get out:

- Obviously, some people just don't earn enough money. It's possible to support a family on under $20,000 a year, but only if you've made all the right choices during the previous years. Frugality is a powerful tool, but it has limits; you can chop your food bill by 50 percent but not by 99 percent. If your income is very low and/or your debts are high, it may make more sense to pour your energy into making more money than into hanging laundry.
- Some people deceive themselves about their overall spending habits. Their letters to me highlight some of their frugal activities (such as baking bread) but omit others (such as their long-distance-calling habits). It's like pointing out the places on a sinking ship that are not leaking. If these people kept a daily log that included all expenditures, no matter how small, they would soon discover where the leaks are and how to patch them.
- Some people abuse credit cards. Sue McCann of Arnold, Maryland, sent me an article about the sharply rising bankruptcy rate in her region. It quotes a bankruptcy attorney who has handled 800 cases and says that improper use of credit cards is the primary reason for his clients' plight.

Obviously, credit cards themselves aren't the problem, it's people's attitudes toward them. Studies have shown that people spend 23 percent more, on average, when they pay with a card rather than with cash. For too many people, paying with a credit card just does not feel like really paying.

If you have problems controlling your use of these cards, visualize pulling the equivalent amount of cash out of your pocket and counting it out, dollar by dollar, before you actually charge a purchase. Those in truly desperate circumstances should stop using their cards altogether.

- Some people don't plan for

their lives to change. Couples may base their debt load on two incomes, but when they have children their expenses increase and their ability to work profitably decreases. Others plan their finances on their current income (which often represents their highest earning potential) and presume they'll always earn the same amount. But history shows us that the economy keeps changing; whole industries vanish while others are created. Everyone should assume their lives can change and spend accordingly.

• Some people marry spendthrifts. Money is the most divisive issue in marriage, so it's not "unromantic" to carefully note his or her spending habits and discuss financial goals *before* marriage. If you're already married, spouse conversion is difficult but possible. An article on this subject appeared in my book *The Tightwad Gazette*.

• Some couples divorce, failing to consider the huge financial impact, particularly when child support is involved. The couple ceases pulling together toward a common financial goal. It's costly to maintain two households, and two frugal parents can raise their kids for much less than the amounts listed in court-mandated support payments. One reader who endured a particularly messy divorce reported that her lawyer fees alone exceeded $12,000. While divorce is sometimes the best alternative, it's often worth the effort to make it work. Only 5 percent of divorced couples get counseling before they split. Counseling fees could easily yield more than the hottest mutual fund.

• Some people have enormous medical bills. According to Gail Merrill, director of education for the Consumer Credit Counseling Service of Maine, this is often a major factor driving families into bankruptcy. While there's no way a family of modest means can easily pay a $150,000 medical bill, Merrill said that in many cases, a more frugal lifestyle could have yielded enough money to buy health insurance and avert disaster. A cheap, high-deductible insurance policy is *much* better than no insurance at all. Further, live right; a high percentage of accidents and illness are completely avoidable.

• Some people have killer debts from buying new cars. In his book *How to Live on Nothing*, Edward Romney puts it in perspective: "New-car prices are now so high that having two new cars is only for the very wealthy." If you're an affluent tightwad and can pay

cash, some new cars may be as cheap as used in the long run. But if you're broke, carefully selected used cars are best. They're cheaper to buy and have lower tax and insurance costs.

• Some people won't abandon cable TV. This may seem like a small point, but to me, cable TV is a sort of barometer. Anyone who is deep in debt and spends $25 a month for cable clearly hasn't "gotten it." A frequent excuse is that "we can't afford any other entertainment, so we feel this one expense is justified." Deeply indebted families should not only cancel cable, but might also sell their TV and use the time they free up for frugal activities or a money-making hobby. They must maximize their use of time to get ahead.

• Some people are unwilling to resort to extreme measures. Once you've covered all of the normal frugal bases, start thinking radical: one or no cars, sell your too-expensive house, ban long-distance calls, limit showers to two minutes, eat less (a good idea for many adults), work opposite shifts from your spouse to avoid child-care costs, and/or move to a cheaper part of the country.

• Some people don't take responsibility for their situation. They blame it all on a spouse, the recession, unexpected bills, and so on. But most financial problems are due to poor decisions and a failure to plan ahead. If they won't own up to past mistakes, it's unlikely they'll change their behavior in the future. It's crucial to honestly confront past mistakes. Then sit down with your family and develop specific plans for doing better.

• Some people have a negative attitude. They view frugal behaviors as restrictions forced on them rather than choices that improve their situation. Eating beans and rice should give you a warm, victorious glow rather than a feeling of deprivation. When money is extremely tight, this can be difficult, but it's crucial.

• Some people see no value in frugality, as it is "too little, too late" to help them. It's true that many tightwad strategies won't get you out of debt overnight, but they *can* help you feel less deprived as you marshal resources to pay down your debt. Rather than suffering because you "can't afford to go out for pizza anymore, don't have new furniture, and can't afford new kids' clothes," you can learn equally good alternatives: homemade pizza, scrounged-and-spruced-up furniture, and yard-sale clothes.

Finally, if you're in a desperate financial situation, contact your local Consumer Credit Counseling Service. The CCCS is a nonprofit group that helps people avoid bankruptcy. As Beckie J. Rogers of Redkey, Indiana, puts it, "They deal with bill collectors for you, and you don't have to worry about nasty calls, getting sued, etc. You make a weekly payment to them instead of sending money to your creditors. CCCS is paid for by creditors; you are charged only for stamps and envelopes. They are a respected organization and can usually get a creditor to lower or even drop the interest rate. It was our first step out of debt and got us started using a budget." To find the CCCS office nearest you, call (800) 388-2227.

GET A WHEEL JOB

Frugality can take time, and a way to gain time is to get your kids to help with chores efficiently. An ongoing hassle in our home has been the equitable distribution of kids' chores. For example, when the four oldest kids put their laundry away, they must also either put away upstairs linen or downstairs linen, or help one of the five-year-old twins put away their clothes. They would complain, "I helped Brad last time!"

I resolved this by making a "job wheel." Using cereal-box cardboard, I cut out 3-inch and 4-inch circles. I marked these into fourths. I wrote a child's name in each section of the larger wheel and a chore in each section of the smaller wheel. I drew arrows to indicate the turning direction. My junk drawer failed to yield a brass fastener, so I attached the wheels with two buttons and string. Now, every time I finish folding laundry, I turn the wheel.

It worked so well that I also made a dinner wheel. In the past, the four oldest kids had rotated setting and clearing the table. However, we hadn't eased them into dish washing or dinner preparation yet. So this wheel's jobs are setting the table, clearing the table, helping a parent with the dishes, and helping a parent prepare dinner. The dinner-helper job follows the dishwasher-helper job because the next night's meal is planned while the dishes are washed and the child can help choose the meal he'll help prepare the next day. Although few parents require children to help prepare meals, I feel this is important so that they learn to cook and may eventually relieve the parents of this job altogether.

Jim was able to prepare meals without help by the time he was 12.

As the kids get older, the twins will be added to the wheel. If you already have older children, the parents and children could be given sections on the wheel and alternate doing adult-type tasks.

Even though these wheels required them to take on additional chores, the kids were quite agreeable, because at last they felt chores were fairly assigned. I also find that when assigning overwhelming tasks to children (such as washing dishes for a family of eight), it's best for the parents to work alongside them. This way the children have a more pleasant experience, and by observing our efficiency they learn how to accomplish tasks quickly.

THE GOLDEN AGE . . . IT'S YOUNGER THAN YOU THINK

Many people are aware of "senior citizen discounts" but think you have to be 65 to get them. "Not true," says Harriett Harrow of Austin, Texas.

"As my husband's 55th birthday approached," she writes, "I researched 'senior' discounts that kick in that early, wrote off for brochures and discount cards, and presented him with all of this information (in rhyming scrapbook form!) as a novel birthday present any tightwad would love. The discounts are offered by banks (no-fee accounts, cheaper safety deposit boxes), grocery stores (10 percent off purchases every Wednesday), bus trips (15 percent off Greyhound regular-price fares), rail travel (in Scandinavia), hotels (some offer twice the standard AARP or AAA discounts), retailers (10 percent off all purchases every Tuesday), haircuts ($2 off at Supercuts), and more. Most discounts are unadvertised—you have to ask! I now always ask every establishment I frequent if they offer special discounts or services to those 55 and up, and I'm often pleasantly surprised!

"P.S. All these discounts made my husband feel a lot better about growing a little older!"

A COOKBOOK QUERY

A newsletter reader from Atlanta, Georgia, writes, "I'm adding my voice to the chorus that I am sure implores: 'Can you please give us a tightwad cookbook?' "

This reader is correct in that we do often get requests from readers for a cookbook. We have discussed writing one, but we realize that doing it really well would be an enormous undertaking. Even if I were to start today, the publication date might be years away.

In the theoretical meantime, how should you fill this gap in your life? In various places in my books I've offered different strategies. The following pulls those strategies together, and offers some new ones:

• You should have a collection of various types of cookbooks. My shelf of cookbooks is over 3 feet long. I don't think I paid retail for any of them. Some were gifts, some were free "review" copies, and some came from used-book stores and yard sales. Most cookbooks have some useful recipes. Your collection should include a few basic books, such as *The Betty Crocker Cookbook.*

When considering books, flip through them and reject ones that lean heavily on convenience foods or exotic ingredients. Specifically look for older cookbooks. These tend to have simpler recipes, such as a chocolate cake recipe that calls for cocoa rather than chocolate squares.

• Select recipes that call for ingredients that are inexpensive to you. Refer back to page 66, "Pantry Principle Update," in which I listed the staples I buy. These are likely to be cheap in your area, too. But because there are regional cost differences, there's a limited number of recipes that are universally cheap to everyone.

• Rather than choosing a recipe and buying the ingredients required, decide what you need to

use up and work from there. On one occasion when I worked at a church supper, I was the only helper who wanted to take home the huge container of leftover cooked carrots. This led me to look for recipes for carrot bisque—a recipe that would use up and disguise a lot of mushy carrots.

• Compare recipes for similar dishes from several cookbooks to get some sense of how much recipes can be successfully varied.

• When you're trying a recipe for the first time and you have all of the ingredients, follow the directions exactly. If you don't like the result, you'll know the recipe is at fault and not your variation. For instance, after I made stuffed tomatoes I found that the recipe called for too much thyme. So I noted in my book to use less next time. When I've tried similar recipes in the same book I've also given them a star rating, so that years later I'll recall which I liked best.

• If you lack a few ingredients for any one recipe, try combining elements of different recipes, such as when I created corn-broccoli casserole (see page 136) from recipes in two books.

• Substitute for ingredients you don't have, as I detailed in "Have-It-Your-Way Seafood Casserole" in the first *Tightwad Gazette* book. If a recipe calls for cream of celery soup, make a white sauce with sautéed celery.

• Make your own cookbook from a loose-leaf binder. Use it to record your experiments, and to copy in recipes from the *Tightwad Gazette* books and other sources. This allows everyone in a multiple-cook household to make the same "family favorite" recipes, and it's handier to have all your favorite recipes in one place.

• Experiment. Food is central to your life, and you will cook nearly every day. Learning to cook is a lifelong process. You should try new recipes regularly; at least once a month. Many of our experiments have become my family's regular favorites.

A final point is that most of the recipes our family uses are for basic dishes that can be found in any number of cookbooks.

DIET, YOU'LL LIKE IT

The weight-loss industry has grown to $32 billion annually. Clearly, many dieters believe they need the aid of clinics, health club memberships, appetite suppressants, expensive healthy foods (fish and fresh salad), and/or expensive "crutch" diet foods (diet sodas, diet shakes, NutraSweet, Weight Watchers frozen dinners, and so on).

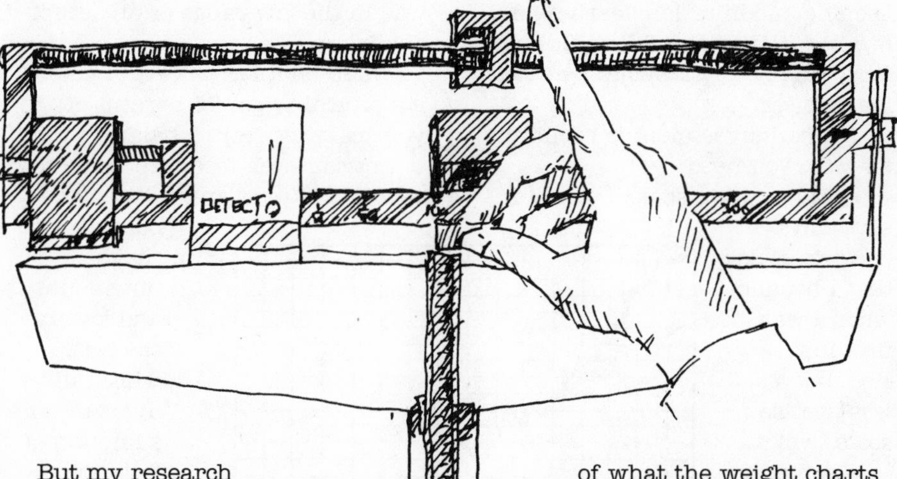

But my research has convinced me that those who want to lose weight can almost certainly do so without spending extra money. Further, if you've mastered frugality, you already possess the parallel skills required.

We interviewed several experts, including John Foreyt, an obesity specialist and director of the Nutrition Research Clinic at Baylor College of Medicine. Foreyt said that despite all the theories, weight loss boils down to one principle: You must use up more energy than you take in. While it's true that genetic factors can make weight loss tougher for some people, if losing weight is important enough to you, you can overcome your genes.

Weight loss is a fairly precise science. To lose a pound you must eat 3,500 fewer calories than you burn. Most adults use about 1,500 to 2,000 calories daily. If you create a daily deficit of 500 calories through eating less and/or exercising more, you should lose a pound a week.

Which brings me to *my* story.

In my early 20s I hit 163 pounds. This was at the upper end of what the weight charts said was acceptable for my height (5 feet, 8½ inches), but I was definitely "chunky." By jogging three to five miles daily my weight dropped to 148, where it stalled. For me, exercise alone wasn't enough. I switched to more moderate exercise and joined Weight Watchers. In four months I lost another 15 pounds. Over the next ten years, despite four pregnancies, my weight stayed between 133 and 138.

But after the birth of the twins five and a half years ago, I'd never dropped below 140 and had averaged about 145. At various times I'd casually tried eating less and exercising more, but I never lost

more than a pound or two. Then, in the spring of 1995, my weight edged up and I was startled one morning when it was over 150. I determined to get serious. I was pushing 40 and wanted to conquer this last unresolved area of my life.

So I decided to use the same skills I had learned from tightwaddery. Like saving money, losing weight can be achieved through unremarkable means. It's about self-honesty, precision, record-keeping, modification, learning a few new tricks, and follow-through. Very simply, I lost weight by counting calories.

A small investment is required for this. You need:

- An accurate scale. I own an expensive doctor's scale that I bought when I was first married, but a less-precise scale will do.
- A food scale (or even a postal scale) to measure food in ounces.
- Measuring cups and spoons to measure food by volume.
- A calorie guide.
- A small notebook to record what you eat. A piece of paper folded in eighths also works as a weekly record; use one section to record each day.
- A piece of graph paper to plot out your progress.

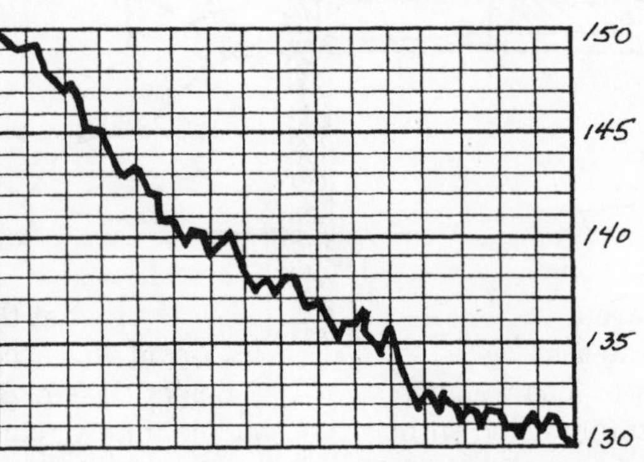

Next, set a daily calorie maximum for yourself. If you need to lose a significant amount of weight, are pregnant or nursing, or have medical problems, discuss this with your doctor.

Otherwise, the calorie maximum you choose is somewhat optional. Most diets are designed at 1,200 calories for women and 1,800 for men. Diets below 1,000 calories for long periods aren't advisable without medical supervision, and diets of 1,500 calories may be too much for many women to lose weight. I chose 1,000 calories and I took a multivitamin. Both Foreyt and a weight-loss physician told me this was in the low range of an acceptable plan.

When on a low-calorie regimen, it's crucial to get 95 percent of your calories from a balanced diet of nutrient-rich foods. You'll tend to eat a lot of fruit and vegetables because they're nutritious and low in calories, while limiting your consumption of fatty and sugary foods. Because protein is important when dieting, I ate the same moderate amounts of meat, eggs, yogurt, and cheese as usual.

Each day I began a new page in my notebook with the date and my weight that day at the top. Throughout the day I wrote down what I ate. I didn't weigh and measure my food before each meal, but instead weighed sample portions of, say, granola, to get an idea of what a 1-ounce portion looked like. I worked out my calorie count before supper and adjusted supper and my evening snack accordingly.

I tallied the total calories each night.

By keeping a notebook I found it very simple and useful to refer back to previous entries, as many of our frugal meals repeat themselves. Eventually I made a one-page calorie list of foods our family commonly eats. In many cases I just estimated as well as I could. I also figured out how many calories were in certain scratch foods by adding up the total calories in the ingredients, noting the volume the recipe made, and doing simple division to determine the calories in a single portion.

Exercise is important while dieting. It burns calories and helps prevent the loss of muscle tissue. Although my life does include some exercise, such as 8-mile bike rides, and physical labor, such as 12-hour house-painting days, it remained about the same as before I dieted.

The result: I lost 20 pounds in 16 weeks. Foreyt said that my rate of loss was excellent. At first you lose weight a bit quicker; then you should lose about a pound a week. If you lose faster than that you'll lose muscle tissue as well.

Foreyt staunchly believes that counting calories, combined with exercise, is the best weight-loss method. People are attracted to diets that save them the work of counting calories, but they will do best if they don't try to skip this brainwork step. Foreyt agreed with my observations about the drawbacks of the following popular weight-loss methods:

• Counting fat grams. Foreyt said he tried having his patients do this because it seemed simpler than counting calories. But he found these patients didn't lose weight consistently, because some foods, such as sugar, are high in calories but low in fat.

• Exercise alone. Foreyt said this doesn't always work. If you exercise, you'll build muscle tissue, and muscle burns more calories than does fat. But a five-mile jog won't help you burn more calories all day long. Your metabolism quickly returns to normal after you stop exercising. Whether they realize it or not, people who maintain weight "through exercise alone" are still balancing the calories they eat with those they burn. In fact, it's amazingly hard to exercise away high-calorie foods. For example, a cup of pudding has about 400 calories. A 150-pound person would need to run about an hour to use up these calories. Most people would find it easier to skip the pudding.

• Relying on "crutch" foods. Diet soda, sugarless gum, Equal, and low-calorie prepackaged foods are a big part of many informal diets and are often used in combination with formal diets. When I was on Weight Watchers, I constantly consumed crutch foods. Because my stomach became used to being fed something frequently, I became obsessed with food and sometimes found myself actually daydreaming about it. By dieting without crutch foods, food eventually became less important to me, almost "utilitarian." I was hungry during the first week while my stomach adjusted, but I chanted my mantra: "Hunger is good." After that, I seldom felt very hungry.

• Eating prescribed, daily portions of certain foods, such as fruit, milk, or fish. Many formal diet programs require this, while others rely on prepackaged diet foods (such as shakes and frozen

dinners) in combination with portions of regular foods. Although this seems simpler than counting calories, it results in the following three problems:

1. It can be more expensive. Some diets require that you eat fish twice a week but limit potatoes to three times a week. They might require a daily citrus fruit, even if your freezer is full of homegrown broccoli, which has much more vitamin C.

2. It's less flexible. Some foods are "illegal," such as pizza made with homemade dough. When I was with Weight Watchers, I could eat English-muffin pizza or Weight Watchers frozen pizza, but since the plan had no provision for homemade pizza dough, eating it was "cheating." This made eating with others difficult. Once I had a family, following a Weight Watchers diet meant either eating different foods than my family or switching everyone over to my diet. In social situations I would have to conspicuously abstain from parts of meals or ask my host to prepare something special for me. But during my calorie-counting diet, I went on vacation for nearly two weeks, went to our annual company picnic, ate at seven birthdays, had overnight houseguests on four occasions, and went to a church supper and an ice-cream social. A couple of people noted when I passed up a second helping, but few people suspected I was trying to lose weight.

3. It doesn't accommodate cravings for specific "illegal" food. When I followed the Weight Watchers diet, I craved illegal foods and binged on several occasions. But counting calories allowed me to eat a few sweets each week yet remain within my limit. Similarly, I've found that I'm rarely satisfied eating "rabbit food" but feel better if I eat the equivalent amount (or less) of calories in a baked potato or muffin. Foreyt said that on the ideal diet, no food is forbidden.

Finally, the problem with myriad diet plans isn't the diet itself, but how to get off it without regaining the weight. This is particularly true of diets based on prepackaged meals and protein drinks. Dieters don't know how much they must eat of regular foods to maintain their desired weight. But if you've kept a record of your calorie consumption, through calculation and experimentation you should be able to pinpoint the number of calories you need to maintain the desired weight.

In the year since I lost this weight, I have easily maintained my weight. I weigh myself every few days. If I find my weight has crept up a pound or so, I simply revert back to the diet for a few days.

One last note: A hidden cost of losing weight is that you may need to replace some of your wardrobe, but this need not be costly. In fact, losing weight can be one of the best tightwad strategies to improve your wardrobe. The secondhand market has a much better supply of clothes for thin people, possibly because people get rid of clothes when they gain weight. Also, thin people almost always look good no matter what they wear. In contrast, some larger women compensate by spending more on hair, nails, and wardrobe. In my case, many of my clothes simply fit better. I had also kept many of my slim clothes, so my wardrobe actually expanded dramatically.

DO YOUR HOMEWORK

Dear Amy,

We saved thousands of dollars when we purchased our home by knowing what the previous owners had paid for it. I merely went to the county assessor's office and asked for the "green sheet." This was a copy of the tax information on the house, including the history of sales of the house. You can also ask for tax information on nearby addresses or similar houses to find out what is a reasonable selling price. Knowing what the current owners paid for it gave us the nerve to offer far less than the asking price. I'm sure we would never have gotten our house for the price we did without knowing this information.

—Debbie Huber
Danville, Illinois

FAMILY FREEBIES

Dear Amy,

Call area attractions you'd like to take your family to and ask if they have any "free to the public" events scheduled or regular "free admittance" times. Our local museums usually charge no admission on the first Monday after each new exhibit opens, and sometimes on school holidays. When my kids were little, the zoo was free on Monday morning before noon. It doesn't hurt to ask!

—Mary T. Graupman
Rochester, New York

EGGSTRA SAVINGS

Dear Amy,

Many people don't take full advantage when eggs go on sale because they don't know that eggs can be frozen. Lightly mix 1 cup of raw eggs (about five large ones) with 1 teaspoon salt and store in an airtight freezer container. Thaw overnight in refrigerator. Properly frozen, eggs will keep for up to six months. Three tablespoons of egg mixture approximates one large-sized egg. They taste good scrambled, in omelets, or in baking.

—Eileen Herman
Seattle, Washington

UNDERFOOT, UNDERPRICED

Dear Amy,

I bought a beautiful 100 percent wool oriental rug by asking a local rug cleaner if he had any that had never been picked up. I had several to choose from and paid only the cost of cleaning.

—Patricia Wyatt
Sunnyvale, California

CHEAPER CHECKUPS

Dear Amy,

I save $50 every other year by creatively scheduling "annual" dental checkups. My dental insurance requires that I pay nearly the entire cost of the first dental visit in any calendar year to satisfy a deductible. The cost of a second dental visit in a calendar year is covered (almost entirely) by insurance. My "annual" checkups are early January and late December of even years (1992, 1994, etc.). The dentist gets the same volume of visits, but I pay less out of my pocket.

—Bob Kastner
Niantic, Connecticut

RENTED, DENTED DEALS

Dear Amy,

Check rental stores for cosmetically damaged or otherwise unrentable items. From two different stores we bought two major-brand color TVs with remotes that work perfectly for $50 each. One had the adjustment-knobs door broken off, the other had a broken rabbit-ears antenna holder (easily fixed). Both were only about a year old. Rental shops frequently have cosmetically damaged or dirty items that they sell *cheap.* They also throw away many repairable or very dirty items. Check their Dumpsters or ask them to call you to unload freebies.

—Anthony K. Colbert
Fort Worth, Texas

SAY IT WITH CARDS

Dear Amy,

I hate using money for flowers when someone dies. Instead, I make up cards and mail one every one to two weeks for several weeks or months. This way, contact is maintained. I've had many people comment to me how much they looked forward to the cards during their time of adjustment.

—Mary Ann Weaver
Paw Paw, Michigan

STU-DENTAL DEAL

Dear Amy,

The local community college offers dental examination, cleaning, fluoride treatment, and X rays, all for $8. The students working on you are usually very thorough because they are being graded and must complete several cleanings in order to graduate.

—Ruth M. Kennedy
Lindenwold, New Jersey

DETERGENT SOLUTION

Dear Amy,

A way to save on dish soap: Fill a small spray bottle with a couple of teaspoons of dish soap and then fill with water. Use one or two squirts for washing. This works great for handwashing one or two items or filling a dirty pot to soak.

—Joan Lasche
Rochester, New York

MINT HINT

Dear Amy,

My husband used a leftover Christmas candy cane to stir his coffee. It gave the coffee a nice minty flavor. It would be good stirred in any hot drink. Then put it in a container for the next time.

—Linda Bukvic
Williamsburg, Ohio

EQUITY IN THE HOME

When we needed to do something about a window that had a broken glass and a rotted section of sash, Jim's first response was to price a new window. He discovered a replacement would cost $150. He decided to fabricate a new wooden-sash section and replace the glass himself.

That situation caused me to wonder why Jim's first inclination had been to entirely replace the window rather than repair the old one. When I asked him about it, he reminded me that while he would enjoy making the new wood section, he loathes glazing (applying putty to hold in a new pane). In fact, he hates it so much that on a few occasions, I later discovered, he had taken a whole sash with a broken pane to a glass-replacement center and paid an extra $5 to have the glazing done there.

Suddenly, I realized that the only reason window-glazing had been Jim's job was because, as a man, it was a skill he'd happened to pick up. I suggested that he teach me how to glaze, as it looked like something I would enjoy and do well. So Jim did a splendid job making a new wooden section from scrap lumber and I happily glazed the window.

Around this time, I happened to catch a talk show (I was sick with the flu) on which couples were squabbling over the allocation of housework. A situation common to two-income couples was presented: The wife did all the housework in the evening while the husband watched television. But another situation was presented in which a husband would come home from his full-time job and was expected to do the housework that his stay-at-home wife should have been able to complete.

Although suggestions were offered, none was as effective as the method Jim and I use. So I felt a discussion of gender roles, and how they relate to frugality, was in order.

Modern families have abandoned the traditional gender responsibilities . . . to some extent. This has usually been the result of changes in the traditional man-as-sole-breadwinner pattern, like dual-income families and stay-at-home dads. But it's still an area of some confusion that often results in poor use of time and therefore dependence on a whole range of expensive luxuries such as restaurant meals and hiring out for cleaning, lawn care, and simple carpentry.

First, let's tackle the allocation of chores on a day-to-day basis. Although it seems obvious to me, it's a solution that wasn't presented on that talk show. Very simply, each spouse must contribute the same number of hours each day to productive activities that directly contribute to the well-being

of the household. How you do this depends on the wage-earner structure of your family.

If your family has two full-time wage earners, and you work the same hours, each spouse must share in the housework during evenings and weekends until it's completed. If one spouse works just part-time, he or she must take on additional housework equal to the hours of extra work put in by the full-time spouse. By working during the same hours, it's easy to see that the share of the work is equal. If a wage earner works a night shift, then instead of working during the same hours each day, the spouses must agree to put in the same *number* of productive hours every day.

If your family has one wage earner, the stay-at-home spouse should expect to work an equal amount of time at home, from the time the wage earner leaves until he or she returns. Any remaining work, including giving kids baths and helping with homework, must be shared equally. During these nine or more hours, the stay-at-home spouse should be able to complete the basic housework and meal preparation, even with caring for young children.

I've been amazed at stay-at-home moms who claim that doing this much is nearly impossible. Few people have as many children as we have, have a larger house than we have, or take on as many do-it-yourself tasks as we do. As a former navy wife, I successfully tended to all the household needs of my family when Jim was away for months at a time, even when I had three preschoolers. Nowadays, we find basic housework (washing dishes, vacuuming, laundry, and so on) can be completed in half a day. Only then do we move on to less essential but still productive tasks, such as weeding the garden, volunteer work, sewing, writing letters, and spending quality time with our children.

If you are a stay-at-home spouse and your daily activities include chatting on the phone, reading romance novels, watching TV (without doing a productive activity simultaneously), etc., you shouldn't expect your spouse to share in the housework when he or she arrives home.

Now that Jim is the stay-at-home spouse, he does for me what I once did for him. It's rare that I come home and find that basic housework has not been completed. When I do come home to an enormous pile of unfolded laundry, I know that he has been busy doing other tasks we both agreed were of a high priority. In fact, we often strike a bargain in the morning: If he'll make wooden "treasure boxes" for kid-gifts, I'll fold laundry when I get home.

(After this article ran in my newsletter, a few readers objected to these points. Some argued that they didn't complete basic housework because they felt that spending their days giving their children most of their time was more important. In response, I would point out that if the wage earner must come home and do basic housework, he or she has less time to give to the children. Others argued that personal time for reading or chatting on the phone was essential in helping them survive the grueling reality of the stay-at-home role. In response, I would point out that being a stay-at-home parent is a *privilege* that many working parents desperately want but have yet to achieve. So, frankly, I have little patience for either sentiment.)

Second, aside from fairness, it's simply more efficient to allocate chores based on each individual's abilities and preferences rather than gender stereotypes.

But what often happens is that, even though we are in the 1990s, jobs still tend to be allocated by traditional gender roles. Frequently readers write to me: "We can't buy a fixer-upper because my husband isn't handy," or "We can't save on our food bill because my wife doesn't like to cook." But the majority of house-painting and renovation on our house has been done by women, either by me or by a crew of female carpenters. And since we've been married, Jim has done most of the grocery shopping and cooking. I've known women who could repair their own motorcycles and a man who taught himself to use a sewing machine because his wife just didn't have the knack for it.

So if your wife avoids a task she intensely dislikes, strike a deal. Teach her to change the oil in the car and have her teach you how to bake bread.

And as for the chores no one likes, a reader summed up the best advice: "You should each do what you like best, and split the rest." There are certain tasks that neither of us loves to do, such as cleaning bathrooms and washing dishes. We're each responsible for cleaning one of the two bathrooms, and we trade off washing the evening dishes.

If I had to list factors that contributed to the financial success of our family, somewhere near the top would be "teamwork."

WAR AND PEAS

Caroline Johnson of Garner, North Carolina, sent me a newspaper clipping that really caught my attention. It told of a single mother who was "struggling" to feed two sons, ages two and four. She worried that her $388 in food stamps wouldn't see her through the month, and her cupboards at home were bare.

This mother's inability to feed her family had several causes. But in reading the story, it was clear that this family's biggest problem was picky eating. The mother preferred sodas and salty snacks. And since she "hates to waste food," she bought microwavable dinosaur-shaped pasta and sugary cold cereals like Apple Jacks for her picky young sons, because they refused to eat cheaper or healthier foods.

Although this story was about a welfare recipient, picky eating occurs regardless of family income. It drives up your food bill, as you either throw away uneaten food or buy more expensive foods to accommodate the picky eater.

Many people regard overcoming picky eating as impossible. But food preferences are largely an acquired habit, and like all habits they can be molded for the better or worse. One of the major reasons our food bill is low is that we have conquered picky eating. We have instilled in our children the "habit" of eating (and, usually, enjoying) the food that is set before them. If you want to chop your food bill, you must conquer pickiness, too.

Picky eating often results from one or all of these parental mistakes:

- The child has not been given enough limits. He dictates what food is bought, and when and how it's served. He may not be required even to sit with the family at mealtimes. He is allowed to eat snacks shortly before or after meals, even when he didn't eat the meal.
- The child's eating has become the entire focus of the meal. The parents continually nag, threaten, or play "down-the-hatch" games. The child learns he has power to manipulate his parents' emotions by being picky.
- One or both parents are picky eaters. They often make negative remarks about meals, or about other foods they think are "disgusting." The child learns that disliking foods is normal. Because of the parents' limited preferences, the child isn't exposed to a variety of foods.

The solutions take a variety of forms, from gentle to firm.

Ellyn Satter, a registered dietitian and family therapist, authored a useful book on this topic called *How to Get Your Kid to Eat . . . But Not Too Much* (Bull Publishing, 1987). She espouses a common professional approach, which I would describe as gentle. If you do at least this much, you'll conquer most of the dinnertime problems.

Satter says that as parents you should choose what food is purchased and selected for meals, how it's prepared, and when it's served. *Never* prepare a special meal for a picky eater or allow an older child to do this for himself. *Never* plan meals around what you know he'll eat. The child must come to the table and sit through meals, but he decides which foods and how much he wants to eat. Whether he eats or not, don't allow him to eat again until the next meal or scheduled snack (which consists of nutritious foods also selected by you). Continue to put some foods on his plate he dislikes, but don't pressure him to eat.

I believe Satter's method can work, but it isn't the most economical way, because wasting food is an acceptable option. The child isn't required to finish his meal, including any seconds he requested. And when one child doesn't eat something, it can have a "domino effect" that magnifies the waste. For example, when Alec, my oldest child, expressed a dislike of mushrooms, his younger siblings also decided they didn't like mushrooms—before they even tried them.

Satter believes that if kids come to the table hungry and are allowed to choose, they'll discover peas are pretty good, sometime in the next ten minutes or ten years. Although I have occasionally observed this in children, I've also seen kids stubbornly hang on to an irrational dislike forever. They refuse to eat sliced beets but will eat julienne-cut beets. Sometimes they decide to dislike a previously liked food as a way to express individuality. Some foods just require practice to like.

Satter believes you should respect your child's individual preferences. I believe that this is like the many situations when your child can override his preference for the greater good of the family. By eating everything, he respects the parent's effort in preparing the meal, he adheres to the family's no-waste ethic, and he participates completely in a shared meal, which I believe contributes to family unity.

Satter believes that pressuring kids to eat generally produces pickier eaters. This has not been my experience.

So here's my "firm" method, which I suspect would never be approved by any modern professional. I agree with Satter until the point where she states that the child gets to choose what he'll eat at meals. We require our kids to clean their plates.

Most children eat well until they are two. Then their growth slows and they require less food. They also begin to challenge authority by not eating foods they already like. Until a kid seems mature enough for firmer measures, we only encourage finishing and put much less food on his plate than I think he'll eat.

When the child reaches two and a half, we begin transitioning him to an understanding that he must

clean his plate. I start by gently reminding the child to eat. Occasionally I may help by feeding him a few spoonfuls. Then he receives mild praise for finishing.

At some point he will simply refuse to eat, even though he hasn't eaten for several hours. I tell him he will be disciplined if he doesn't, and remind him of this a few times during the meal.

If, after everyone else has eaten and left the table, the child still refuses, he is disciplined. The key point here is that the child has been warned but has not controlled my attention throughout the meal. It's crucial to be 100 percent consistent in following through with discipline.

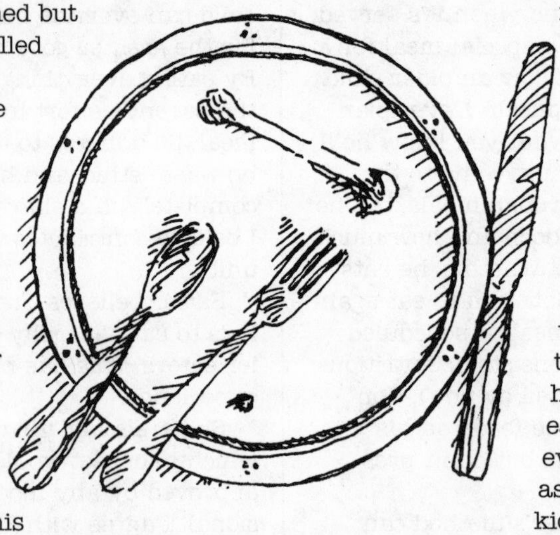

The form of discipline depends on the child's age, what is effective for this child, and what type of discipline is accepted in your home. Discipline can provide a choice for your child. If you tell an older child he can't watch TV for a week unless he eats the fish sticks, you've given him the options. In the rare case when the fish sticks will truly make him ill, he can opt not to eat, and you haven't caved in. But the right discipline is almost always effective.

With each of our six kids we had from one to six showdowns that led to discipline. Sometimes the episodes occurred over foods a three-year-old liked but decided not to eat that day. Other times they balked over certain foods they disliked. I respected their dislike by giving them very small portions, but they had to eat that portion.

Once kids accept that they must eat some foods they don't like, it's not traumatic. Without prodding, they valiantly work their way through the small portion as if it were any other undesired task I ask of them. Frequently this occurs as they continue to chat and laugh. In our home, we revere the ability to eat disliked foods just as we revere other skills. Later, I might hug a child and say, "You did a good job eating the turnip. I know it's not your favorite."

It doesn't work to have the child sit for hours until he eats. Small kids eventually fall asleep. Older kids miss their school bus. Pokey eating (chewing a bite of oatmeal for an hour) is treated the same as not eating.

Because it's a given that the kids will eat at mealtimes, we've found it isn't necessary to schedule snacks to ensure hunger at supper. We discourage snacking within an hour of the meal, and the kids must ask for permission, but I let them choose their snacks because almost all of the food in the house has nutritional value. I place limits only on juice and some more-expensive foods I'm saving for lunch boxes.

Kids, like parents, should not

make negative comments about foods. I resolved the previously mentioned mushroom problem by leaning toward Alec and whispering, "If you say one more bad thing about the mushrooms, I'm going to fish around in the casserole and find you a few more."

It's commonly believed that forcing kids to eat will cause obesity. In a telephone interview, Satter said she knew of no studies that confirmed this. I believe asking your kids to eat ¼ cup of peas when they haven't eaten during the previous two hours won't make them fat. My kids all tend to be lean—in the 90th percentile for height and 75th percentile for weight.

What are the results of each method? With Satter's method, she says school-age kids may still eat a limited number of foods. If you don't pressure them, they will gradually accept more.

With my method, all my kids eat 100 percent of the meals set before them without problems, and they like 95 percent of the foods offered. Neal, who once loathed asparagus, now "almost" loves it. Jamie's onetime dreaded food, bean soup, is now like any other to her. Many mealtime guests have watched in amazement as our children ate.

Parenting isn't an exact science. If my method doesn't work or feel comfortable for you, use Satter's method.

Is cracking down on picky eating mean? I consider it to be a tough-love kindness. The short period of discipline required to conquer this problem seems like a worthwhile tradeoff to gain 15 years of harmonious mealtimes.

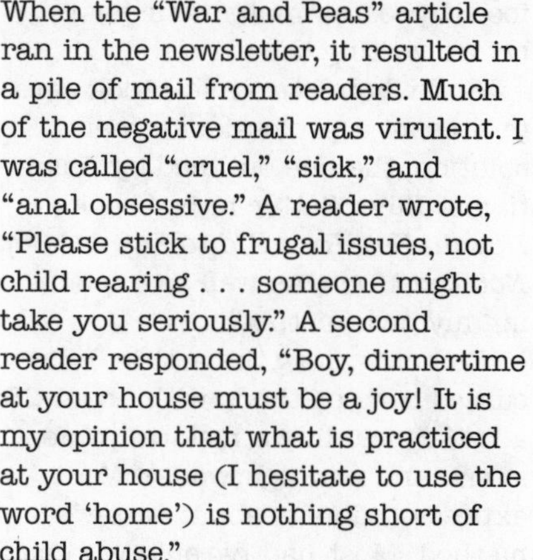

WAR AND PEAS UPDATE

When the "War and Peas" article ran in the newsletter, it resulted in a pile of mail from readers. Much of the negative mail was virulent. I was called "cruel," "sick," and "anal obsessive." A reader wrote, "Please stick to frugal issues, not child rearing . . . someone might take you seriously." A second reader responded, "Boy, dinnertime at your house must be a joy! It is my opinion that what is practiced at your house (I hesitate to use the word 'home') is nothing short of child abuse."

But the positive comments outnumbered the negative ones and were often just as charged with emotion. Readers said the article was "fabulous," "profound," and "the only way to go." Marlene Yanchus of Wilkes-Barre, Pennsylvania, wrote, "Bravo! Finally, a parent who doesn't take orders from children!" Karen Poulson of Los Angeles, California, said, "Everything we serve has a nutritional purpose. Just as we do not allow children to take medication at will, they may not choose what they eat at mealtimes." Vicki Robin, president of the New Road Map Foundation, a group that promotes frugality, wrote, "The latest issue is great. I continue to refer all people who are economic hostages of their children to you."

Obviously, people have differing—and very strong—opinions about what constitutes good parenting. Further, although my system was common a generation ago and works beautifully for my family, I know that it isn't generally accepted by modern child-rearing professionals. That's why, although I have always believed that picky

eating is one of the chief reasons that Americans spend too much on food, I procrastinated four years before writing the article.

And when I wrote it, I took care to present a professional, "gentle" solution, the one outlined by nutritionist Ellyn Satter in her book *How to Get Your Kid to Eat . . . But Not Too Much,* as well as explaining my own method.

Before writing the article, I discussed both methods with about 25 adults (including a medical professional and non-tightwads). Most expressed doubts about Satter's method. Most had parents who had used a clean-your-plate system, and/or they used it with their own kids. Only one objected strongly to my method. Had I presented Satter's method alone, I believe that *many* parents would have disputed the article.

Some readers suggested I was too compulsive in worrying about the cost of a small portion of peas. But picky eating often begins with small amounts wasted and can increase to where as much as one third of the food on the child's plate is wasted, even when the child is allowed to choose what's put on his plate. I know, because I have seen this. Parents often tell me that their food bills are out of control because their older children refuse to eat low-cost foods. They sigh and regret they weren't firmer when their kids were young.

It's also significant that in over 400 pages, Satter's book didn't devote a single sentence to the cost of wasting food. When I asked her about it, she indicated that she didn't feel it was an important issue.

While child abuse is a serious problem, I feel our culture has become so oversensitized to it that some have begun to use the term indiscriminately. I have, for example, been accused of "child abuse" because I dress my kids in yard-sale clothing. By my discussing discipline at the dinner table, people presumed that Jim and I do it constantly and that all of our mealtimes are tense and grim. But, as the article stated, I disciplined each kid an average of three meals. This means that from ages 3 to 18, each child will eat 16,422 meals in which he is not disciplined and food is not wasted.

Mealtimes in our house are *happy* times, precisely because the expectations are clear, and we are free to get beyond constant battles over food and talk and laugh together as a family.

A WHISKER'S DIFFERENCE

A newsletter reader from Bellevue, Washington, asks, "Have you ever done a study comparing electric razors versus shaving with a blade?"

No, but now's as good a time as any. All comparisons below are based on a man who shaves daily. Women (usually) shave less often and will have to adjust the figures accordingly. As you'll see, there are too many variables to give unequivocal guidelines.

Electric razors (priced at a discount department store in nearby Auburn, Maine) cost from $35 to $169, and, according to *Appliance* magazine, last an average of four years. A Norelco representative told me that the heads of their razors should be replaced annually, at a cost of about $25. Jim, who has a light beard, says he once had an electric razor that today would cost about $75. It died after six years and he never needed to replace the heads. So the annual cost of using an electric razor might be as high as $67.25, but Jim's annual cost was the equivalent of $12.50.

As for blade shaving, store-brand one-piece disposable razors cost $1.39 for 12. Used carefully, one razor can last a month, so this is a year's supply. Jim uses a $1.59 can of shaving gel each month. So his annual cost for blade shaving is $20.47, but this cost could be lowered.

Canned shaving cream is not the only option. David Sumner of Muncie, Indiana, wrote that he uses a free shaving mug (an old coffee cup) and a $5 brush. The shaving soap, he said, costs $1 per bar and lasts much longer than a can of shaving cream.

To this, I would add a couple of black-belt tightwad comments from my male staffers. First, you need not use special "shaving mug" soap. Any hunk of bath soap will work. And if you shower every day, you may not even need shaving cream at all. The purpose of the cream is to make whiskers wet and soft, but a hot shower has virtually the same effect. Immediately after showering, dry everything but your face and shave with no cream. You may be surprised at how well it works, particularly for men with light beards. And there is no annoying soap goop to rinse off.

Use a mug-and-brush and the annual blade-shaving cost drops to under $5.00. Use no shaving cream at all and the annual cost is $1.39.

So those in pursuit of all-out economy should probably opt for some variation of blade shaving. But given that the annual cost variation may be fairly small, and that men shave every day, I feel this matter should be left up to personal preferences.

TOYS FROM TRASH

The following is a collection of toys made from everyday objects.

Meat-tray blocks. Make building blocks from meat trays by cutting off the rounded edges, leaving only the flat part. Cut slits in the trays ¼-inch wide (or the thickness of the tray) and as deep as you want. Cut trays into circles, squares, and triangles. Kids can use these to build a variety of structures. (Sent in by Julie Lewis, Decatur, Arkansas.)

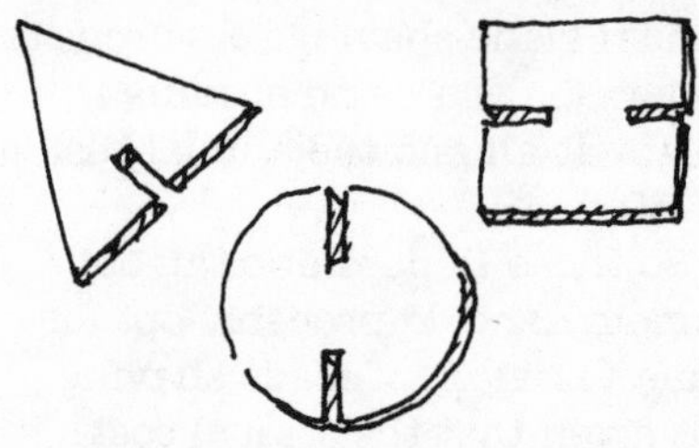

Hockey game. You need the bottom of a large box, markers, small round and flat objects such as checkers or poker chips, and small rulers. Draw on the playing lines and cut out two holes on the opposite sides of the box to make goals. Use the round object for a puck and rulers for hockey sticks. (Sent in by Susan Finley, Albuquerque, New Mexico.)

Box easel. Cut the corner off a sturdy, appropriately-sized box. To attach paper, use tape or push pins. (Sent in by Earlene Giglierano, Iowa City, Iowa.)

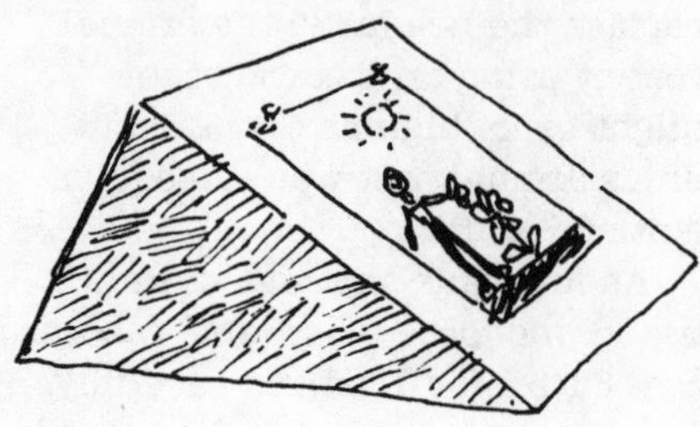

Pull toy. You need five large soda bottles, four washers, a piece of string, and a coat hanger. Remove the hard-plastic bottom from four bottles. Cut off the rounded inner bottom, turn it around, and reinsert it into the plastic bottoms (certain brands, like 7-Up and Pepsi, work best). Make four holes in remaining bottle and make holes in the four plastic bottoms. Cut the hanger to make two axles and assemble the pull toy. Put a washer on each end of the axles and bend the wire end so that the washer can't come off. Poke a hole through the cap, thread the string through it, and screw it back on the bottle. (Sent in by Ruth Palmer, Glendale, Utah.)

Ribbon dancer. Advertised on TV for $12.95, this can be easily made. Tape an 8-foot crepe-paper streamer (party leftovers work fine) to the end of a dowel or paper-towel tube and let the kid swirl it around as he/she dances. Can also be made using a paint stirrer and more than one streamer. (Sent in by Sharon Mitchell, Camillus, New York.)

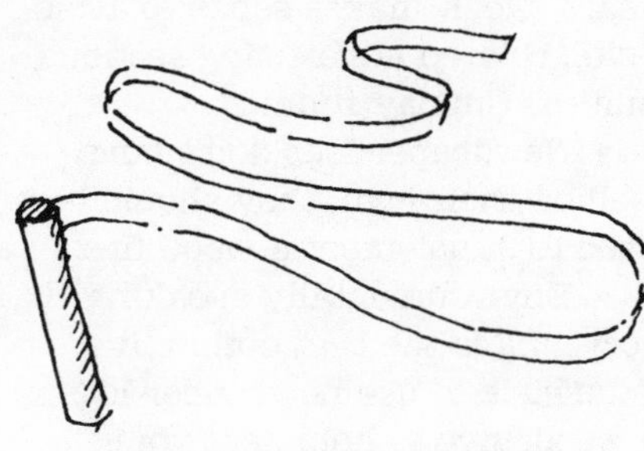

Skip it. Toy stores sell a version of this for $13.95. It helps a child count. To make one, you need a plastic coffee-can lid, masking tape, a tuna can, and 3 to 4 feet of twine. Cut away the inside of the plastic lid, leaving a hoop. Wrap the hoop with masking tape so that it won't chafe. Poke a hole in the bottom of the tuna can, knot one end of the twine, thread it through the hole in the tuna can, and tie the other end of the twine to the hoop. The child puts the hoop over her ankle, swings the can in a circle so she can skip it, and counts herself.

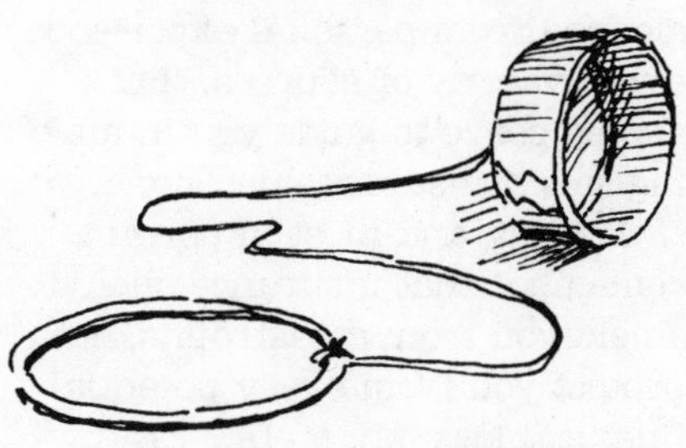

Flickers. Bread tabs can be used to make interesting projectiles. Break the tab as shown. Place tab on fingertip. Use your thumb to hold finger back as you flick the finger forward. The bread tab will sail surprisingly far—about 20 feet. The tabs work best on smaller fingers, so your ten-year-old may accomplish this better than you; and it does pinch a bit. Encourage kids to shoot at a target rather than at each other. These entertained the Dacyczyn children for hours.

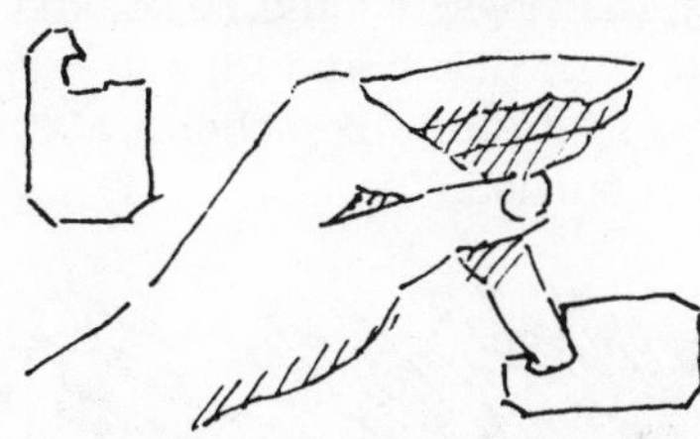

Giant loom. Back in the '60s, we made pot holders by weaving nylon-stocking loops on little square frames. The same idea can be enlarged. Cut a square frame from a piece of plywood, put finishing nails around the sides about ¼ inch apart, and weave loops cut

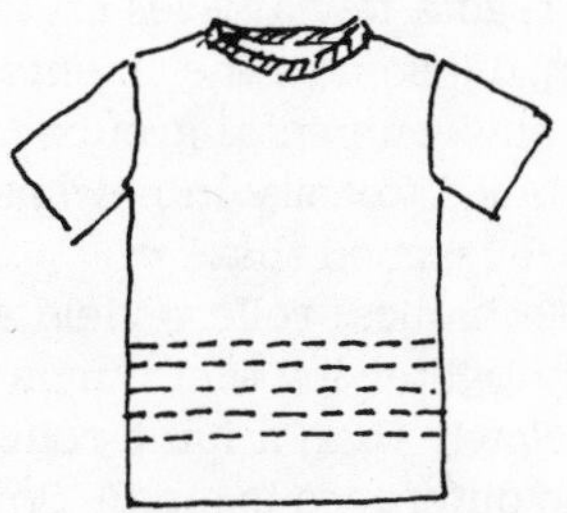

from the bodies of old T-shirts. The resulting squares can be used for placemats, chair seats, blocks for a rug, pillows, hot mats, etc. (Sent in by Lita Wallace, Boise, Idaho.)

HOT OFF THE PRESS

A frugal way to supplement a dwindling woodpile is using rolled-up newspapers as logs. A 10-inch-high bundle of newspapers can put out as much heat as 18 pounds of coal. But some people are discouraged from trying this, as they have heard or read that: The newspapers must be rolled on an expensive, mechanical roller; to burn properly, the "logs" should be soaked in water and dried; and inks in newsprint emit toxic chemicals when burned.

We read a few articles on this subject, did some experiments, and called environmental groups that had studied toxicity in newspaper inks. We learned that:

- Mechanical rollers yield a slightly tighter log that burns a bit more slowly than a hand-rolled log, but the difference is small. So just hand-roll a 2-inch-high stack of papers as tightly as possible. Secure with coat-hanger wire, which can be fished from the ashes and reused.
- Soaked logs take up to three months to dry, yet there's no appreciable difference in their burning quality compared to unsoaked logs.
- Though chemicals used in colored inks contain fewer toxic heavy metals than they did ten years ago, it makes sense to avoid using colored advertising sections and the Sunday funnies.
- Newspaper logs don't burn well on their own; they should be used to supplement a wood fire.
- Environmentally speaking, recycling is the best option. It's defensible to use newspaper logs in a woodstove to help heat your home, but newspapers should be recycled rather than burned in a heat-wasting fireplace.

INSURANCE PHILOSOPHY

Insurance is a complex subject. We've covered aspects of it in previous *Gazettes*, but thumbing through some huge books on insurance has persuaded me that we can never cover all of the specific ins and outs. Consequently, I thought it would be useful to write about insurance *philosophy*. So here are some general ideas, gleaned from personal experience and a variety of sources, that should serve to guide you in making smart insurance decisions.

1. First, and most important, remember that insurance should shield you from catastrophe, not protect you from every potential financial loss. My staffer Brad was chuckling the other day

because he bought a $19 calculator at a local store and the clerk tried to sell him a $6 service contract to go with it. (A good rule of thumb: *Never* buy a service contract.) If you try to insure everything to avoid going broke, you *will* go broke from the cost of insuring everything.

2. When it comes to areas of your life where insurance is essential, such as for your home or medical care, set the deductibles high. As in point number 1, your goal should not be to pay nothing in the event of misfortune, but simply to avoid unbearable financial pain. What "unbearable" means is an individual decision that each family must make. But keep in mind that the savings that come with high-deductible policies can quickly grow into a substantial emergency fund. Always have an agent quote you rates for a wide range of deductibles.

3. Comb through existing policies and cancel unnecessary coverage. In reviewing our auto insurance policy, I found that we were covered for the cost of a car rental in the event our car went in the shop. But we would never have used this because we have two personal vehicles and a business vehicle; and it's an expense we can afford, anyway. So we canceled this part of the insurance and saved a little money. Make sure you understand every provision in every policy.

4. Shop around. Price differences of over 100 percent for precisely the same coverage are common. You can compare rates on the phone, though Bob Millar, an independent agent we interviewed, pointed out that agents have considerable discretion in pricing policies, and in some cases can offer you a better rate if they meet you in person and get to know you. Don't forget to call independent agents; to some extent, they can do the comparing for you. But be aware that extremely low rates may indicate that a company is shaky and/or has a bad payout record. A reputable independent agent is probably the best source of information on the trustworthiness of a particular company.

5. Shop around again. Every few years, rates change, so you should do your phone survey at least once every three years.

6. Get discounts. Breaks on premiums are offered for all sorts of things: marriage, graduating from a driver's course, not smoking, having several policies with the same company, having antitheft devices in your car, and so on. Agents may not list these for you, so be sure to ask.

7. Think term. Unless you are wealthy, term life insurance is generally a better deal than whole-life. Whole-life combines insurance and tax-sheltered investing, and the investment component is usually a good deal only for those who are in the highest tax bracket *and* have already put the maximum allowed in other tax-sheltered retirement accounts. So most people should stick with term insurance, which is cheaper, and invest the surplus in other ways.

8. Change your insurance when your life changes. Once a car is over five years old, it often makes sense to drop collision and comprehensive coverage. As children leave home, your need for life insurance may decrease or vanish.

9. Don't rely solely on your agent's advice to save money. Even

good agents tend to overinsure tightwads, because they are accustomed to providing coverage for average, debt-ridden, on-the-financial-brink Americans, not disciplined people who have stashed substantial emergency funds. *You*, and not an agent, are in the best position to decide if your coverage is adequate.

MIDWIFERY: A BIRTH OPTION TO EXPLORE

Although I've written before on how to spend less on infant care, Andrea Sims of Providence, Rhode Island, suggested what could be the biggest baby-related saving strategy of all: having a certified nurse-midwife (CNM) handle the birth. Andrea writes, "Women's and Infants' Hospital in Providence, Rhode Island, estimates the hospital cost for a mother and baby attended by a CNM at $2,000. For a mother and baby attended by an obstetrician, the hospital estimates the cost at $3,400."

To learn more, I called the American College of Nurse-Midwives (ACNM) in Washington, D.C., and received a large packet of information. I also interviewed Deanne Williams, director of professional services for the ACNM, and Mary Gabay of Public Citizen, a consumer-research group.

A CNM is a registered nurse who has completed a graduate-level midwifery program and passed an examination administered by the ACNM. There are over 4,000 CNMs practicing throughout the United States, and in 1993 they attended nearly 5 percent of all U.S. births. They can provide the following: prenatal care, labor and delivery care, postpartum care, well-woman gynecology (including breast and pelvic examinations and Pap smears), normal newborn care, family planning, medication and/or vitamin prescriptions, preconception care, and health maintenance counseling. In general, they charge less for all of these services than an M.D. would. Service by CNMs is covered by most private insurance companies and by the federal CHAMPUS and FEHBP programs.

About 95 percent of CNM-attended births are in hospitals, where doctors are immediately available in case of complications. But some CNMs also attend home births. Like doctors, CNMs carry professional liability insurance.

Along with the financial advantages, many women prefer this alternative because they feel CNMs are generally more attentive and more oriented toward natural childbirth. A Public Citizen survey revealed that CNMs are much more likely to walk with laboring patients, give them fluids, and suggest alternative birthing positions than are OB/GYNs. I've had six kids with five different OB/GYNs, and in one case a midwife also happened to be present. Although my experience is just anecdotal, I agree that a few OB/GYNs were annoyingly inattentive, but the midwife seemed like an angel to me, offering a level of support that I had never experienced from an OB/GYN.

The study also found CNMs' success rate with vaginal births after a previous C-section is 68.9 percent, far better than the national rate of 24.9 percent.

Several studies have backed up the effectiveness of CNMs. An article in the *American Journal of Public Health* judged by birthweight and newborn-health-index scores that "mothers and babies have distinctly better outcomes when births are attended by midwives, either in or out of hospitals." In 1992, Kaiser Permanente, a California HMO, reported that CNMs managed 70 percent of the low-risk patients there and had lowered the C-section rate to 12 percent, compared to the national average of 23.5 percent. The success rates of CNMs may be at least partially due to their tendency to specialize in low-risk births, but Public Citizen's survey revealed that 87 percent of CNMs also comanage high-risk patients with obstetricians.

Williams told me that in England, where the infant mortality rate is lower than it is in the United States, the Royal College of Midwives has about 36,000 members, while there are only about 3,000 OB/GYNs. Midwives handle over 80 percent of births in England.

To find a CNM, look in the Yellow Pages under "Midwives," ask if one is associated with your local hospital or clinic, or call the ACNM at (202) 728-9860.

THE MATCH GAME

Ever since we moved to Maine seven years ago, I've wanted to get cross-country skis for our family. We need an outlet for exercise during the long winter months, and we are ideally situated, surrounded by countless acres of snowy woods and fields.

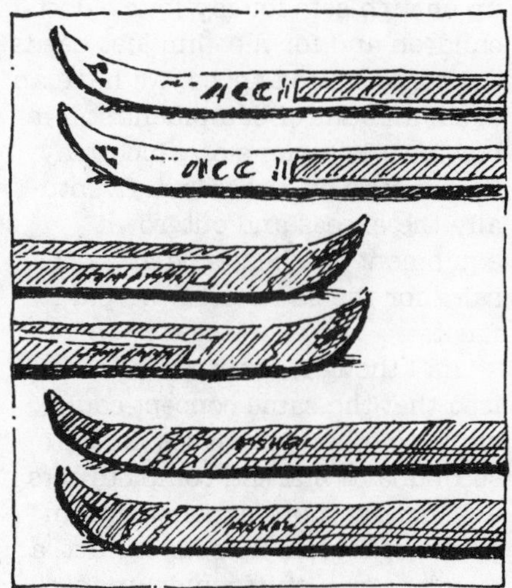

So I began to look for skis at yard sales. I found that the minimum price for a complete outfit (skis, shoes, and poles) was $25—cheaper than used-sporting-goods-store prices, but still much more than I wanted to pay. Sold individually, unmatched ski equipment was much cheaper, say, $1 for a pair of shoes. But the problem was that there are about three types of bindings. This, compounded with the need to buy for six family members, kept me from purchasing anything for fear I could never use it.

Finally, in the summer of 1995 it occurred to me that my approach to the problem was wrong—unmatched stuff was so cheap that

I could afford to take some risks. I began to buy *all* of the inexpensive unmatched equipment I found at yard sales (eventually I made an inventory to avoid buying duplicates).

By the end of the summer I had spent a total of $50. Then we began to look for matches, and to swap bindings from one ski to another when needed. We matched up enough sets for my four oldest children and for me. Jim just needs the correct-sized shoes. We have an equal amount of equipment still in our barn loft, some of which may fit someone at some time. Eventually the excess and outgrown equipment can be resold at yard sales for the same price we paid for it.

As I thought about this, I realized that the same concept could apply to other purchases. In the secondhand market, complete sets are usually more expensive than pieces of broken-up sets. In fact, a major reason stuff winds up in trash-pickable piles is that it is missing some part. But some risk-taking, hoarding, and imaginative combining can yield big savings.

Examples:

- Last summer, I trash-picked a small lampshade for which I did not have a lamp. An hour later I found a shadeless yard-sale wall lamp for 10¢. The combination made a perfect reading light over Alec's bed.
- People often don't buy an individual article of clothing because they don't have anything to match it. But if the item is cheap enough, it's worth the risk. If you don't buy the first item, you won't have anything to match the second item when it comes along.
- We often buy up makes of small appliances that are similar to the ones we have. For instance, we often see blender base-units without jars, and jars without base-units, at yard sales. We've found if we always buy items from the same maker, they'll match. We've replaced two jars, and recently replaced the base-unit.
- Children's games often have missing pieces. The game Mousetrap, for instance, is worthless if it lacks a single piece. You can get spare parts directly from the manufacturer. But if a game is very common, it's generally cheaper to buy a second game with missing pieces to make one whole game.

HEARTBREAKING HINT

Dear Amy,

I've found that chocolate candy in the shape of hearts, bunnies, pumpkins, etc. can be purchased after the holidays for up to 90 percent off. These are easily broken into chunks or melted down for use in recipes. Calculate the cost per ounce to be sure it is cheaper than buying baking chocolate.

—Nancy Melough
South Windsor, Connecticut

FIT FOR A QUEEN

Dear Amy,

After buying a "new" queen bed at an auction, I looked for bedding at garage sales. I found that you can use king-sized sheets and cut off enough to make two pillowcases.

—Barbara Janish
Scotland, South Dakota

BUT NOT THE *GAZETTE*!

Dear Amy,

I have a small business that requires me to ship my product. I bought a $70 shredder and now have all the packing material I'll ever need by shredding all of my unwanted mail, newspapers, and catalogs.

—Susan Stone
Los Lunas, New Mexico

A WORD ABOUT CURDS

Dear Amy,

Your yogurt article (see page 140) mentions "yogurt cheese" made by draining yogurt in a coffee filter or a cloth-lined colander. I've found that a pinch of salt stirred in before draining greatly improves the flavor. Also, the liquid that drains out is whey, which is very nutritious. I've used whey instead of milk as the liquid in muffins and other baked goods.

—Karen Lee
University City, Missouri

FROM DOGS TO HOGS

Dear Amy,

My kids love "Pigs in a Blanket." I stir up half a batch of biscuits, roll them out, cut them into thin strips, and wrap the strips around hot dogs. Half a batch is enough for a package of ten hot dogs. I bake them at 400 degrees for 12 to 15 minutes.

—Jeannette Kiper
Forest, Ohio

ZAP DOGS

Dear Amy,

Instead of dog treats, microwave hot dogs sliced into small pieces until you have little shriveled treats. Freeze in Ziploc bags and use for rewards, training, etc. An animal trainer told me these are more nutritious than commercial treats, cheaper, and dogs love them!

—Karen Yochim
Sarasota, Florida

BEYOND THE PALE

Dear Amy,

Last year we bought a $20 gallon of paint for $2 at a yard sale. It was very light blue. Our local paint store colored it for us to a lovely dark gray, at no charge. The man there said that if the paint is light in color, he could tint it to almost any color we wanted.

—Lynda F. Ward
Searsport, Maine

(Your paint store may not provide free tinting, or may refuse to do it to paints they don't sell. Check this out before stocking up on yard-sale paint. FZ)

BUDGET BRIDGE

Dear Amy,

We have a 30-foot-wide creek and needed a "cheap," very sturdy bridge. The city was widening a street about two miles from our home and I noticed that they were putting in new power-line poles. I called the electric company, and they gave the old poles to us free and even delivered them free. We used cheap landscape timbers for the deck of the bridge.

—Linda Fiedler
Arlington, Texas

A DYE TO TRY

Dear Amy,

My daughter and I came up with a new twist for your home-made play-dough recipe [given in the first *Tightwad Gazette* book]. We were low on food coloring, so we used Kool-Aid instead. It is spectacular. It makes a great color, and it is the best-smelling play-dough we've ever had. We used three packages per batch of dough. You can add it to the dry ingredients, or to the liquid before mixing.

—Patty Wheeler
Waverly, New York

DON'T DESPAIR, REPAIR

Dear Amy,

I recently spilled bleach on a favorite black shirt. I took some black fabric paint and rubbed it on the spot. This covered it perfectly. You can also salvage yard-sale and hopelessly stained kids' clothes the same way. This works best if rubbed in rather than brushed on. I got the paints on sale for 49¢ for 2 ounces. Only a few drops are needed for each repair.

—Cynthia Linkous
Amherst, Ohio

THE CITY TIGHTWAD AND THE COUNTRY TIGHTWAD

Recently, I was amused by a suggestion that I write a "city" version of the *Gazette* to complement the current "country" version. While the specific suggestion was new, this sentiment has been expressed before. I'm often seen as a "rural tightwad," someone who saved all her money by gardening, canning, and squirreling away bulk-purchases in a large house and a big barn.

The truth is that although I grew up in rural areas, I've lived most of my adult life in cities and suburbs. I went to art school in Boston, and I lived in either Boston or neighboring Cambridge until I was nearly 30. Then Jim and I lived in suburban areas of Virginia and Maine. We moved to the country when we bought our current home in 1989.

None of the money we saved to buy our house was saved when we lived in the country. This is important to understand. Many people have said to me, "Gee, I try to be frugal, but it's harder because I live in the city." But frugality is not necessarily easier in the country, the city, or the suburbs. Each setting has advantages and disadvan-

tages. To save money, you must exploit the advantages and minimize the disadvantages.

Living in a city has numerous pluses for tightwads, including:

• Cheaper transportation. Mass transit, and being within walking or biking distance of many amenities, make it possible to get by with one or even no cars. Even if you choose to own a car, it does not have to be a top-notch, reliable one, because you aren't so dependent upon it. However, if you do own a car, it will cost you more to park and insure it.

• More resources for cheaper goods. A downside of living in Maine is that there are only two major supermarket chains here, and real price wars are unknown. Conversely, where my father-in-law lives in Massachusetts, a half-dozen grocery chains compete for a slice of the market. Stores there typically slash prices and offer double and occasionally even triple-coupon sales. This can hold true for other consumer goods. For instance, there are literally hundreds of consignment and thrift shops in the Philadelphia area; so many that there's actually a guidebook devoted to them. In contrast, there are only about five such shops within a 30-minute radius of my home. I've found that everything from gas to consumer electronics is cheaper in cities.

• More cheap housing options—if you're flexible. Single people and couples without kids who are willing to live in small spaces and/or less-desirable neighborhoods can have very low housing costs in the city. Singles, in particular, can exploit the phenomenon of "group houses" and live in relatively elegant—albeit crowded—homes for minimal rent. Studio apartments are roomy enough for two-career couples before kids come along. Few people would opt for these living arrangements permanently, but the city does offer more of these short-term, low-cost housing options than can be found in the suburbs or the country.

• Better trash. A resourceful New Yorker can furnish an entire apartment from stuff that has been discarded. A San Francisco antique dealer told me that her best supplier was a trash-picker. Trash disposal in cities is expensive and inconvenient. This leads urbanites to leave good stuff out on the curb.

• Free cultural entertainment. The Washington, D.C., area is perhaps the best example, with several gigantic, free Smithsonian museums that would require years to fully explore. But most cities offer at least some free or inexpensive entertainment: free outdoor concerts, free days at the children's museums, street entertainers, and large libraries with a variety of programs and offerings.

The country offers different advantages:

• The ability to garden. This can lower food bills, though even in the case of our family of eight, gardening saves us only about $500 a year. We also have greater access to pick-your-own orchards and farms.

• Cheaper family-type housing and cheaper land. Our house and barn on seven acres cost $125,000 in 1989. Though it was a great deal, even for here, a comparable property near a large city could cost well over $250,000. And housing in rural Maine is very expensive compared to some other rural areas. In the Midwest, in particular, country ranch houses go for as little as $30,000.

• More utility options. Building a solar home, or heating with wood that you cut and haul yourself, can dramatically lower heating costs. Similarly, a well and septic system can cost less in the long run than city water and sewer service . . . *if* the systems are maintained properly.

• The ability to stockpile. Food, clothing, lumber, and furniture that are purchased cheaply can be set aside for later. I stockpiled when we lived in city apartments, but I can definitely store much more now.

• More lifestyle freedom. Theoretically, cities are bastions of tolerance and individuality. But my experience is that practicing black-belt frugality has been easier since we moved here, because our family is more isolated. If my kids lived in the city or suburbs, I think the fact that they never eat junk food, aren't swamped with toys, and don't own a Nintendo would seem odder and less comfortable to them than it does in the private world we have here. Although they see junk food in school, they are not confronted by material excess once they come home.

What about the suburbs? The 'burbs combine both the advantages and disadvantages of city and country life, but they do have some frugal advantages all their own:

• Better schools. Inner-city schools are often so poor that parents who can afford it tend to send their kids to private schools. Schools in the country can be either good or bad, depending on the particular district. We have been happy with our school, but also know that the incidence of parents resorting to home-schooling in other rural Maine communities (indicating a dissatisfaction with public schools) is significantly higher than it is in our district. While there are certainly exceptions, suburbs generally have the best public schools.

• Access to yard sales. When Jim and I lived in the city, we never encountered yard sales, so they were not part of our saving strategy. Now that we live so far out in the country, going to yard sales requires conscious effort and a lot of driving. However, when I lived in the suburbs I could find more than enough yard sales within a few blocks.

• Low cost of keeping a car in combination with many resources. While there are many resources in the heart of larger cities, it can be inconvenient to get to them if you are relying on public transportation. In the country, while we have cars, it is often inconvenient to drive far to get to the resources.

• Carpooling. This is generally a suburbs-to-city phenomenon, as it's unlikely that two country people would work for the same employer on the same shift. So though many ruralites commute over an hour to a good-paying job, I know of just one man in my area who carpools.

One last point: Despite all of these dissimilar advantages, frugal behavior generally should not change depending on your location. City, suburban, and country people should all cook from scratch, negotiate, sew, cooperate, buy used, cut their children's hair, "do-it-yourself," and so on. Most *Gazette* articles apply no matter where you live . . . which is why I have no plans to start a "city" edition.

ADVICE OVER AIRWAVES

When a friend's car began making a chicken-bone-in-a-garbage-disposal noise and lost 90 percent of its power, he was in a quandary. The car had 166,000 miles on it, a slow brake-fluid leak, and a fair amount of rust, so it seemed likely that this engine problem spelled the car's demise. There was a small chance that it would be cost-effective to fix it, but if he took it to a mechanic, he'd have to pay for a diagnosis of the problem; chances are, all he would learn was that it should be junked.

Then inspiration hit. The success of the National Public Radio show "Car Talk" has spurred the creation of local versions. Sure enough, each weekend, a local radio show called "Auto Answers" is hosted by one of the top mechanics in Portland, Maine. My friend called the host and together they figured that the problem was a blown valve-cover gasket. My friend spent $300 to get it fixed, and has since put another 20,000 miles on the car.

Reader Nancy Dietz and her husband have extended this concept into other realms. Not only do they call the auto repair show in Baltimore, Maryland, they also regularly quiz the host of their local "Garden Club" radio show.

In fact, as Nancy writes, "for over a year now, we have been taping the gardening program each Saturday. During the week, I type up notes from the show on our computer in alphabetical form, from 'Acid Soil' to 'Zoysia Grass.' There are now over 70 pages in the computer that my husband and I can refer to. I feel as if I'm getting a degree in horticulture at no cost!"

Aside from cars and gardening, common themes for local call-in shows include home repair, medical treatment, pet care, and investments. Such programs are usually on "all-talk" AM radio stations. For a listing,

check your Sunday newspaper or call the station directly. While you can get advice free from other sources, radio shows are unique in that, generally, the hosts are not trying to sell you something. And don't worry about getting through. Unlike national shows, local shows are generally desperate for callers, and a line is usually open.

CHECK UP ON CHARITIES

Kim Strom of Coeur d'Alene, Idaho, asks, "What are your thoughts on large charitable organizations such as CARE, Children's Defense Fund, St. Jude's Hospital, etc? Is there any way to find out who gets the most value for my dollar?"

Kim's question applies not only to big charities like the ones she lists, but to any organization or person that accepts donations. It's a real dilemma for tightwads. While frugality will naturally create surplus funds, and most of us understand the moral obligation to give, will the recipients of our money use it as wisely as we would? It's a question with which I personally wrestle.

Here are some of the methods that Jim and I use to ensure the money we give is put to the best use:

• Never give to a person or organization you don't know. Early in my urban life, a clean-cut young man approached me with a convincing story about how he had just run out of gas and had no money. I believed him but was carrying almost no cash. The following day, not recognizing me, he approached me again with the exact same story. I also worked in an inner-city convenience store and recall selling to some panhandlers who were carrying serious amounts of cash. Following these experiences, I never again gave money to strangers, no matter how honest or down-and-out they appeared.

Similarly, there are many fake charitable organizations that use names similar to those of legitimate organizations, and that use telemarketing techniques and door-to-door sales pitches to raise money.

So play it safe. If you want to help a street person, give directly to a shelter. If you give to an organization, check it out first. Get material, in writing, that satisfies you before you give. Make checks out to organizations, not to individuals, and mail the check in. Don't give out your credit card numbers to strangers. Don't make commitments over the phone.

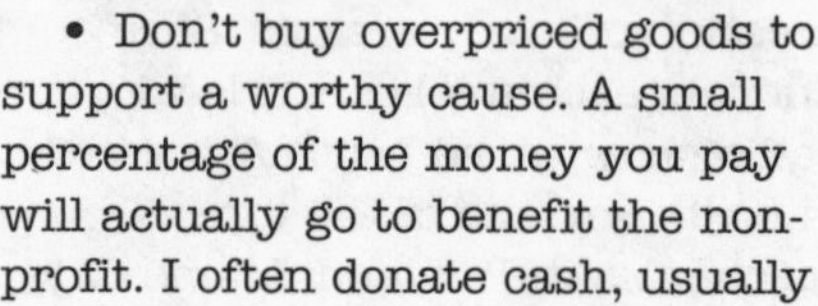

• Don't buy overpriced goods to support a worthy cause. A small percentage of the money you pay will actually go to benefit the nonprofit. I often donate cash, usually

a smaller amount than the cost of the item being sold, directly to the organization.

• Give to local organizations. You are more likely to know the work of the specific organization and/or personally know the individuals who run it.

• Give directly to people you know personally. In my case, I prefer to help elderly individuals, because regardless of financial mistakes they might have made in the past, they are often unable to change their current circumstances. In contrast, I rarely encounter "needy" young people who are doing everything possible to improve their current situations.

Giving to people you know personally can be tricky. In one case, I learned of a specific need in my community and made arrangements with a local organization to operate as a go-between so that the recipient would not know that the help came from an individual.

• Give something other than cash. I always save my deposit bottles for Scouts and other organizations conducting bottle drives. I give baked goods and other items to local fund-raiser auctions. While I could sell outgrown clothing at yard sales, I prefer to donate ours to our church's clothing center, which resells it at yard-sale prices. High school auto shops need used cars (this can be a smart option when a car is worn out and unsellable; most school auto shops will provide you with a form that allows you to take a tax deduction for the car's fair value). Also remember to give of your time. Meals on Wheels needs drivers, Habitat for Humanity needs builders, and schools need classroom and field-trip helpers.

• When giving to large organizations, check them out first. The leading evaluator of national and international charities is the National Charities Information Bureau.

Dan Langen, NCIB's director of public information, told me that his organization, which has been in operation since 1918, collects information on over 400 charities. The NCIB evaluates many factors, including the charity's specific purpose, the makeup of its board of directors, and the percentage of contributions that actually goes to programs rather than to fund-raising or administration. (NCIB says at least 60 percent of funds should go directly to programs.)

All of the information is distilled into the NCIB's *Wise Giving Guide.* I received a copy of the winter 1995–96 issue and found it quite impressive. It contains a listing of 200 charities that meet all nine of the NCIB's standards for quality. The current copy of the guide is available free on request from NCIB, 19 Union Square West, New York, NY 10003, (212) 929-6300. The NCIB is now also on the World Wide Web at http://www.give.org.

Another source of information on large charities is the Philanthropic Advisory Service of the Council of Better Business Bureaus, 4200 Wilson Boulevard, Arlington, VA 22203. The group's website is http://www.bbb.org/bbb. Its publication *Give, But Give Wisely* is free with a self-addressed stamped envelope.

A final point: I have come to understand that almost no individual or group uses money as carefully or efficiently as I do. If I held everyone up to my own frugal standards, I might never give any

money. Further, there's a limit to how much I can find out about how my contribution will be used. Ultimately, for a tightwad to make a contribution, there comes a time when he or she must simply swallow hard, sign the check, and hope for the best.

ECONOMIC RE-PRESSION

Dear Amy,

Pressed powder compacts often fall apart before they are half used. I salvage them by breaking up the remaining chunks, adding a small amount of rubbing alcohol, and mixing to a paste. As the alcohol dries, a solid cake forms again. The drying takes a few hours, but hands-on time is only a couple of minutes.

—Kathy Kritzberg
Santa Cruz, California

TIGHTWADS IN TAFFETA

Dear Amy,

A local high school recently held a consignment sale for prom dresses. For every dress sold, $25 went to the donor and $5 was kept by the school for the prom fund. It was a great way for people to get money for used dresses, and it was a bargain for the buyers.

—Laura Schenk
Newton Lower Falls,
Massachusetts

SALING WITH THE RICH

Dear Amy,

My yard-sale secret is to hit the sales in expensive neighborhoods. These people rarely go to yard sales themselves, which means they are not always aware of yard-sale prices. Sometimes, the prices are very high, but I offer less and say, "I usually see these for $2 at yard sales." More often, they assume yard-sale prices are even lower than they actually are (or they don't care) and I find wonderful bargains.

—Kathleen Clary-Cooke
Centerville, Oklahoma

LOSERS TAKE ALL

Dear Amy,

A group of friends has found a frugal and fun alternative to expensive weight-loss clinics. The "Chubby Buddies" meet once a week, not just to weigh in but to share our mutual experience. Everyone puts a dollar in the "piggy" bank and the buddy that loses the most weight takes it home at the end of the month. The $25 prize may not be the lottery jackpot, but it sure is fun.

—Sarah Severns
Kensington, Ohio

BUDGET BABY BYPASS

Dear Amy,

A Cooperative Method of Natural Birth Control by Margaret Nofziger [Book Publishing Co., 1991] is a short, well-written book explaining how to use fertility awareness to avoid pregnancy. I've found the method easy and empowering. I found the book in the public library, so the only cost is the price of a basal body thermometer (about $7).

—Eve Abraham
Columbia, Maryland

SHOWER POWER

Dear Amy,

Instead of buying distilled water (which protects against mineral buildups) for my iron, I collect rainwater and it serves the same purpose.

—Lori Buckley
Grayslake, Illinois

PAGES FOR PENNIES

Dear Amy,

Library sales are a huge help to my family's home-schooling budget. This fall we are studying composers, art history, and American history. We selected books on these subjects and took home a shopping cart full of literature, much of it priced at 25¢ per book.

—Diane Gasaway
Troy, Ohio

ORANGE YOU THRILLED?

Dear Amy,

I love orange marmalade but don't have the patience to follow usual recipes. So I cut up an orange with the skin on and place it in the blender with about 1 tablespoon water. After blending, pour into a pan along with ½ cup sugar and boil for 15 minutes. Cool and refrigerate. Keeps for several weeks.

—Lois Venzke
Streamwood, Illinois

(If possible, use an organic orange for this recipe. Otherwise, be sure to scrub the orange peel thoroughly. FZ)

PERM YOUR PRESENTS

Dear Amy,

If you cut strips of wrapping paper, you can curl it with the edge of a pair of scissors, just like ribbon. Be careful, as it tears if you're too rough. This is a gorgeous topping for a gift.

—Sheri Youngquist
Newark, California

MOM TARTS

Dear Amy,

Here's a quick homemade "toaster pastry" recipe that's better and cheaper than store-bought. Make a pie crust. Roll it out flat on a cookie sheet. Score with a knife into squares. Bake until almost done. Spread with jelly or preserves. Bake about three minutes longer. Top some squares with other squares, jam-sides touching. Yum!

—Mary Swerens
Dunkirk, New York

PARSIMONIOUS P.S.

Dear Amy,

When I start a letter to my son, I leave it out on the kitchen table. I encourage my daughter, younger son, and husband to each add a paragraph. If a grandmother or aunt stops by, I have them add a note. It keeps our son up to date with all his favorite people and all for the price of one postage stamp.

—Lynda F. Ward
Searsport, Maine

E-MAIL BONDING

Dear Amy,

Many people are using E-mail these days. They communicate through computers via Prodigy, America Online, or even free networks. We know people all over the country and exchange Christmas cards each year. This year, we are having a rubber stamp made up with our computer address on it, which we'll use to stamp each Christmas card. This will allow those who are "on-line" to send us E-mail anytime they wish. This will save a lot of money on phone calls and it is quicker than the mail.

—George W. Hadley
Lincoln, Rhode Island

SAVING LACE

Dear Amy,

When we get used little-children's shoes, they almost always need new shoelaces. I've not been able to find shoelaces for little shoes, so I take a long, flat nylon lace, cut it in half with a diagonal cut, and then melt the end with a match or candle flame. This makes it pointed, so it goes through the holes.

—Mrs. Wendell Filbrun
Hamilton, Ohio

SAVING SOFTLY

Dear Amy,

We live in a high-altitude area of North Carolina. We have a great deal of rain. The dehumidifier runs almost constantly. Our washer is close by. We empty the water collected into our washer. It's nice soft water in which to do your laundry.

—Shirley W. Craft
Sapphire, North Carolina

A PROCLIVITY FOR PRODUCTIVITY

Imagine you're on a tropic isle. Sipping a "Coco Loco," you recline on a beach chair and watch the gulls lazily wheeling overhead. The azure sea, warm as bathwater, laps at your toes. There is absolutely nothing to do, day after day, but relax on this white-sand beach. Sure, it has cost you a bundle, but you are living out the fantasy that's promoted in dozens of travel ads.

There's only one problem. You don't get it. "What," you wonder, "is the big deal?"

The scene described above actually happened to me. When I was in my early 20s, I visited the Caribbean island of St. Thomas. I saw sun worshippers similarly reclining and inert and simply could not fathom the attraction of it.

To live a successful, frugal life, you should develop a very critical attitude toward what seems to be our new, national goal: lying around doing nothing. Being busy, being productive, doing things that improve your family's long-term prospects should not be seen as drudgery to be endured until you reach the cherished goal of utter inactivity. The happiest and most successful people I know have realized a crucial truth: The *act* of doing things is more fun than doing nothing. If this is not your current attitude, you should work to acquire it.

If an efficiency expert followed Jim and me around for a day, he would find that most of our time is filled with productive activity: making pies, refinishing furniture, painting bedrooms, sorting clothes, yard-saling, cutting hair, and so on. We enjoy the fact that each of these tasks helps us financially; but there is also a satisfaction that comes from being absorbed in the task itself.

Wise people throughout the world have long understood this. Playwright George Bernard Shaw said, "The secret of being miserable is to have the leisure to bother about whether you are happy or not." Former British prime minister Margaret Thatcher said, "Look at a day when you are supremely satisfied at the end. It's not a day when you lounge around doing nothing; it's when you've had everything to do and you've done it."

Similarly, in stories in *People* magazine and *60 Minutes*, gracious-living guru Martha Stewart said that she doesn't enjoy nonproductive activities such as playing games and sailing. She washes her car or does a craft for fun. We can debate the relative usefulness of covering lampshades with moss,

but the point is that Martha Stewart is a professionally successful person, and preferring productivity over leisure is a hallmark of successful people.

If you remain unconvinced—if your dream is still to loll endlessly on Aruba's sands—it may be because you have approached your work or chores around the house incorrectly. Here are some keys to enjoying a life of productive activity:

• Plan. One reason people find their activities unrewarding is that they are nagged by the notion that they are doing the wrong thing. They can't concentrate on painting the hall because they feel they should be canning beans.

Scott and Helen Nearing, the famous New England homesteaders, began each day by surveying the weather to determine if they should work indoors or outdoors. Then they made a precise schedule of the day's activities. Similarly, before we go to bed each night, Jim and I each decide what we are going to do tomorrow. Secure in the knowledge that we are doing the right thing at the right time, we are able to concentrate on it. (Incidentally, if the beans are ripe, can them now and paint the hall later.)

• Understand your own clock. Mike Harper, a management consultant and author of the book *Hope Is Not a Method,* points out that people's internal clocks differ, and their energy peaks at different times. Morning people should tackle their most daunting tasks early in the day; afternoon people should begin with simpler chores.

• Do what you like to do. As I pointed out in "Equity in the Home" (see page 238), as much as possible Jim and I divide up chores on the basis of what each of us prefers to do. Jim likes to cook, can, and garden. I like to refinish furniture, paint, and tackle big cleaning tasks. We split the chores that neither of us enjoys.

• Involve the family. Increasingly, "quality time" with kids is seen as doing what the kids want to do: playing video games, cruising the mall, etc. But quality time can just as easily be centered around productive tasks. Our kids make baked goods, pick strawberries, and help with painting. Involving kids in household chores can be fun, teaches them responsibility, (usually) increases the amount of work that gets done, and imparts skills that they will need to get along on their own. Above all, it gives kids the right attitude about productive activity. Those who learned the pleasure of productivity as children tend to go on to be productive, happy adults.

• Do it well. If you resolve to do a task to the best of your ability, you will find that you enjoy it more. This is true even when doing something well requires more time. For example, replacing a zipper on a jacket is a time-consuming challenge for any seamstress. Some hope the task will go quickly so they can move on to "fun" activities; when the job takes longer than planned they become frustrated. I approach the same task knowing that it will be time-consuming and that each seam may not come out right the first time. But ultimately, it's satisfying to replace a zipper and have it look as good and function as well as the original.

• Reflect on the basis of happiness. In his 1951 book *How to Stop Worrying and Start Living,* Dale Carnegie lists many cases of people who pulled themselves out of despair simply by being productive. For example, he tells of a man who lost two daughters to disease and saved himself from insanity by going from room to room in his house and compiling a list of 242 items that needed attention; everything from broken storm windows to leaky faucets. He spent over two years fixing them one by one, and he also joined the school board, attended adult-education classes, and collected money for the Red Cross. "I am so busy now," he said, "I have no time for worry."

All of this is not to imply that tightwads should never goof off. But I have found that a distinguishing characteristic of successful frugal people is that they tire rather quickly of nonproductive activities and long to do something that shows concrete results. If you follow the recommendations listed above, you should find your definition of "fun" expanding to include activities that provide you and your family with long-term benefits.

You may not go as far as I would, but if you at least see some sense in the following statement, you are on the right track: I would—honestly—rather scrape paint off my barn than lounge around on a Caribbean beach.

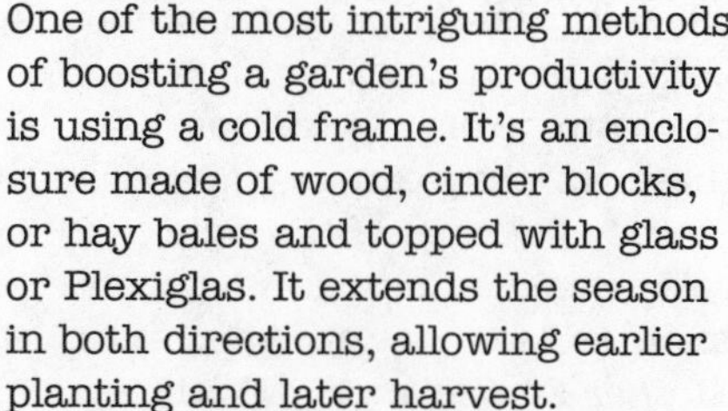

GARDEN-FRESH YEAR-ROUND

One of the most intriguing methods of boosting a garden's productivity is using a cold frame. It's an enclosure made of wood, cinder blocks, or hay bales and topped with glass or Plexiglas. It extends the season in both directions, allowing earlier planting and later harvest.

Until recently, I had thought of cold frames as aids to extending the spring seed-starting season. But Eliot Coleman's book *Four-Season Harvest* (Chelsea Green, 1992) points out that the real advantage of cold frames comes in the fall. He writes, "Only the harvest season, not the growing season, needs to be extended."

The distinction is important because extending the growing season more than a month or two is a difficult technological feat, while extending the harvest season through the whole winter is easy with a cold frame; it simply protects plants in their dormant state. In Harborside, Maine, where lows can hit minus 20 degrees, Coleman harvests 18 kinds of vegetables from his cold frames up until spring.

The cold frame is among the simplest handyman projects. Don't use costly, kiln-dried lumber. Lacking large pieces of used lumber, my staffer Brad built three cold frames from rough-sawn, green, 2-inch-by-10-inch hemlock he bought at a local sawmill for about one third the price of equivalent kiln-dried lumber. He used 3-inch screws for assembly; three at each corner. He avoided having to cut tricky bevels by assembling the frame upside-down on a flat sur-

face. When flipped right side up, the uneven edges are on the underside and are buried in the soil when in use. Coleman recommends nailing 1-inch-thick scrap pieces to the bottoms of cold frames; as these rot, they can be replaced.

The challenge of the tightwad cold frame is finding inexpensive materials for the top. Articles in *Mother Earth News* and other publications blithely recommend "old storm windows." These may work in some climates, but around here the weight of snow tends to break them. Further, storm windows don't shed water properly; it pools around the crosspieces. If you are very lucky, you may be able to find used tempered glass (such as from a salvaged sliding-glass door) or Plexiglas for a reasonable price.

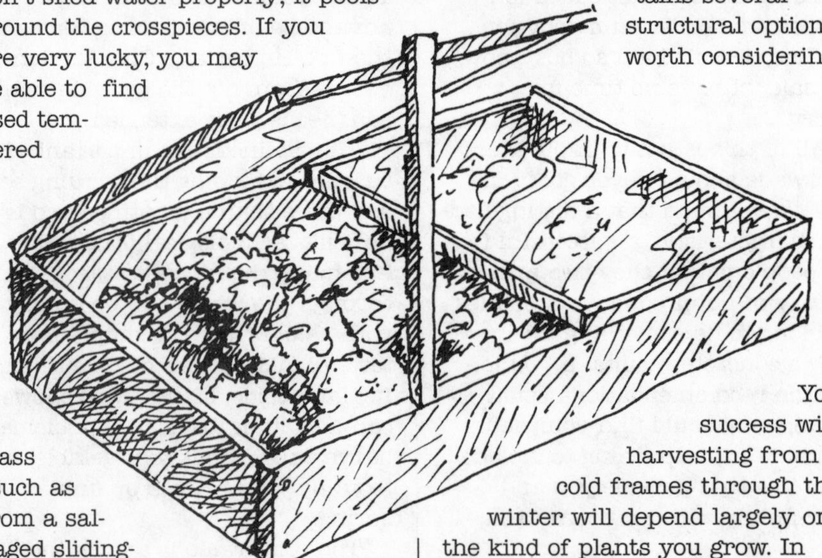

Probably the best choice among new materials is a space-age transparent polycarbonate called Polygal. It seems expensive—the best price we could get is $1.85 a square foot. But this is only one third the price of new tempered glass (which is what Coleman uses). Further, it is guaranteed to lose less than 6 percent of its transparency in ten years, and it is 200 times more impact-resistant than regular glass. Its double-layered, air-channel construction means it has about twice the insulating ability of regular glass. To find a distributor in your area, call (800) 537-0095.

Because Polygal is so light, you should enclose its edges with a wooden frame to lend it weight and rigidity. This frame should be open at the bottom to allow rain and melting snow to run off. If you live in an area with high winds, use hinges to attach the Polygal's frame to the cold frame. Coleman's book, available at libraries, contains several structural options worth considering.

Your success with harvesting from cold frames through the winter will depend largely on the kind of plants you grow. In general, leafy greens are the most cold-hardy plants. Coleman says in his area, any of the following can be planted in the late summer and harvested right through until the following spring: arugula, claytonia, Italian dandelion, kale, kohlrabi, lettuce, parsley, radicchio, scallion, sorrel, spinach, Swiss chard, and sugar-loaf chicory. A cold frame filled with straw can even overwinter root crops such as carrots.

In the late spring and early fall,

a cold frame can be a bit fussy to use. You must be sure to prop it open by early afternoon on sunny days to avoid overheating. Place a thermometer inside and make sure that the temperature inside does not exceed 80 degrees. In the depths of winter simply leave it closed, except when harvesting. Brush off snow, but don't worry if it accumulates for a week or two while you're away. Remember, the plants are dormant.

I've seen elaborate watering systems proposed for cold frames, but it's generally simplest just to water with a mister attached to a hose. Once the plants stop growing in winter, no further watering is required.

Should you use cold frames? If you build with new materials, a 4-foot-by-8-foot cold frame will cost about $75. A cold frame this size might grow 50 heads of lettuce. So you would have to figure that a cold frame might take a year or two to pay for itself. But for those who love fresh, homegrown produce and who enjoy gardening, cold frames are a reasonable investment. They allow those with little gardening space to extend their season and get two harvests where they previously got one.

Our situation is somewhat different. With our 8,000-square-foot garden, Jim and I don't need to maximize our land's productivity. Further, our garden space is often on the other side of a 3-foot snowbank, so fetching food from a cold frame for supper could be a bit of a chore. However, fresh is nice, and we may place a few cold frames next to our house so that we can have a small quantity of greens for wintertime salads.

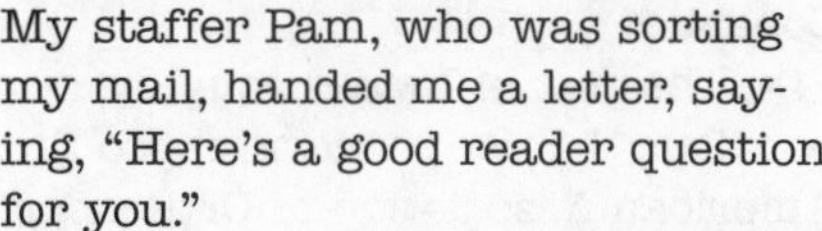

THE STRAIGHT TOOTH

My staffer Pam, who was sorting my mail, handed me a letter, saying, "Here's a good reader question for you."

Suzanne Johnson of Lawrence, Kansas, asked, "Have you considered an article on dental braces? It's a major expense that seems to have become an acquired need. Are we depriving our children by refusing to spend $3,000 for cosmetic corrections? It's hard to stand firm when half the eighth-grade class seems to have braces."

After reading this, I turned to Pam, smiled broadly to exaggerate my crooked-toothed overbite, and said jokingly, "Geez, why do you suppose she's asking *me* this?" Kidding aside, I realized I could offer a unique perspective on this question.

I grew up in a home with modest financial resources, and spending money on nonessential dental care was never considered by either child or parent. To be perfectly honest, it was something to which I never gave a thought. I'm living proof that it's possible to be successful and happy despite having an imperfect smile. Like Suzanne, my initial reaction to this expense is that the notion that everyone must have perfect teeth is a bit misplaced.

I also feel it's important to distinguish between a child's desire for braces and her desire for better-looking teeth. Braces were despised when I was a kid, but nowadays they are less obtrusive and some kids actually like how they look. Braces are much too expensive—not to mention painful—to be used solely as a fashion accessory.

However, persuasive arguments can be made in favor of braces. Consider:

• The cost of braces roughly parallels the need. According to the American Association of Orthodontists, minor corrections can be achieved for as little as $1,500. Corrections for the most serious medical or cosmetic problems can cost up to $5,000. Due to improved materials and techniques, the cost of braces has actually increased much more slowly than the inflation rate.

• Unlike the temporary benefits derived from designer clothes and trendy haircuts, braces are an "investment" purchase. When you consider haircuts, nail care, makeup, and wardrobe, most women spend at least $1,000 annually on temporary improvements to their appearances. A $2,000 orthodontist bill, spread out over 60 years, is just $33 annually.

• In many areas of our budgets, tightwads can spend far less than everyone else while achieving the same level of quality. But braces are an either/or thing. You can't "do-it-yourself" with paper clips, rubber bands, and duct tape. When there are no economical options and I determine that the benefit is worth the cost, I shop for the best price and don't sweat it any further.

To sum up: If affording braces for a minor cosmetic problem means making difficult financial trade-offs for the family, I think it is appropriate to ask the child if she is willing to forgo store-bought clothes, allowances, and family vacations. Is she willing to take on more housework and give up after-school activities so that her parents can work overtime to earn the money required? An eighth-grader is old enough to peek into the family ledger to gain a clear understanding of what the entire family must give up to accommodate her desire. If she's unwilling, it isn't that important to her.

On the other hand, if the child has a fairly serious, noticeable cosmetic problem, I feel it can be appropriate for a frugal parent to insist that the child get braces even if he doesn't want them. Boys, in particular, are often completely oblivious to their physical appearance, but as adults they will thank their parents for making them wear braces. In either case, make sure the child understands the hassle and possible pain involved in braces. For some people, braces can involve months of soreness to gums and teeth—even to the point of tears. Braces also require special care in brushing, and avoiding certain types of food.

One of my children does have a minor cosmetic problem and does want braces. I said yes.

HAVE A BLOCK PARTY

Wooden blocks are among the best toys for young children. They're simple, durable, and foster imagination and coordination.

I find that commercially made wooden blocks, which can sometimes be purchased at yard sales, are usually too small to make the impressive structures kids enjoy building. Larger blocks are obviously a possible do-it-yourself project, but how, exactly, should they be made?

David G. Fielder of Akron, Ohio, provided the answer. He wrote that short pieces of 2 × 4 can always be found around building projects. With the builder's permission, take these home. The thickness and width are already fine, so they need only be cut to length and sanded.

David's block sets (he's made 12 so far) consist of three sizes. First is a square, the second size is twice that long, and the third size is three times that long. That makes them 3½ inches long, 7 inches long, and 10½ inches long respectively. The fact that they are all based on the same basic 3½-inch unit is important because it makes many structures possible.

David says he tries to provide at least 20 blocks of each size in a set, and perhaps a few extra of the smallest size. These can be made with a handsaw, but a circular saw makes the job much easier. Easiest and most accurate is a radial-arm saw, or a motorized miter saw (commonly called a chop saw). Virtually all carpenters have one or both of the latter saws; beg, borrow, or barter access (and ask for a lesson—these are serious tools).

Sand by hand or with an orbital or belt sander.

For variety, I would also add "ramp" pieces in several sizes. These are made by cutting some of the basic-sized blocks diagonally (safest for older kids). You can also use a coping saw, scroll saw, or jigsaw to cut a semicircle out of the longest side of the longer blocks to make arches. Finally, you can cut 1½-inch-thick dowels in 3½-inch, 7-inch, and 10½-inch lengths to make columns.

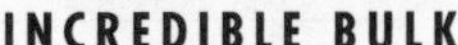

INCREDIBLE BULK

Dear Amy,

To buy in bulk, don't be afraid to contact manufacturers directly. I saved 33 percent (includes shipping) off the price of some specialty honey for gift baskets . . . delivered to my door! All I did was call and inquire about buying a case of 12 and they were glad to help.

—Heidi and James Kushlan
Harrisburg, Pennsylvania

CHEZ CHEAPSKATE

Dear Amy,

Work in a restaurant or get friendly with someone who does. My college roommate worked in a high-class steak house. Every night she'd bring home a steak not cooked to order, or a cracked lobster, or broken crab legs, which they were not allowed to serve to customers. We also got day-old pastries and slices of cake that didn't cut prettily or had smeared icing. The restaurant was closed on Mondays, so on Sunday nights we got whatever vegetables and salad fixings remained on hand. Our grocery bill was negligible and our friends were envious when we'd moan about being tired of eating lobster.

—Karen M. Campbell
Sacramento, California

PEANUT POINTER

Dear Amy,

It is important to recycle the Styrofoam peanuts that are often used for packing these days. Contact your local private mailing service (such as Mail Boxes U.S.A.) and ask if they accept them. Some services will give you a discount in return for giving them your old peanuts.

—Gloria Pomykala
New Kensington, Pennsylvania

REBIRTH OF THE BLUES

Dear Amy,

To rejuvenate worn denim garments, we buy RIT denim dye and use it in an entire wash load of denim items. They come out looking like new.

—Linda Santa Maria
Phoenixville, Pennsylvania

DELIGHTFUL DISCARDS

Dear Amy,

A friend of mine cleans houses for a living, and her clients include at least one landlord. Renters will sometimes move out and leave their units a blessed mess, abandoning furniture, housewares, and especially clothing. Sometimes the tenants owe back rent, so they leave quickly and quietly and don't take anything they can't fit in their cars. (Using a U-Haul might attract attention.) In addition to her hourly wage, my friend gets her pick of what is left behind. If you are interested in this kind of work, check city/county records for rental owners and solicit their business by phone or mail.

—Elizabeth Case
Belfair, Washington

CROWNING ACHIEVEMENT

Dear Amy,

You mentioned the savings you can get from student dental assistants cleaning your teeth. Well, we are fortunate to have a full-fledged dental school here that trains both

future dentists and orthodontists. I recently got a crown that would have cost $500 for $135 by signing up with the University of Texas Health Science Center Dental School. You pay fees for the materials used.

—Janet Whitehouse
San Antonio, Texas

LOW-TECH LOAVES

Dear Amy,

If I make homemade yeast bread, I use my Crock-Pot. You can order a metal canister insert for bread or cake baking from the manufacturer for $9. You have to do the mixing yourself, but otherwise it works as well as a bread machine.

—Deborah Black
Grandview, Missouri

SLICK OIL TIP

Dear Amy,

In your newsletter you wrote that one reason you do not use homemade mixes is that the recipes call for shortening. I, too, prefer to use oil and have made my own biscuit mix for years. I substitute two thirds the quantity of oil for the amount of shortening called for in the recipe. In fact, I do this for all my baking. I entered a batch of my scratch biscuits at the local county fair and won first place!

—Nadine Bryan
Sidney, Ohio

WEED IT AND REAP

Dear Amy,

A plant that is nutritious, free, and abundant is the dandelion. It is very good for everyone to eat and contains many vitamins.

—Robyn Quaintance
Sidney, British Columbia

(Pick these from your own yard to be sure they have not been sprayed. All parts are edible. They are less bitter if picked before they flower. FZ)

WATER WORKS

Dear Amy,

I used to shampoo and condition every day. Then I read a "star's" hint in a magazine. She shampoos every other day with some expensive product, then just washes with water on the other days. Tried it. Works great.

—Kathy Terrill
New York, New York

BISECT YOUR BIRD

Dear Amy,

When buying a frozen turkey and you don't want to or can't use it all at one time, ask the meat cutter to saw it in half or quarters. They will do this for a few cents, or sometimes for free.

—Bish Wolf
Lebanon, Pennsylvania

BATTERY BONANZA

Dear Amy,

Many hospitals are sending patients home overnight with cardiac, respiratory, and brain-wave monitors. These are battery run; 9-volt, C, and AA cells are the most common varieties used. Frequently, new, industrial-grade batteries are used, and are thrown away after a single overnight use. They are mine for the asking at the local hospital.

—Jeffrey P. Hazzard
Valrico, Florida

PUREE SAVES THE DAY

Dear Amy,

I have been using your suggestion to replace half the fat in cookies with applesauce. When making some cookies, I didn't have applesauce, but I had pumpkin puree. I used that in place of half the fat. The cookies were delicious! Pumpkin puree is cheaper for me than applesauce.

—Laurie Lentz-Marino
Belchertown, Massachusetts

SWINGING INTO SPRING

Dear Amy,

As springtime approached last year, my husband and I began pricing gym/swing sets. To purchase even a kit plus lumber was way out of our budget. While driving through a nearby town we noticed one in someone's backyard that was exactly what we had wanted. It was clearly no longer being used (the beautiful lawn around it gave that away). We got our courage up and knocked on the door. We offered to remove the set, fill the holes, and reseed their lawn. The owners agreed. We saved about $500.

—Francine Fazio
Schenectady, New York

GOING WITH THE GRAIN

Here's another universal recipe, and I hope it helps put to rest the silly notion that frugal eating cannot be healthy. This "Universal Pilaf" represents state-of-the-science nutritional excellence; it is low in fat and cholesterol and high in fiber, vitamins, and complex carbohydrates. Depending upon the options you choose, it also ranges from extremely to moderately cheap.

My thanks to Andrea J. Albert and David E. Gurzynski for sending it in. They say these proportions make a meal for two with leftovers for lunch the next day. For my family I would at least triple the recipe.

Grain: One cup of uncooked brown or white rice, bulgur, couscous, or other favorite grain.

Fat: Two tablespoons of olive oil, butter, vegetable oil, or other favorite oil.

Base vegetable: Two to three cloves of diced garlic and one of the following, cut up: one small onion, three shallots, or one small leek (white part only).

Liquid: Two cups vegetable broth, chicken broth, cooking water from boiled vegetables, or water.

Meat or protein (omit if using the pilaf as a side dish): From ½ to ⅔ cup skinned chicken (may be diced and boned or left whole), tuna, cooked white or red beans, white fish, hamburger, or cheap steak cut into cubes.

Additional vegetable: About ½ cup frozen or fresh peas, cut-up carrots, frozen corn, green peppers, celery, and/or any other favorite vegetable except for leafy greens and potatoes.

Seasoning: Salt, pepper, chervil, parsley, whatever works well with chosen ingredients.

Directions: Heat fat in a large cast-iron or nonstick skillet. When hot, add the base vegetables and fry until golden and translucent. Add the meat and brown (but if using tuna, don't add it at this point). Add the grain and fry for a minute or so to coat it with the fat. Add the liquid and bring to a boil (add tuna now). Add the other vegetables, season, stir, return to a boil, lower the heat so it just simmers, and cover. Check it often; if using whole grains, it will take up to 40 minutes to cook, while white rice takes only about 15 minutes. Don't stir too much. When the liquid is completely absorbed, it is done. Stir, season to taste, and serve.

INVESTIGATION 101

Most people know how to research timeless questions such as how to lay tile or do upholstery: Simply read library books. But judging by my mail, many people are stumped when it comes to researching "new deals." These deals—discount grocery offers, phone deals, and network-marketed doodads—supposedly save you money; others are touted as income opportunities. Each type can cost you money if you don't do proper research. But because they're new, you can't learn about them in library books.

Sometimes I do investigate such offers and publish the results, but there are too many to report on them all. And I don't like to devote space to bad deals that few people would hear about anyway.

In such cases, readers have to

do their own research. So I thought I would pass along a few basic consumer-research methods. Many of these are also useful for digging up other sorts of information, such as answers to safety, legal, or health questions.

When investigating, gather several kinds of information, such as: the company's history, what consumer reporters have written about it, whether certain claims the company makes are true, and so on. This information can be gathered from a variety of sources. Here are some we typically use:

• The Better Business Bureau. I usually call the BBB first, because whenever my research ended after a single call, it's been when I found the BBB had received complaints. But no record of complaints is not necessarily a sign of a good company. For example, if a bad company has been doing business in that BBB's area for less than a year, it may not have received complaints yet. BBBs can also tell you a company's history and the type of business it does. To find a local BBB, call information in the town where the company is located. If there is no BBB in that town, ask the operator for the nearest branch. Some BBBs charge a small fee for information provided over the phone but will give you the same information free if you write.

• The company itself. Call the company and ask questions! It's crucial that company officials provide a satisfactory answer to every question you have. If they refuse, give contradictory answers, are never available to take your call, or simply can't make a good case for their deal, odds are it's a bad risk.

Also, ask companies for all the free literature they'll send you. Often if you read all the fine print and do the math, you can determine if the deal is bad. If it looks good, keep investigating. And *don't* rely solely on the information and references of happy customers provided by the company.

• On-line resources. Subscription-based on-line services offer a wealth of information. CompuServe, for example, gives you access to complete texts of articles from some 400 magazines and dozens of major newspapers over the last several years. Some large, well-financed city libraries provide similar access for free. Smaller libraries may offer stripped-down versions. Basically, you enter a keyword or words, such as "affinity credit cards," and every article that contains those words is listed; you then select the ones you want to read. Two caveats: There's often a fee. CompuServe, for example, charges $1.50 per article retrieved. And be aware that most consumer reporters lack the critical tightwad perspective. For example, when I wrote about telephone debit cards, I read dozens of articles that raved about the potential savings, but *none* that explained when these cards would cost more to use than calling cards. Negative reviews are generally more reliable than positive ones, perhaps because a negative story requires more careful research to avoid lawsuits. An exception to this is *Consumer Reports,* which tends to be extremely thorough and accurate whether its conclusions are positive or negative. All articles, regardless of their accuracy, can provide other leads, such as names of experts or companies that offer similar deals.

• Reference librarians. They can help locate experts to verify the claims of a company. These claims might include medical or nutritional benefits, scientific facts, or the feasibility of a marketing plan. Librarians can tell you the names and addresses of industry associations, which periodicals track this industry, government sources, contacts in major corporations, and so on. Many of these have toll-free numbers. You need not travel to the library, as reference librarians will field queries over the phone. As an example of just how specialized experts can be, before running a bird-feeder idea I called the National Bird-Feeding Society. If an expert can't answer your questions, ask for suggestions of who you might call.

Investigations usually require both time and money, but how much depends on how thorough you want to be. In most cases, if a deal is bad, only a few phone calls are needed to become sufficiently skeptical to pass on it. It can take a lot of work to definitively prove a deal is either bad or good. Weigh your time and research expenses against your potential savings or investment.

If, for whatever reason, you are disinclined to investigate, simply walk away. In the 16 years that I have been a tightwad, I've rarely seen a new, nationally marketed, ongoing deal that was genuinely amazing. Great deals are usually local and/or limited, such as the odd great find at a yard sale, salvage store, or in the freebie section of the classifieds.

RELOCATION CALCULATION

It's common knowledge that housing is cheaper in some parts of the country than in others. This insight leads many people who want to get ahead to consider moving from expensive-housing to cheap-housing areas.

But often these people hesitate. Why? Because they believe that salaries in these cheap-housing areas are correspondingly low. Consequently, they believe that one region is no more affordable than another. In fact, this is not true. Some regions of the country are *much* more affordable than others.

To make a state-by-state comparison we obtained a 1990 Census Bureau report on median house values. These figures are based on estimates homeowners put down on their census forms and tend to be lower than market prices. We also obtained a 1993

Bureau of Labor Statistics survey that details average per-worker income, which includes all workers covered by unemployment compensation. The terms "median" and "average" are different, but a Census Bureau statistician told us that for the purposes of our comparison, it's valid to compare the two. As far as we could determine, these are the best state-by-state numbers available.

We divided the median house value by the average annual pay and came up with a ratio and a ranking. Theoretically, the lower both of these numbers are, the more affordable the state is.

There's a lot of variation in housing affordability because housing prices vary widely; but salaries don't. For example, we have friends in California who have been unable to buy a home there and are considering a move to Michigan. The chart indicates that they might lose $1,208 in annual income, but could save $134,900 on the cost of a home. So this would be a very wise financial move for them. Although Maine is relatively unaffordable, moving

	MEDIAN HOUSE VALUE	AVERAGE ANNUAL INCOME	INCOME/ HOUSE RATIO	RANK BY STATE
Alabama	$53,700	$22,786	2.36	11
Alaska	94,400	32,336	2.92	30
Arizona	80,100	23,501	3.41	36
Arkansas	46,300	20,337	2.28	7
California	195,500	29,468	6.63	50
Colorado	82,700	25,682	3.22	33
Connecticut	177,800	33,169	5.36	47
Delaware	100,100	27,143	3.69	39
District of Columbia	123,900	39,199	3.16	32
Florida	77,100	23,571	3.27	35
Georgia	71,300	24,867	2.87	27
Hawaii	245,300	26,325	9.32	51
Idaho	58,200	21,188	2.75	21
Illinois	80,900	28,420	2.85	26
Indiana	53,900	24,109	2.24	5
Iowa	45,900	21,441	2.14	3
Kansas	52,200	22,430	2.33	10
Kentucky	50,500	22,170	2.28	6
Louisiana	58,500	22,632	2.58	17
Maine	87,400	22,026	3.97	41
Maryland	116,500	27,684	4.21	43
Massachusetts	162,800	30,229	5.39	49
Michigan	60,600	28,260	2.14	1
Minnesota	74,000	25,711	2.88	28
Mississippi	45,600	19,694	2.32	8
Missouri	59,800	23,898	2.50	14
Montana	$56,600	$19,932	2.84	25
Nebraska	50,400	20,815	2.42	12
Nevada	95,700	25,461	3.76	40
New Hampshire	129,400	24,962	5.18	46
New Jersey	162,300	32,716	4.96	45
New Mexico	70,100	21,731	3.23	34
New York	131,600	32,919	4.00	42
North Carolina	65,800	22,770	2.89	29
North Dakota	50,800	19,382	2.62	18
Ohio	63,500	25,339	2.51	16
Oklahoma	48,100	22,003	2.19	4
Oregon	67,100	24,093	2.79	22
Pennsylvania	69,700	26,274	2.65	19
Rhode Island	133,500	24,889	5.36	48
South Carolina	61,100	21,928	2.79	23
South Dakota	45,200	18,613	2.43	13
Tennessee	58,400	23,368	2.50	15
Texas	59,600	25,545	2.33	9
Utah	68,900	22,250	3.10	31
Vermont	95,500	22,704	4.21	44
Virginia	91,000	25,496	3.57	37
Washington	93,400	25,760	3.63	38
West Virginia	47,900	22,373	2.14	2
Wisconsin	62,500	23,610	2.65	20
Wyoming	61,600	21,745	2.83	24
Average of all states	79,100	24,803	3.19	

here from even less affordable Massachusetts made the difference in our being able to buy the house we wanted and still live on one income.

In viewing the chart, there are a few points to bear in mind:

• I ranked the states in affordability based on the ratio of income to house value. In a few cases, the ratios in two or three states were the same, although the incomes and house values varied. In these cases I gave the higher-income states a better rating, assuming that you're always better off earning more money.

• The fact that we are dealing with average numbers for entire states leaves out the important differences between cities and rural areas. For instance, our chart indicates that New York has a high 4.0 ratio, but that number is pushed up because of New York City; rural New York State is probably approximately as affordable as neighboring Pennsylvania.

• In our comparison we're assuming that your income and your housing costs are the two biggest factors in your financial picture. Obviously, there are other factors. Utilities costs, local taxes, and insurance can vary widely from state to state. Consumer goods and groceries are less variable.

• The differences in average annual pay in your particular profession may vary more widely than does overall average pay. Further, there may be far fewer employment opportunities in certain professions in one state versus another. It's seldom a good idea to move unless you actually have a job lined up.

• Moving is in itself expensive, so if you plan to move to gain an economic advantage, try to do it just once.

• People whose incomes would not vary regardless of where they live, such as retirees and owners of mail-order businesses, should pay more attention to the house-values column. The ratio of income to house values is of little importance to them.

Given these points, this exercise is intended to provide a rough guideline for affordability and is in no way a substitute for the thorough research required before you pack your bags.

APPROVAL, THEN REMOVAL

Dear Amy,

I called our city hall about an abandoned house, hoping I could remove the small plants for landscaping. They gave me five addresses and told me how to contact the owners. While three declined, the two who gave permission owned old farms. I got rose bushes, bugle vines, hydrangeas, and enough of a fieldstone retaining wall to make a walkway.

—Annette Weber
Eden Prairie, Minnesota

A GRATITUDE ATTITUDE

Dear Amy,

During all our years of scrimping and saving, I resented being poor. Then, *The Tightwad Gazette* entered our life. We began doing many more frugal things, but the real change was in my attitude. It hit me after I dropped off a boot at the local shoe-repair place. One year before, I had dropped off the other boot because it was coming apart. At that time, I felt sorry for myself that I was having to repair five-year-old boots rather than buy new ones. But this year was different. As I walked home, I felt triumphant that I was making it through one more year with these boots. The burden of always wanting things has been lifted, and I feel good about what we do have. So thank you from the bottom of my heart.

—Laura Honan
Whitewater, Wisconsin

GOOD CUP, BAD CUP

Dear Amy,

I honestly didn't know that I didn't need to put dishwasher detergent in both cups for the regular wash cycle! Unless my machine is set to a prewash cycle, such as pot-scrubber, detergent placed in the open cup is wasted. It's amazing what you learn when you *read the manual*!

—Name withheld by request
Bakersfield, California

BUT HOLD THE MUSTARD!

Dear Amy,

This is a fun snack idea my kids like, and it is also a use for overripe bananas. It's called a banana dog. Spread peanut butter on a bun or bread, place the whole peeled banana on the bun/bread, and eat like a hot dog.

—Lori Kimbley
Bellevue, Nebraska

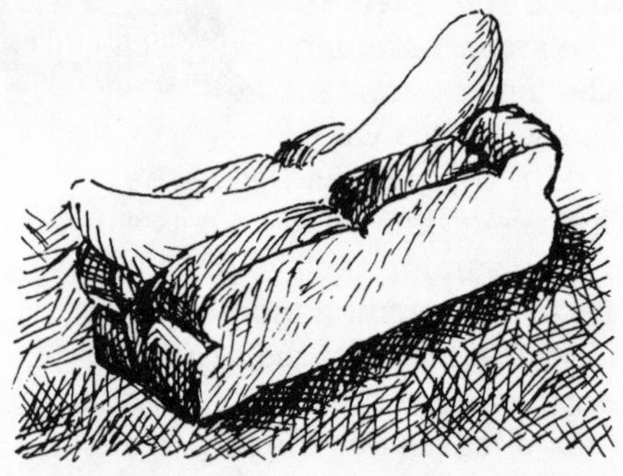

FRUGAL FUNGI

Dear Amy,

My grocery store sells huge bags of "tarnished" mushrooms very cheap. I buy the bags and sauté the mushrooms, sliced, 2 cups at a time, in 1 tablespoon butter or oil for about 3 minutes. I freeze them immediately in little bags. The mushrooms are very flavorful (no comparison to canned!) and make a frugal gourmet addition to soup, casseroles, etc.

—Ruth Laura Edlund
Bellevue, Washington

CHART SMARTS

Dear Amy,

For wrapping some of our gifts, we use obsolete aviation charts. They are often very colorful and unique. We have always gotten positive responses from the receivers. I'm a commercial pilot and am required to update my charts many times per year. Any active pilot should be able to supply you with obsolete charts.

—Stephen Craven
Edgewood, Kentucky

(Stephen sent a sample, and he is right—the charts do have an appealing, technical look. Older children, in particular, would appreciate these as wrapping, wall art, or for study. FZ)

SOAK FOR SUCCESS

Dear Amy,

I have five small, active children. It seems that every load of laundry includes dozens of stained items. I used to spend a lot of time pretreating and scrubbing spots. Now I just throw them in, turn the washer on, let it run for a few minutes, then turn it off and let everything soak for 15 to 20 minutes. They come out just as clean (except for tomato-based stains, which still need a good scrubbing). Saves pennies on pretreatment and lots of time.

—A grateful reader
Huntsville, Alabama

FROZEN ASSET

Dear Amy,

Keeping yeast in the freezer will prolong its life nearly indefinitely. Make sure it is in a well-sealed, moisture-proof container.

—Tammy Janelle
Caledonia, Mississippi

THE UNEMPLOYMENT OPPORTUNITY

Back in 1990, when I had been publishing the newsletter for just three months, I got a call from a man who said, "You should send copies of your newsletter to the New Road Map Foundation in Seattle. Your ideas are similar to theirs." I followed his advice. That was the start of a friendly relationship I've had with the foundation's founders, Joe Dominguez and Vicki Robin, ever since.

At that time, their ideas were available in a cassette-tape program. Since then, the same material has been published in a book called *Your Money or Your Life: Transforming Your Relationship with Money and Achieving Financial Independence* (Penguin, 1992). I weaseled a "review copy" of the tape program and spent a day listening to Joe while scraping paint off my porch.

His personal story is fascinating. Years ago, while employed as an investment counselor on Wall Street, he realized he was tired of working hard and spending his money on things that meant little to him. It occurred to him that if

he stopped spending in this way he could save the difference and become financially independent. He experimented with lowering his budget to the minimum level that felt comfortable to him. He began investing the surplus in supersafe treasury bonds. When he had saved about $100,000, this yielded an annual income of about $6,000, which happened to be the same amount he could live on. He quit his job in 1969, at the age of 31, and has lived on the same $6,000 per year ever since. To do this, he now shares housing and transportation and buys high-deductible health insurance. In the last 25 years he has devoted his time to working on various causes that are important to him. All of the proceeds from his tapes and books have been distributed to various causes through the foundation.

It was then that I first understood that financial independence wasn't exclusively for the super-rich—that it was possible for at least some frugal people with average incomes. But I doubted that it could apply to us. "What an amazing concept," I wrote back to Joe, "if you don't have kids." I pointed out that, at that time, we had four small children, and a year earlier we had bought a large fixer-upper that would consume most of our surplus cash for some time. Jim would be retiring from the military the following year and it was likely our income would be smaller. It had taken us seven years to save $49,000 at a time when we had relatively few expenses. We'd be hard-pressed just to pay off our mortgage early, much less save for an early retirement.

But since then, I've realized that financial independence is possible for a surprisingly broad range of people, including us. It's important to realize this, since the first, crucial step in achieving financial independence—or FI, as Joe and Vicki refer to it—is believing that you *can* reach it.

I'll concede that given the "strikes" we had against us, FI was possible only through a financial fluke. Within a year of its founding, the newsletter gained phenomenal national media coverage, and with the resulting income we were able to pay off our mortgage and could have just barely survived on Jim's pension, making us technically financially independent. In the last few years, we've saved for large future expenses.

I'll also concede that a great many of my readers have so many strikes against them that achieving FI early is very unlikely. While virtually any reader can put frugal strategies into practice, financial flukes are exceedingly hard to come by.

Nevertheless, FI is very relevant to some readers. I frequently encounter people who could achieve FI . . . and don't realize it. If at least some of the variables below describe you, you might be a candidate:

- You have no children, or your children will be grown by the time you are in your forties.
- You don't have excessive debts.
- You have a significant amount of disposable income. Single people with average incomes can achieve FI in five to ten years.
- You have low-cost housing, such as a paid-for, low-maintenance ranch house.
- Your work offers an early retirement option. Downsizing cor-

porations often offer attractive early-buyout deals, and military people can retire and receive a pension after 20 years.

• You have a financial windfall, such as an inheritance (it happens).

• You and your family members are reasonably healthy. Unfortunately, people with expensive preexisting conditions who receive medical coverage through their jobs may need to work simply to keep the coverage.

• You're young. Even if many of the above variables don't describe you, if you start early, you can overcome many obstacles.

Of these variables, not having children seems to be the one most crucial for achieving FI at a young age. As an example of one FI success story, I just received a letter from a 40-year-old single reader (who requested anonymity) from Phoenix who'll retire in December. Her net worth is nearly $180,000. Over the last few years she has saved 52 percent of her income.

Although families with children have achieved FI, it's far more rare. If you have kids and an average income, you can still shoot for retiring early; say, in your 50s.

Another with-kid option is achieving an increased freedom from the need to earn money. Consider my staffer Brad. Brad was the journalist who sold the story about us to *Parade* magazine, converted to tightwaddery, and then a year later came to work for me part-time. Frugality enabled him to leave his newspaper job (which he disliked) and build a successful freelancing career. This allowed his wife to quit her job (which she disliked); she's considering new career options. Recently, they paid off their mortgage. With one school-aged child, they now need about $15,000 per year to get by. Although not yet FI, Brad can be very selective about the freelance assignments he accepts. This in-between phase of *increased* FI is an option for virtually anyone.

FI through frugality is an important concept for anyone who ever said or thought, "I make so much money I don't need to be frugal." Typically, such people save 10 percent of their income and blow the remainder. They're assuming their desire to work and ability to generate income will be the same until they are 65. Striving for FI is a way to anticipate that these variables are likely to change.

Still, some people are cool to the idea of FI because it would be "boring." Work is the best part of their lives—either because they love

their work or because their home life offers little to keep them busy. The work-till-you're-65 thinking is so deeply ingrained in our culture that the question most frequently asked about my retirement is, "But what will you do?" Others assume I'm going to immediately gear up for another career. But with six kids, a huge house, a gigantic garden, many hobbies, and numerous volunteer opportunities, I will never be "bored." I can't imagine any job could be so attractive as to lure me into an away-from-home commitment anytime in the next decade.

Joe and Vicki point out that most who achieve FI have fewer at-home commitments than I do, and devote their newfound free time to a variety of volunteer jobs. They say that, given the hard work and discipline needed to achieve FI, they have never met anyone who achieved it and then sat around doing nothing.

In my view, the point of aiming toward FI isn't necessarily to never again work for money. Rather, it's to acquire the freedom to choose when, where, what, and how much work you do. I often reflect on something Vicki once said to me that seemed to sum up so much: "I buy my freedom with my frugality."

Index

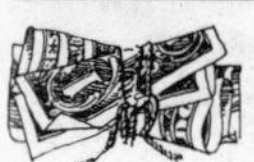

Z

ABOUT THE AUTHOR

AMY DACYCZYN published a newsletter called *The Tightwad Gazette* from June 1990 until December 1996. Amy is now retired from her writing career. The Dacyczyns and their six children live happily and frugally in Leeds, Maine.

NOTES

NOTES

NOTES

NOTES

NOTES

NOTES

NOTES